Let Nature Do the Growing

inch — — — — — — 2.54 cm
Foot — — 12 IN. 0.3048 m
Yard 3 Ft. 0.9144 m.

Conversion factors
1 centimeter = 0.39 in.
1 meter = 39.4 in

2015
From aunt norma lundberg.

Let Nature Do the Growing

The Fertilizer-free Vegetable Garden

by Gajin Tokuno

 Japan Publications, Inc.

The original Japanese-language editions published by Marge-sha Publishing Co., Tokyo in 1980 and 1984 in two volumes.

Published by JAPAN PUBLICATIONS, INC., Tokyo and New York

Distributors:
UNITED STATES: *Kodansha International/USA, Ltd., through Harper & Row, Publishers, Inc., 10 East 53rd Street, New York, New York 10022.* SOUTH AMERICA: *Harper & Row, Publishers, Inc., International Department.* CANADA: *Fitzhenry & Whiteside Ltd., 195 Allstate Parkway, Markham, Ontario L3R 4T8.* MEXICO AND CENTRAL AMERICA: *HARLA S. A. de C. V., Apartado 30–546, Mexico 4, D. F.* BRITISH ISLES: *International Book Distributors Ltd., 66 Wood Lane End, Hemel Hempstead, Herts HP2 4RG.* EUROPEAN CONTINENT: *Fleetbooks, S. A., c/o Feffer and Simons (Nederland) B. V., 61 Strijkviertel, 3454 PK de Meern, The Netherlands.* AUSTRALIA AND NEW ZEALAND: *Bookwise International, 1 Jeanes Street, Beverley, South Australia 5007.* THE FAR EAST AND JAPAN: *Japan Publications Trading Co., Ltd., 1–2–1, Sarugaku-cho, Chiyoda-ku, Tokyo 101.*

First edition: December 1986

LCCC No. 86–080219
ISBN 0–87040–668–X

Printed in U.S.A.

Preface

Many of the fruits and vegetables currently commercially marketed have been raised with artificial fertilizers, weed-killers, and insecticides and then subjected to some other chemical treatment. Furthermore, as is often pointed out, agricultural chemicals and the various additives found in modern foods can contribute to the emergence of such grave illnesses as cancer and degenerative disorders.

In the past few years, home-gardening has become so increasingly popular in Japan that a number of how-to guide books on the subject have appeared on the market. Most of them, however, blithely recommend the use of the same kinds of chemicals and fertilizers widely employed in commercial agriculture. And this has the effect of exposing to grave danger of soil pollution home-gardens, which by nature ought to be free of such peril. In other words, chemicals developed for use in profit-oriented agriculture are being introduced into gardens whose primary concerns should be freshness, goodness, and safety.

Until fairly recently, the Japanese Ministry of Agriculture and Forestry has demonstrated no interest in organic agriculture. In 1986, however, it initiated actual investigations into the matter and seems at last to be taking seriously the influences chemical agriculture can have on the body, the way chemicals are retained in vegetable products, and the environment-polluting effects of such substances. This indicates realization of the danger of chemical fertilizers and insecticides and a willingness to reassess the agricultural system employing them.

But, today many home gardeners, whose numbers are said to be greater than those of commercial farmers, are daily spreading chemicals on and around the plants they grow. Taking a disparaging view of home-gardens as purely individual undertakings, society at large remains largely ignorant of the danger these activities pose. Stimulated by an awareness of the peril, I have written this book in the hope of helping large numbers of people raise harmless, safe-to-eat vegetables.

Though they grow fast and are large and handsome, vegetables raised according to the chemical system exert a bad influence on the ecology. To combat this, I recommend avoiding chemicals and relying on the great forces of life inherent in the natural world itself to raise vegetables that are delicious, nourishing, and safe.

This book, which originally appeared in two Japanese-language volumes entitled *Nōyaku o tsukawanai yasai-zukuri* (Raising vegetables without agricultural chemicals; vol. 1 published in 1980 and vol. 2 in 1984, both by Marge-Sha Publishing Co.), began as a record of natural, organic gardening on a plot of land only 46.2 square meters in area, located in the city of Zama, in Kanagawa Prefecture, not far from Tokyo and about in the middle of the Japanese archipelago.

The system set forth in this book is geared to the climate of this region, which may be described as follows. On the coldest days of the year, which occur from the middle of January to the beginning of February, temperatures at night drop to minus 1–4 degrees centigrade (30–25 degrees Fahrenheit). The cherry trees bloom in early April. Spring is a busy time for gardeners. The rainy season lasts for about a month, beginning in the middle of June. Hot summer—temperatures of 30–33 degrees centigrade (86–91 degrees Fahrenheit)—lasts throughout August. Then from September until November occurs autumn, which is as busy a time for gardeners as spring. After first frosts, in the middle of November, days grow increasingly cold. Usually 5–20 centimeters of snow will fall three or four times a winter.

At all seasons except winter, my field is completely obscured by a green covering that gives the impression of being insufficiently tended. Closer examination, however, reveals scarcity of insect damage, healthy vegetables, and lively insects and small animals in a green garden that beautifully preserves the natural balance.

Of the seventy-eight plant varieties contained in this book, only two—prickly ash and *fuki*—are native to Japan. All the others have been introduced and acclimated at some time in history.

I made drawings for the illustrations, while gardening, over a period of about ten years and tried to ensure that as many of the pictures as possible would be actual size in order to facilitate better understanding by beginning gardeners. Production demands, however, necessitated illustration-size reductions in the English-language edition, which has been amended and corrected in a number of places.

In conclusion, I should like to express my profound gratitude to Iwao Yoshizaki, president of Japan Publications, Inc., whose warm understanding and encouragement made possible the issuing of the translated edition, and to the members of his staff responsible for the translation, editing, and production.

August, 1986

Gajin Tokuno

Contents

8

Chapter I Basics

1. Nature, Not Man, Makes Things Grow

Soil is alive with countless microorganisms and other small life forms existing in a common ecology shared with all the other life forms on the earth. Furthermore, all of these life forms are organically interrelated. Nothing in the world of nature is without its use and function. Everything exists in some kind of connection with everything else. And this is why such things as weeds, insects, and birds are essential to the cultivation of the vegetables human beings use for foods.

Nature, not man, makes thing grow: human beings only help a little. In the past, people raised vegetables solely for their own consumption; and the cultivation method was to allow them to grow like weeds, naturally, in a way that took advantage of local soil and climatic conditions. Under such a system, plants were little affected by disease or insects. It was only when cultivators ceased regarding the vegetables they grew as destined for their own tables alone and began thinking of them as commercial products that resort was made to agricultural insecticides and chemical fertilizers. A society oriented toward the pursuit of profit evaluates vegetables with criteria different from those of a society based on the idea of production for self-sufficiency alone and tends to consider beautiful those products that have been cosmetically doctored by means of chemicals. But this view is difficult to endorse, because the method it prescribes calls for the application of chemicals that destroy essential microorganisms in the soil and is therefore unsafe.

Originally used only in commercial operations, this dangerous system of cultivation has now penetrated to the small family vegetable garden. Writers of handbooks and other texts on home gardening all advocate the credulous and irresponsible use of agricultural chemicals and in this way put all of us who want to raise food for ourselves in a perilous position.

The home garden needs neither insecticides nor chemical fertilizers. The gardener who avoids them and grows vegetables the natural way will learn many things. First he will see how useless agricultural chemicals are. Second, he will be astounded afresh by the surprising relations connecting insects, small animals, and plants. Human beings have traditionally regarded weeds as a nuisance, but the natural cultivator takes a different view and ceases seeking to destroy them with chemicals.

In growing plants, the wisest way is to interfere little and leave things up to the providence of nature. The true fascination of raising vegetables lies in recognizing the rotational cycles of nature and devising ways to work for harvests without the use of insecticides and fertilizers.

2. Sunlight, Temperature, and Water

Plants use the energy of the sun and the carbon dioxide in the air together with the moisture in the soil to carry out a process called photosynthesis, which releases the oxygen essential to all animal life. Indeed animal life on the surface of the earth would be impossible without the photosynthesis carried out by plants.

Sunlight

Plants vary in sunlight requirements. Those demanding strong sunlight grow well from spring into autumn and do best in places that are exposed to the south and get plenty of sun all day long. Those requiring less sunlight grow well in the period from autumn till early spring on the north sides of buildings or in shaded regions. It is safer, however, to avoid seasons of weak light or shaded places for the cultivation of plants that do not grow without adequate sun. In general, in fact, most plants need adequate sun. And this is why it is a first prerequisite to locate vegetable patches or fields in areas open to the sky.

Temperature

Because of the strong influence exerted on them by local climates, plants are sensitive to temperature and must be given the degrees of warmth they require. Those native to hot climates will not do well without great heat, and those native to cooler zones cannot tolerate extremely high temperatures. Care must be taken to select varieties suited to the local climate and not to attempt to force plants to grow under unsuitable conditions.

Humidity too is a decisive factor. In high humidity, plants tend to be weak and straggling and to fall victim easily to insect damage. Such vegetables as eggplants tend to bloom and form fruit badly when humidity is high. In regions with extended rainy seasons, plants may be damaged. The only way to deal with this is to let nature run its course.

Water

Ideally plants should be given suitable amounts of water at the right intervals. Care must be taken, however, to adjust the amounts of water to the needs of the variety being cultivated. Some plants require more and some less water, and overwatering or underwatering has harmful effects.

In dry soil, ample organic compost retains moisture and at the same time prevents excess and helps maintain a suitable water content. Weeds too prevent soil drying. A vegetable field without weeds dries out under even short exposure to strong sunlight. Home gardeners who cannot obtain straw can cut the tops of weeds, leave the roots and lower parts in place to retain moisture, and spread the cut leaves and stalks on the soil for compost. Understanding the symbiotic relation between food plants and weeds makes clear how much time can be wasted in weeding.

Location

People who have gardens may choose a sunny spot and make a vegetable garden. Even if this takes space that might have been used to raise flowers, a vegetable garden gives the pleasure of a crop. Moreover, many vegetable plants have charming blooms. The flowers of *komatsuna*, *daikon* radish, snow peas, broad beans, eggplant, flat chives (*nira*), squash, okra, sesame, and red chili peppers are especially appealing.

City dwellers without gardens may sometimes rent fields in suburban or rural areas for the cultivation of vegetables. But, without going to this extent, it is possible to raise plants even on very small city plots. Ideally, plenty of sunlight should be available; but, some plants will grow in semishaded areas.

Once the plot has been selected, it should be spaded and the soil freed from all such potentially harmful foreign objects as bits of concrete block, glass fragments, empty cans, and so on. If the soil has weeds on it and worms in it, without fertilizing, it should be ready for planting in a month. If the soil is poor and lacks weeds, for a starter, it should be mixed with commercially available dried guano, pressed soy meal, or organic compost. It should then be ready for planting in from two to three weeks.

Vegetable scraps and other clean kitchen wastes piled in a corner of a lot and allowed to rot make excellent compost. People who rent their garden space may find the soil in bad condition from the insecticides and chemical fertilizers previous users may have applied to it. As a consequence, in the first stages insects and illness may cause considerable trouble; but, as the soil gradually comes to wholesome life, it will permit excellent cultivation.

Light

Strong light	Grow well	Chinese cabbage, *mizuna*, kohlrabi, tomatoes, miniature tomatoes, eggplant, cucumbers, bitter melon, white melon, green beans, green soybeans, peanuts, *sanjaku* cowpeas, corn, squash, okra, strawberries, burdock, taro, sweet potatoes, potatoes, *ensai*, Indian spinach, Chinese wolfberry, comfrey, flat chives, sesame, green bell peppers, red chili peppers, sweet green chili peppers, sage
	Grow moderately well	edible chrysanthemums, *okahijiki*, yellow mustard, leaf mustard, cabbage, kale, Boston lettuce, sunny lettuce, endive, snow peas, turnips, *tacai*, Shaoxing cabbage, bok choy, *qing-gen-cai*, Java spinach, scallions, Bermuda onions, *wakegi*, garlic, wild rocambole, *fuki*, ginger, prickly ash, coriander, fennel
	Grow poorly	spinach, *komatsuna*, *caixin*, *hengcaitai*, parsley, basil
		komatsuna, edible chrysanthemums, *okahijiki*, yellow mustard, Boston lettuce,

Weak light	Grow well	sunny lettuce, endive, *daikon*-radish sprouts, *caixin*, *hengcaitai*, bok choy, *qing-gen-cai*, beefsteak plant, prickly ash
	Grow moderately well	spinach, Chinese cabbage, *mizuna*, leaf mustard, cabbage, strawberries, *tacai*, Shaoxing cabbage, Chinese wolfberry, comfrey, garlic, wild rocambole, *fuki*, ginger, basil
	Grow poorly	kohlrabi, tomatoes, miniature tomatoes, eggplant, cucumbers, bitter melon, white melon, green beans, peanuts, *sanjaku* cowpeas, squash, okra, *daikon* radishes, icicle radishes, burdock, taro, sweet potatoes, potatoes, *ensai*, Java spinach, Indian spinach, scallions, *wakegi*, sesame, parsley, green bell peppers, red chili peppers, sweet green chili peppers, sage

Temperature

Heat tolerance	Very tolerant	edible chrysanthemums, *fudan-sō*, tomatoes, miniature tomatoes, eggplant, bitter melon, peanuts, okra, burdock, taro, sweet potatoes, *ensai*, Java spinach, Indian spinach, Chinese wolfberry, comfrey, scallions, flat chives, sesame, beefsteak plant, ginger, green bell peppers, red chili peppers, sweet green chili peppers, basil
	Moderately tolerant	kohlrabi, endive, white melon, green beans, green soybeans, *sanjaku* cowpeas, squash, *daikon* radishes, *daikon*-radish sprouts, carrots, bok choy, *qing-gen-cai*, prickly ash, sage, fennel
	Moderately intolerant	spinach, *komatsuna*, *aburana*, *taisai*, *bitamin-na*, *okahijiki*, kale, cucumbers, corn, strawberries, turnips, *caixin*
	Very intolerant	Chinese cabbage, *mizuna*, yellow mustard, leaf mustard, cabbage, Boston lettuce, sunny lettuce, snow peas, broad beans, radishes, potatoes, *tacai*, *hengcaitai*, *wakegi*, garlic, wild rocambole, *fuki*, parsley

Cold tolerance	Very tolerant	spinach, *komatsuna*, *aburana*, Chinese cabbage, *santō-sai*, *taisai*, *bitamin-na*, yellow mustard, cabbage, kale, snow peas, *tacai*, Shaoxing cabbage, *hengcaitai*, scallions, Bermuda onions, garlic
	Moderately tolerant	leaf mustard, kohlrabi, sunny lettuce, endive, strawberries, *daikon* radishes, carrots
	Moderately intolerant	edible chrysanthemums, *mizuna*, turnips, bok choy, *qing-gen-cai*, wild rocambole, parsley, sage, fennel
	Very intolerant	tomatoes, miniature tomatoes, cucumbers, bitter melon, white melon, green beans, green soybeans, *sanjaku* cowpeas, corn, squash, icicle radishes, burdock, taro, sweet potatoes, potatoes, *caixin*, *ensai*, Java spinach, Indian spinach, Chinese wolfberry, comfrey, *wakegi*, *fuki*, sesame, ginger, prickly ash, green bell peppers, red chili peppers, sweet green chili peppers, basil

Soil Dryness

Moist soil	Grow well	edible chrysanthemums, *okahijiki*, *mizuna*, cabbage, kale, kohlrabi, Boston lettuce, green beans, *sanjaku* cowpeas, okra, *daikon*-radish sprouts, icicle radishes, turnips, carrots, taro, *tacai*, Shaoxing cabbage, *caixin*, *hengcaitai*, bok choy, *qing-gen-cai*, *ensai*, Java spinach, Indian spinach, Chinese wolfberry, comfrey, Bermuda onions, garlic, *fuki*, beefsteak plant, ginger, prickly ash, fennel
	Grow moderately well	spinach, *komatsuna*, *aburana*, Chinese cabbage, *santō-sai*, *taisai*, *bitamin-na*, *fudan-sō*, yellow mustard, leaf mustard, sunny lettuce, endive, tomatoes, miniature tomatoes, eggplant, cucumbers, bitter melon, white melon, green soybeans, strawberries, sweet potatoes, parsley, green bell peppers, red chili peppers, sweet green chili peppers, basil

	Grow fairly poorly	flat chives, wild rocambole, sage, coriander
	Grow poorly	snow peas, peanuts, squash, potatoes, scallions, *wakegi*, sesame
	Grow well	peanuts, corn, squash, potatoes, flat chives, sesame, sage, coriander
	Grow moderately well	*aburana*, *santō-sai*, *taisai*, *bitamin-na*, *fudan-sō*, snow peas, green soybeans, sweet potatoes, comfrey, scallions, wild rocambole, prickly ash, red chili peppers, basil
Dry soil	Grow fairly poorly	*komatsuna*, cabbage, kale, Boston lettuce, sunny lettuce, endive, tomatoes, *daikon-radish* sprouts, Chinese wolfberry, *fuki*
	Grow poorly	spinach, Chinese cabbage, *okahijiki*, kohlrabi, eggplant, cucumbers, bitter melon, white melon, green beans, broad beans, okra, strawberries, *daikon* radishes, turnips, carrots, taro, *ensai*, Indian spinach, Bermuda onions, *wakegi*, garlic, parsley, beefsteak plant, ginger, sweet green chili peppers

3. Soil

Rich soil is alive with the activities of innumerable microorganisms and other life forms including bacteria, yeast fungi, primitive animals, and algae. As a consequence of conditions connected with oxygen quantities, temperature, moisture, sunlight penetration, and soil quality, different microorganisms inhabit different soil depths. Analysis has shown that, at a depth of about ten centimeters from the surface of the earth, the level at which they are most numerous, there are hundreds of millions of bacteria in one gram of soil. At deeper levels their numbers decrease.

At death, these small life forms rot and become nourishment absorbed by plants, which, when they wither, are broken down to become food for microorganisms. (The action of bacteria accounts for the complete disappearance of many of the birds and small animals that die in the world of nature.)

Soil conditions required by microorganisms—good ventilation, suitable warmth and moisture, and from neutrality to slight acidity—are the same conditions required for the cultivation of vegetables.

Kinds of Soil

Soil may be roughly classified into the following three types:
1. Sand—in which the grains of soil are coarse.
2. Loam—in which sand and clay are mixed at a ratio of two to one. A higher percentage of sand produces what is called sandy loam; and a high percentage of clay, what is called clayey loam.
3. Clay—in which the grains are very fine.
    Though well-ventilated, sand tends to dry out quickly. It becomes very warm during the day and cools off at night. The higher temperatures stimulate the action of fertilizers, which are, however, easily leached out because sand drains too well. And this speeds the aging of vegetables.
    Clay tends to pack tight and to hold water well and therefore can become too moist. It retains fertilizers a long time, but is poorly ventilated. Whereas it does not warm much during the day, it also does not cool sharply at night.
    Since it is both well-ventilated and moisture-retaining, loam is used for the cultivation of many vegetables. If the land you are going to work is either mostly clay or mostly sand, its quality can be adjusted by hauling in loads of the kind of soil in which yours is deficient. But selecting vegetable species that grow well in the kind of soil you have and then devising ways of watering and draining it and applying plentiful organic compost to it for two or three years will ensure success.

Preparing the Soil

In the present context, the term *preparing the soil* does not mean introducing large quantities of chemical fertilizers and artificially forcing plant growth. Instead, it refers to the process whereby the multiplication of microorganisms is stimulated in order to produce the kind of natural soil in which plants grow well.
    In preparing soil that has been packed firm by human feet and that supports no growth of weeds of any kind, it is necessary to improve soil ventilation by hoeing and then artificially to enrich the soil with the addition of natural organic compost.
    Weeds need no cultivation to flourish in the same places each year. This is because their roots loosen and ventilate the soil with countless small holes and their leaves fall and rot and are broken down through the action of microorganisms to become enriching organic nutrients. For this reason, when it is necessary to cut weeds and in harvesting vegetables that permit it, leaving the roots in the ground and cutting off only above-ground parts contribute greatly to natural improvement of the soil.

Soil Acidity

Many plants, for instance spinach and broad beans, dislike acid soil. Excessive soil acidity often results from using chemical fertilizers.
    In addition, tilling disrupts the delicately balanced natural ecology of plant roots and microorganisms and in this way increases soil acidity. Soil that has been naturally cultivated without weeding or tilling maintains the slight acidity suited to crop

growth. Moreover, this kind of agriculture prevents leaching of natural soil lime and renders additional dosage unnecessary. Indeed, heavy doses of lime applied to neutralize acidity caused by fertilizers render soil even more inorganic.

The system of agriculture that uses no chemical fertilizers or insecticides and that avoids tilling and weeding prevents excess acidity and destruction of the ecology, stimulates the activities of important earthworms, and through the enriching effects of rotting vegetable matter and of microorganisms keeps soil soft and in a condition of warmth and vitality.

Soil Characteristics

Sandy soil	Grow well in sand	*okahijiki*, peanuts, okra, potatoes, Java spinach, *ensai*, comfrey
	Grow well in sandy loam	*komatsuna*, edible chrysanthemums, *aburana*, *bitamin-na*, *fudan-sō*, cabbage, kale, kohlrabi, miniature tomatoes, corn, squash, radishes, turnips, carrots, scallions, sesame, basil, sage, coriander
Suited to loam		*komatsuna*, edible chrysanthemums, *aburana*, *santō-sai*, *taisai*, *bitamin-na*, *fudan-sō*, cabbage, Boston lettuce, sunny lettuce, endive, tomatoes, miniature tomatoes, bitter melon, white melon, snow peas, broad beans, peanuts, *sanjaku* cowpeas, okra, strawberries, icicle radishes, burdock, *tacai*, *caixin*, *hengcaitai*, bok choy, *quig-gen-cai*, *ensai*, scallions, Chinese wolfberry, *wakegi*, flat chives, wild rocambole, parsley, sesame, ginger, prickly ash, green bell peppers, fennel
Clayey soil	Grow well in clayey loam	spinach, *komatsuna*, Chinese cabbage, *mizuna*, yellow mustard, leaf mustard, cabbage, tomatoes, eggplant, cucumbers, bitter melon, turnips, *ensai*, Indian spinach, scallions, Bermuda onions, *fuki*, parsley, beefsteak plant, ginger, green bell peppers, sweet green chili peppers, *Fushimi* peppers
	Grow well in clay	sweet potatoes, garlic, broad beans

Acidity tolerance

Intolerant	spinach, *fudan-sō*, tomatoes, eggplant, bitter melon, snow peas, green beans,

	broad beans, *sanjaku* cowpeas, scallions
Moderately intolerant	cabbage, kohlrabi, miniature tomatoes, cucumbers, white melon, green soybeans, radishes, icicle radishes, turnips, carrots, Bermuda onions, garlic, flat chives, parsley, ginger, green bell peppers, sweet green chili peppers, *Fushimi* peppers
Moderately tolerant	*komatsuna*, edible chrysanthemums, *aburana*, Chinese cabbage, *santō-sai, taisai, bitamin-na, okahijiki, mizuna*, yellow mustard, leaf mustard, sunny lettuce, endive, peanuts, corn, squash, okra, *daikon* radishes, turnips, *tacai*, Shaoxing cabbage, *caixin, hengcaitai*, bok choy, *qing-gen-cai, ensai*, Java spinach, Indian spinach, sesame, beefsteak plant, red chili peppers, basil, sage, coriander
Tolerant	strawberries, potatoes, Chinese wolfberry, comfrey, wild rocambole, fennel

4. Weeds

Seeded by the wind, surviving winter colds, and each year putting out fresh buds and leaves in their various seasons, weeds play a vital role in cultivation because their roots, some of which penetrate deep and some of which remain at shallow depths, loosen the soil and vitalize it with oxygen and enrich it with nutrients when they themselves wither and rot. In other words, not merely taking from it, they return nutrients to the soil. Consequently, when weeds are plentiful, soil is rich in organic material and alive with the activities of microorganisms, earthworms, insects, and small animals.

A covering of weeds protects crop plants from the damage and possible contagious diseases that result from their being splashed with mud in rain storms. Stripping the ground of weed cover, produces a dusty, dense upper crust that hardens, reducing ventilation, strangling crop roots, and thus necessitating further tilling.

Seeding themselves yearly, weeds thriving among vegetable rows in gardens or in open farm fields illustrate the vigor possible as long as natural ecological balance is preserved. And in fields where organic materials are naturally accumulated as the result of the operations of weeds, vegetable crops too get the requisite amounts of sunlight and, absorbing abundant nutrients from the soil, thrive.

In the summer, from June to August, the once low weed cover grows tall enough to compete with crops for sunlight and comes to require cutting. The weeds should not be uprooted, however, but should instead be cut at the ground line. Their above-ground parts may be spread around plants to serve as compost and to prevent evaporation of ground moisture. Since they constitute a kind of immature compost, however, cut weeds must not be mixed with the soil.

Once summer weeds have been cut, crop seeds may be sown. As autumn weeds do not grow tall, the seedlings will have plenty of latitude to grow fairly large before cold weather sets in. Low winter weeds surrounding them cover the earth and protect crops from cold.

Leaving weeds in place has a number of good effects; it reduces evaporation of ground moisture thus protecting plants from the damage caused by aridity and it protects roots by blocking strong sunlight and thus lowering ground temperatures in summer. In addition, while stimulating their appearance in large numbers, weeds give insects something other than crop plants to eat and in this way reduce insect damage.

In short, instead of regarding them with hostility, it is wiser to realize that weeds loosen the soil and provide important nutrition and to allow them to grow together with vegetables in a natural ecological system.

5. Repeated and Rotated Cultivation

Planting the same crop year after year on the same plot—repeated cultivation—can result in the abnormal thriving of harmful bacteria that are especially strongly attracted to the kind of vegetable being grown there. In nature, the world of plants and the world of animals, including microorganisms, preserve a delicate balance. Without human intervention, a similar balance obtains between the harmful and helpful microorganisms in the soil. Heavy use of chemical pesticides and fertilizers, however, upsets this balance by killing the microorganisms that normally would feed on the harmful bacteria. To prevent this, it is necessary to ensure adequate organic matter in the soil through the use of plenty of mature compost.

Another step that should be taken to reduce this kind of damage is to avoid repeated cultivation of plants that are highly susceptible to damage from bacteria and to rotate them on the plot with some other crop.

In rotational planting, several different kinds of vegetables are grown in succession on the same land. The cycle returns to the first kind of vegetable after from two to five years. In other words, first, vegetable A is planted. The following year, vegetable B, and not vegetable A, is grown on that same plot. B is replaced in successive years with vegetables C, D, and E. And, then, the cycles begin again with vegetable A.

A cultivation plan is easy to arrange if the longest resting period is allowed to vegetable A and other vegetable crops are carefully combined with it.

Legumes and members of the nightshade (*Solanum*) family are especially prone to damage from repeated cultivation, which should be avoided not only for individual plant types, but also for members of the same family. The tomato, the eggplant, green bell peppers, and potatoes are all members of the nightshade family and therefore should not be cultivated successively on the same piece of land. For instance, if eggplant is grown one year, none of the other members of the nightshade family should be raised on that ground for from four to five years. Since growing eggplant on all of a small plot one year means no eggplant crops from that plot for four or five years, it is best to subdivide fields into small patches to make possible rotation and successive harvests of these vegetables without damaging the soil. The same thing is true of the legumes.

The following methods help minimize damage from repeated cultivation. After raising corn (maize), which drains the soil of nutrients, on the same plot the following year raise beans, which require less nutrition. Since beans enrich the soil, follow them on a piece of land with leafy vegetables requiring no fertilizing. From the standpoint of loosening the soil, it is effective to follow crops of shallow-rooted plants like turnips and cucumbers with spinach, tomatoes, and okra, the roots of which sink deep. Instead of planting a whole field in one crop only, subdividing and planting small areas in a variety of crops reduce damage from insects. In short, natural cultivation using plenty of mature compost and effective rotation prevents the kinds of damage that result from repeated cultivation.

Repeated Cultivation

Plants lending themselves to repeated cultivation	spinach, *komatsuna*, edible chrysanthemums, *aburana*, *santō-sai*, *taisai*, *bitamin-na*, *fudan-sō*, *okahijiki*, *mizuna*, yellow mustard, leaf mustard, corn, squash, okra, *tacai*, *caixin*, *hengcaitai*, bok choy, *qing-gen-cai*, Java spinach, Indian spinach, Chinese wolfberry, comfrey, flat chives, wild rocambole, *fuki*, sesame, beefsteak plant, prickly ash, basil, sage, coriander, fennel
Plantable in two-year cycles	peanuts, *daikon* radishes, *daikon*-radish sprouts, radishes, icicle radishes, turnips, burdock, sweet potatoes, *ensai*
Plantable in three-year cycles	Chinese cabbage, cabbage, kale, kohlrabi, Boston lettuce, sunny lettuce, endive, cucumbers, bitter melon, white melon, green soybeans, strawberries, carrots, Shaoxing cabbage, scallions, *hanegi*, Bermuda onions, *wakegi*, parsley, ginger
Plantable in four-year cycles	tomatoes, miniature tomatoes, potatoes
Plantable in five-year cycles	eggplant, snow peas, green beans, broad beans, *sanjaku* cowpeas, green bell peppers, red chili peppers, sweet green chili peppers, *Fushimi* peppers, taro

6. Fertilizer

The natural ecology is a communal entity of mutually and variously interrelated animals, plants, and microorganisms. And it is the variety of these beings that prevents the balance of the world of nature from crumbling. The whole ecological structure, in which all creatures live together, each in its own realm, is far too wonderful for the human intellect to grasp.

What we call vegetables are in effect no more than plants that, originally thought of as weeds, have been selected by human beings for the ease with which they can be eaten and have therefore been gradually improved. Agricultural fields first came into being when human beings began raising a single kind of vegetable on a given plot of land. In land where weeds grow the soil contains the requisite nutrients; and plants bud afresh each year. But fields that have been weeded lack nutrients and, as might be expected, require fertilizing.

The natural method of cultivation takes into full consideration the importance of microorganisms, weeds, and insects and, avoiding chemical pesticides and fertilizers, strives to raise vegetables in a natural state, together with weeds. Indeed, vegetable crops grown in this way have the zestier tastes of wild plants and are richer in nutrients than those that have been poisoned with agricultural chemicals and insecticides.

There are no vegetables that cannot thrive without chemical fertilizers. Unless it has been sterilized with pesticides and other chemicals, natural soil is constantly producing its own nutrients as countless microorganisms break down plant and animal remains. Leafy vegetables and beans will grow well in soil that has been enriched in no more than this natural way.

But a virtually total lack of nutrients will not support vegetable life and growth. And such plants as tomatoes, eggplant, and okra require supplemental fertilizing if they are to bear well. In organic farming, mature compost is used as the supplement.

Some plants—tomatoes and cucumbers—thrive and bear very well if fertilized with guano or pressed soy meal (the product left when oil is pressed from soybeans). But these materials cannot be used with complete safety since, when broken down by microorganisms in the soil, they generate heat and noxious gases that attack plant roots and stunt growth. Seedlings that have been weakened in this way fall victim to insect damage readily. Consequently, when they must be used directly, mix dried guano or soybean waste with the soil at least three or four weeks prior to sowing or to final planting to give the breakdown and fermentation processes time to take place. The use of mature compost—that is, material that has been fermented so that its nutrients may be returned to the soil—is the safest way to avoid mistakes in organic cultivation.

The following elements are required by plants.

Nitrogen.   Nitrogen contributes to good leaf and stalk growth. In overabundance, however, it reduces plants' resistance to illness and can impede fruiting in beans and other vegetables.

Phosphorus.   Phosphorus strengthens roots and seeds, increases power to generate roots, strengthens plant tissues, and improves resistance to disease and insects. In addition, it improves blooming, increases sugar content in fruits, and enhances flavor.

Potassium.   Especially important to beans and other seed-bearing plants and to root vegetables, potassium improves resistance to cold and heat. Administered in large quantities, however, it causes deficiencies by suppressing intake of lime and magnesia.

Calcium.   Calcium neutralizes acids formed in plants, strengthens tissues, and neutralizes soil acidity.

Magnesium. Magnesium improves intake of phosphoric acid and contributes to the production of chlorophyll. This is why magnesium deficiency results in poor leaf color.

In addition to these, plants require a number of trace elements, which are naturally present in the soil and which are connected with the prevention of disease and insect damage.

As has been indicated, natural soil is beautifully balanced and is of the utmost importance in vegetable cultivation. Consequently, when nutrition must be added to a field, it should be fully fermented—that is, mature—compost. Once the soil has come to life again and is rich in organic matter, fertilizer-free cultivation may be practiced with assured results.

Compost Preparation

Compost is prepared in order to avoid applying organic fertilizers directly to crops. It has no ill effects on plants since fermentation has already taken place in it. It is prepared from dried grasses or straw with which cow dung or guano plus earth, lime, and water have been mixed.

Two or three weeks after the mixture has been prepared, it must be well raked and turned to stimulate the action of microorganisms. The raking and turning should be repeated once or twice. The compost will be mature within three months in summer and within six months in winter. There are many ways of preparing compost; but merely heaping up cut summer grasses and weeds and exposing them to the weather for a period of time produces good, natural nutritional material.

Characteristic Features of Organic Cultivation Using Compost
• In contrast to chemical fertilizers, which harden the soil, impede drainage, and contribute to the accumulation of harmful substances, compost improves both drainage and ventilation and stimulates the activity of the aerobic bacteria that assist plant growth. Loose soil stimulates root growth and, because of its high water-retaining ability, prevents dryness.
• Soil fertilized in this way harbors many earthworms, which have a further enriching effect. Chemical fertilizers acidify the soil, making it inhospitable to earthworms.
• Soil to which organic compost has been added is warm because it retains the heat of sunlight. In summer, however, it protects roots from direct sun.
• A human way of returning soil to a natural condition, fertilizing with compost is safe and greatly reduces damage from disease and insects.
• Because they are strong, vegetables raised in such soil are nutritious and delicious.

Production of compost for a vegetable garden approximately 33 m² in area
(materials set down in October)
• Ingredients

Guano or cow dung	40 kg
Pressed soy meal	3 kg
Rice bran	10 kg
Bone meal	3 kg

Ground limestone such as dolomite   1.5 kg
Cut weeds and grasses (dried or green) from an area of about 16 m²
• About two hours are required for preparation.

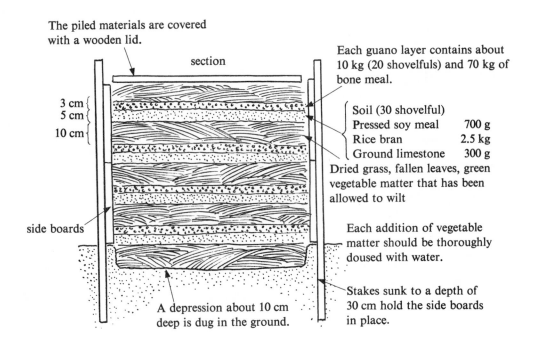

The piled materials are covered with a wooden lid.

section

3 cm
5 cm
10 cm

side boards

A depression about 10 cm deep is dug in the ground.

Each guano layer contains about 10 kg (20 shovelfuls) and 70 kg of bone meal.

Soil (30 shovelful)
Pressed soy meal   700 g
Rice bran   2.5 kg
Ground limestone   300 g
Dried grass, fallen leaves, green vegetable matter that has been allowed to wilt

Each addition of vegetable matter should be thoroughly doused with water.

Stakes sunk to a depth of 30 cm hold the side boards in place.

It is a good idea to make a frame for the compost in the following way. But, if materials are lacking, the kitchen wastes may simply be piled on the ground and covered with a sheet of some kind or with dried weeds.
• Materials
stakes   8 thick stakes about 1.2 m long
boards   8 boards about 1 m long and 30 cm wide

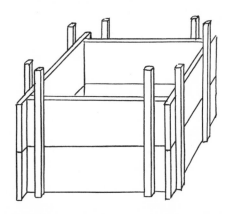

Compost from kitchen waste
Unpolluted vegetable and animal scraps from the kitchen, mixed with pressed soy meal or fallen leaves and soil, are allowed to stand to produce compost.

Preparing plant and wood ash
Ash may be made by burning thoroughly dried weeds, leaves, branches, and twigs. Paper and other materials containing potentially harmful substances should be avoided. The materials should not be burned in agricultural fields or vegetable patches since fire kills beneficial microorganisms.

Elements readily available in compost materials

Material	Nitrogen	Phosphorus	Potassium	Major constituent elements
dried guano (chicken)	O	O		mainly phosphoric acid and nitrogen
dried cow dung				elements present in smaller quantities than in dried guano
dried guano (quail)		O		elements present in larger quantities than in chicken guano
pressed soy meal	O			a nitrogen fertilizer that contains phosphoric acid
rice bran		O		mainly phosphoric acid
bone meal		◎		a phosphoric-acid fertilizer containing lime
fish meal	O	O	O	a potassium fertilizer containing lime
wood ash			O	a potassium fertilizer containing lime
grass ash			O	contains less potassium than wood ash
dried (green) grasses				includes trace elements of nitrogen and potassium

7. Insect Pests

Having decided that it is harmful, human beings destroy certain kinds of insect life with pesticides. At the same time, however, they kill insect life that, beneficial as an important part of the ecological system, prevents the abnormal proliferation of harmful creatures. By eating wholesome foods and maintaining powers of resistance, we human beings stay in good health in spite of the many pathogenic bacteria existing in our bodies. When resistance drops, however, some of those bacteria cause sickness.

The situation is similar with plants, which are nourished by such organic elements in the soil as the decomposed bodies of various microorganisms and of many other kinds of creatures broken down by the action of bacteria and fungi. The richer the soil in organic material, the healthier the plants and the stronger their resistance to harmful bacteria. When resistance is low, however, illness brought on by those bacteria causes great damage.

By devouring them as food, beneficial bacteria keep down the numbers of pathogenic bacteria, which, however, multiply in excess when, for some reason or another, numbers of beneficial bacteria decrease. Clearly a major cause of such decrease is the use of chemical fertilizers and insecticides, which destroy microorganisms that, as nutrients in the soil, are intimately connected with the rules of the natural cycles.

The damage done by chemicals is readily apparent to our eyes. They destroy microorganisms and thus weaken plants by cutting off their supply of nutrition. In addition, they destroy beneficial bacteria, thereby stimulating the abnormal proliferation of harmful bacteria, which have remarkably strong and apparently annually escalating powers of resistance to pesticides.

In the world of nature, a field without insects is unthinkable; and plants are safer and more natural for being somewhat insect-eaten. As long as the ecological system remains largely undisturbed, such predator insects as praying mantises and spiders will keep the number of pests that damage crops to a reasonable limit.

The excess use of nitrogen fertilizers and immature compost increases the numbers of aphids, grubs, and other harmful insects that damage crops. An excellent way to deal with many of these pests is to plant in the garden varieties of flowers and vegetables that produce smells or have other characteristics that insects do not like. Some of these are garlic, sage, mint, marigolds, icicle radishes and so on. This kind of communal planting has the additional benefits of inhibiting the development of harmful bacteria and of promoting efficient use of limited garden space. In planning, however, it is important to consider the characteristics of the plants to be grown together. Plants with deep roots should be grown with shallow-rooted ones. Tall plants should be combined with low ones out of consideration for sunlight, and so on.

In the past, extraordinary emergence of insects in vast numbers has been rare. Even the notorious plagues of locusts and grasshoppers are said to have been the outcome of massive doses of agricultural chemicals that killed off the birds that naturally would have fed on the insects. It would be a grave error to perpetrate the vicious circle by spraying the insects with pesticides that could then be brought into vegetable gardens.

Insecticides infiltrate the roots, stalks, leaves, and fruits of plants. No matter how the vegetables are prepared in the kitchen, the permeating insecticides cannot be removed. Furthermore, there is no way for us to ascertain the extent of their residue. Consequently, for the sake of our own safety and to regulate the numbers of insect pests in our gardens, it is best to follow the natural system of cultivation. In short, as long as the soil maintains good balance and the crops are healthy, numbers of harmful insects will be restricted. Natural cultivation with compost is the best and smoothest way to achieve these aims.

Chapter II Raising Your Own Vegetables

Year-round Work Flow Sheet

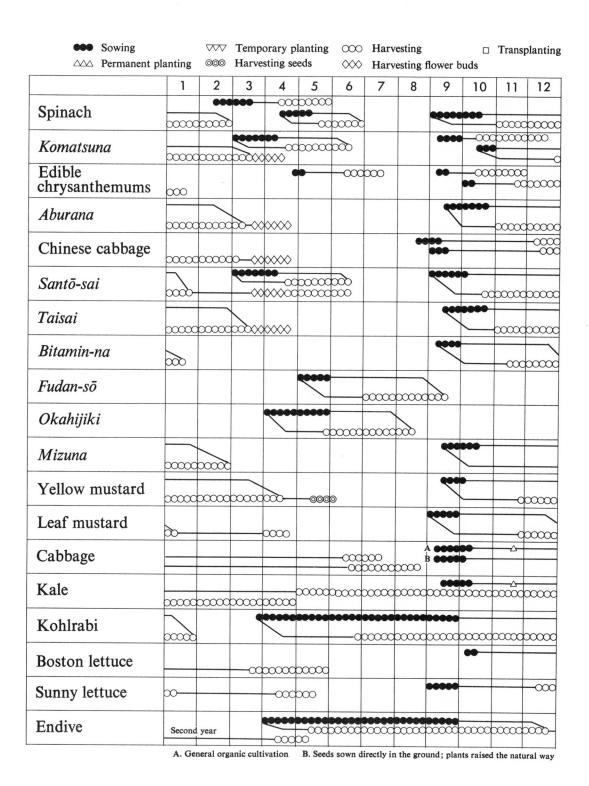

	1	2	3	4	5	6	7	8	9	10	11	12
Tomatoes					Sowing Seedlings							
Miniature tomatoes												
Eggplant					Sowing Seedlings							
Cucumbers												
Bitter melon												
White melon												
Snow peas												
Green beans (String beans)				Vines No vines								
Green soybeans												
Broad beans												
Peanuts												
Sanjaku cowpeas												
Sprouts					— — —Any time— — —				— — —Any time— — —			
Corn (Maize)												
Squash												
Okra												
Strawberries		Later than second year										
Daikon radishes												
Daikon-radish sprouts												
Radishes												
Icicle radishes												
Turnips												

	1	2	3	4	5	6	7	8	9	10	11	12
Carrots								3 inch / 5 inch				
Burdock	Second year											
Taro												
Sweet potatoes												
Potatoes												
Tacai												
Shaoxing cabbage												
Caixin												
Hengcaitai												
Bok choy												
Qing-gen-cai												
Ensai												
Java spinach												
Indian spinach												
Chinese wolfberry	Planting roots / Later than second year			Any time								
Comfrey	Planting roots / Later than second year			Any time								
Scallions												
Hanegi												
Bermuda onions							Early variety / Medium variety					
Wakegi												
Garlic						Moderately warm region / Warm region						
Flat chives (*Nira*)	Second year / Later than third year											

	1	2	3	4	5	6	7	8	9	10	11	12
Wild rocambole	Later than second year											
Fuki (Wild coltsfoot)	Later than second year — Flower heads			Planting roots								
Sesame												
Parsley												
Beefsteak plant (Shiso)	Naturally germinating											
Ginger							Sprout		Root			
Prickly ash (Sansho)	Later than second year			New leaves			Green berries		Mature berries			
Green bell peppers	Sowing / Seedlings											
Red chili peppers	Sowing / Seedlings											
Sweet green chili peppers												
Fushimi peppers												
Basil												
Sage	Later than second year											
Coriander												
Fennel	Florence / Florence											

Spinach

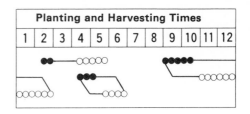
Apparently in Japan, heavy rains leach alkaline elements from the soil, which therefore tends to acidity. The use of chemical fertilizers has aggravated the situation. But natural organic cultivation calls for neutral or slightly acid soil, since these conditions are most conducive to good crop growth.

Because spinach reacts badly to acid, it is essential to use lime to neutralize the soil. But it must be remembered that excessive lime too can inhibit growth.

Sowing: A hard seed shell accounts for the low germination rate of spinach seeds, unless they are sown under optimum conditions. The best time is immediately after a rain. In dry weather, thoroughly water the soil in the seedling bed before sowing. Thereafter, water moderately and maintain suitable moisture without allowing the soil to dry out.

Insects: Spinach can be attacked by cutworms or *Barathra brassicae*, which, though inactive during the day, chew through leaf petioles at night. Signs of the presence of these insects at plant bases are wilted shoots and leaves that have dropped after having been chewed off. To protect plants from the danger of total destruction, these insects must be carefully removed, without resort to chemical pesticides. Spinach is, however, much less susceptible to insect damage than many other plants.

Fertilizers: Spinach may be grown without additional fertilizers in fields in which organic material is abundant. In the case of fields on which nothing has been grown for a long time, however, fertilize as shown in the accompanying diagrams. Vegetables grown without fertilizer resist illness better and are much better-tasting than those raised with chemicals. In spring, spinach may be harvested from forty to fifty days after sowing; in autumn, fifty days after sowing.

One Month before Sowing

Digging deep and working it into the soil thoroughly, add 100 g of lime to every 1 m² of the plot.

Two Weeks before Sowing

Spread a bucketful of mature compost evenly over the soil and work it in thoroughly to a depth of 20–30 cm. If you have not prepared mature compost, three weeks before sowing mix 1 kg of well-pulverized guano with the soil.

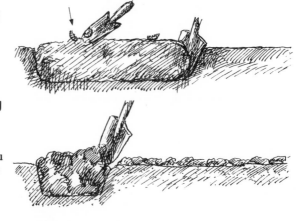

Remove all insects from the soil.

After the soil has been prepared, make a furrow the size shown in the drawing and flatten its top.

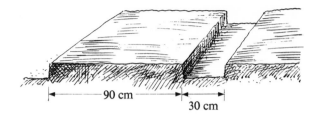

90 cm — 30 cm

If spinach has grown poorly in the field to which you have annually added lime, results will improve if you stop these additions. Excess of lime has a greater inhibiting effect on spinach growth than acidity.

Spinacia tetrandra   *Spinacia oleracia*

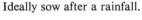
—spinach seed —
(actual size)

Sowing

Turn the upper layers of the soil over to check for such insect pests as *Barathra brassicae* or *Anomala rufocuprea*, which lurk not far from the surface.

Ideally sow after a rainfall.

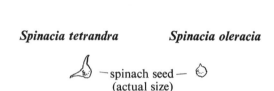

Water the soil before sowing.

Prepare troughs for either row sowing, which produces large harvests, or scatter sowing. Water beforehand and sow throughout the troughs at an interval of 1–2 cm.

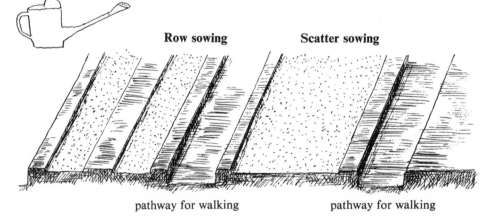

Row sowing   **Scatter sowing**

pathway for walking   pathway for walking

Cover the seeds with a layer of soil 2 or 3 times as deep as they are thick and press it lightly. Dryness is one cause of poor germination of spinach seeds. But, by inhibiting oxygen intake, excess moisture too can inhibit germination. After sowing, the soil should be maintained in a state of suitable moistness—ideally, a degree of moisture permitting seed cases to dry gradually.

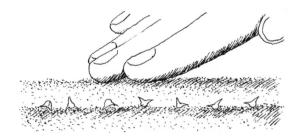

Germination

Growth is slow until 2
true leaves have emerged.

The natural staggered germination of spinach
seeds has the advantage of lengthening the
harvest period.

true leaves

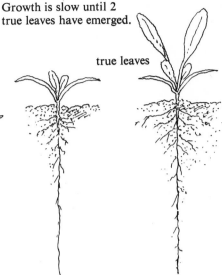

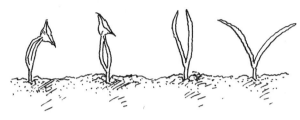

A certain amount of crowding is good
since it increases the harvest. There is no
need to thin the plants even if they overlap.

The main root penetrates straight
and deep. It and the innumerable
lateral rootlets keep winter plants
robust.

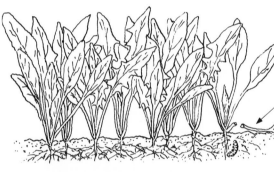

Fallen leaves cut at the bases and shriveled
shoots are certain signs of the presence of
cutworms or *Barathra brassicae* at the
roots. Unless they are removed, small
seedlings will be completely devoured.

Slender, straight-standing
leaves are developing well as
can be expected if seeds were
planted after a rain and if
sunny weather continues
thereafter.

When eight, large, fully open
leaves have developed, it is
time to harvest some plants
and, in the process, thin.

Thinning

When thinning, make sure plants remain close enough to each other to prevent their leaves from drooping to the ground. Press the soil around the base with the fingers of the opposite hand as you pull the plant from the soil.

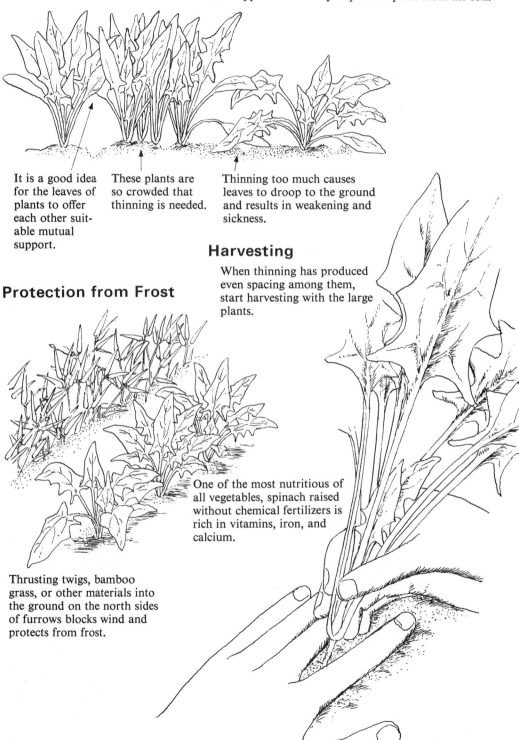

It is a good idea for the leaves of plants to offer each other suitable mutual support.

These plants are so crowded that thinning is needed.

Thinning too much causes leaves to droop to the ground and results in weakening and sickness.

Harvesting

When thinning has produced even spacing among them, start harvesting with the large plants.

Protection from Frost

One of the most nutritious of all vegetables, spinach raised without chemical fertilizers is rich in vitamins, iron, and calcium.

Thrusting twigs, bamboo grass, or other materials into the ground on the north sides of furrows blocks wind and protects from frost.

Komatsuna

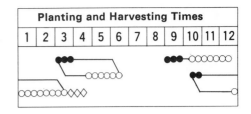
In Japan, this leafy vegetable is popular for home vegetable gardens because it is not finicky about soil and can be raised in the same ground for several years in a row. Because it is tolerant of both cold and heat, *komatsuna* can be raised year round. But, owing to insect damage, when following the natural organic cultivation system, it is best to avoid the summer. *Komatsuna* raised in the winter is little harmed by insects, delicious, and of good quality.

Various gardening manuals advocate, as a matter of course, the use of organic fertilizers accompanied by chemical fertilizers and insecticides. Although I concur in the need for organic matter, I consider the use of chemical fertilizers and pest killers far more harmful than useful in connection with the quality of the soil. For that reason, in the case of leafy, quick-maturing vegetables like *komatsuna*, I recommend using no fertilizers at all. They grow well as a follow-up on land where the preceding crop has been legumes or fruiting plants. The organic fertilizers left in the soil from the crop of the preceding year or even from the year before that is sufficient for leafy vegetables.

Preparations of the Seedling Bed

Sowing

Use 3 or 4 shovelfuls of organic compost for each 1 m² of plot and mix well.

Water the soil before sowing seeds.

When natural organic compost is unavailable, mix dried guano 200 g per 1 m² with 3 or 4 handfuls of vegetable ash and spread this in the bottom of the trough made as shown in the drawing. Cover this with soil.

sowing trough

furrow width

—50 cm—

15 cm

50 cm

covering soil

fertilizer

15 cm

seed rows 10 cm apart

Make a shallow trough in the soil 15 cm wide. In this make 2 rows of seeds 10 cm apart. Cover the seeds with a layer of soil 2 or 3 times as thick as the seeds.

In soil that is enriched by being maintained in a natural condition, these vegetables thrive without fertilizer and suffer from little insect damage. In the early stage, *komatsuna* grows slowly but soon picks up speed and, raised free of polluting chemicals, produces glossy, well-fleshed leaves.

Germination

Three to four days after sowing.

Thinning

After 1 or 2 true leaves have developed, thin from over-crowded regions, beginning with damaged or long, straggling seedlings.

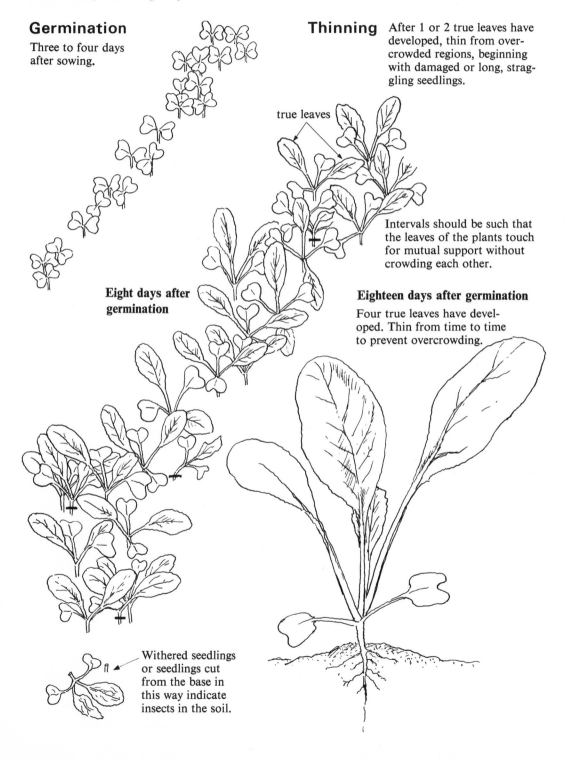

true leaves

Intervals should be such that the leaves of the plants touch for mutual support without crowding each other.

Eight days after germination

Eighteen days after germination

Four true leaves have developed. Thin from time to time to prevent overcrowding.

Withered seedlings or seedlings cut from the base in this way indicate insects in the soil.

Harvesting

Plants from seeds sown in the middle or late September in soil treated with organic fertilizer may be harvested thirty days after germination. In the early stage, plants raised in unfertilized soil grow slowly but begin to develop more rapidly from about mid-November and produce thick, delicious leaves with little insect damage. It is better to allow *komatsuna* to mature fully instead of rushing harvest.

In the spring, *komatsuna* sends out stalks and blooms. Like those of a number of other leafy vegetables, *komatsuna* buds, plucked before blooming, are considered a great springtime delicacy in Japan.

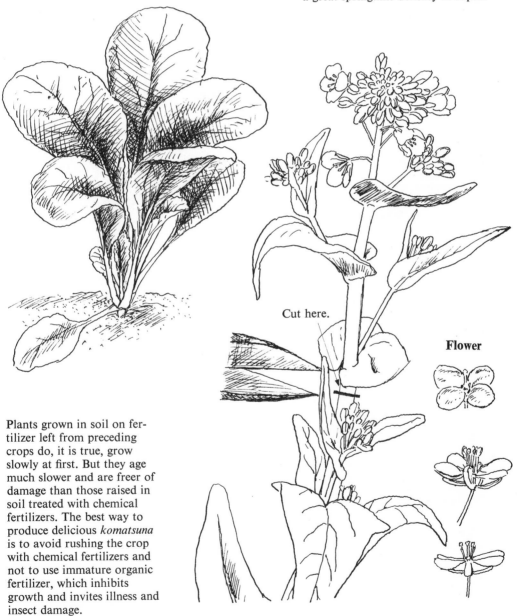

Cut here.

Flower

Plants grown in soil on fertilizer left from preceding crops do, it is true, grow slowly at first. But they age much slower and are freer of damage than those raised in soil treated with chemical fertilizers. The best way to produce delicious *komatsuna* is to avoid rushing the crop with chemical fertilizers and not to use immature organic fertilizer, which inhibits growth and invites illness and insect damage.

Harvesting Seeds

After blooming, allow large, robust plants to remain in the ground as a source of seeds.

Select sturdy plants free of insect damage.

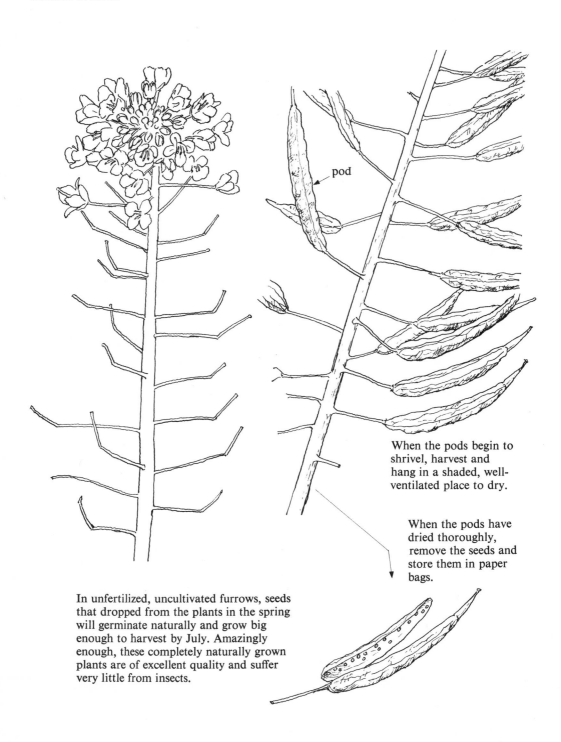

pod

When the pods begin to shrivel, harvest and hang in a shaded, well-ventilated place to dry.

When the pods have dried thoroughly, remove the seeds and store them in paper bags.

In unfertilized, uncultivated furrows, seeds that dropped from the plants in the spring will germinate naturally and grow big enough to harvest by July. Amazingly enough, these completely naturally grown plants are of excellent quality and suffer very little from insects.

Edible Chrysanthemums

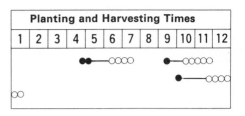

Planting and Harvesting Times											
1	2	3	4	5	6	7	8	9	10	11	12

It is said that once people invariably raised their own edible chrysanthemums, which wilt too quickly to withstand transport to distant markets and therefore have no commercial value a fairly short time after they have been harvested. Nonetheless, they are delicious when eaten fresh and are a good home-garden crop because they may be planted several years running on the same plot, are subject to little insect damage, and thrive on no more fertilizer than what remains in the ground from preceding crops.

Sowing: Like spinach seeds, edible-chrysanthemum seeds are covered with a thick case. For best germination, this case should first be softened by the moisture in the soil. Too much moisture, however, like that of a heavy rain immediately after sowing, saturates the case, thus virtually suffocating the seeds and inhibiting germination. Shock too plays a part in the lowered germination rate of seeds subjected to heavy rain immediately after having been sown.

Ideally, these seeds should be sown after a rain and should then be given a dry period until germination. In Japan, the best time is from the middle of October until early November. Seeds sown at this time have the longest harvest period. Since, even under good conditions, their germination rate is low, edible-chrysanthemum seeds should be fairly heavily sown.

Sowing

After a rainfall, plant seeds in 2 rows about 10 cm apart. Cover with a layer of soil 1–2 cm thick and press lightly. Sow fairly heavily.

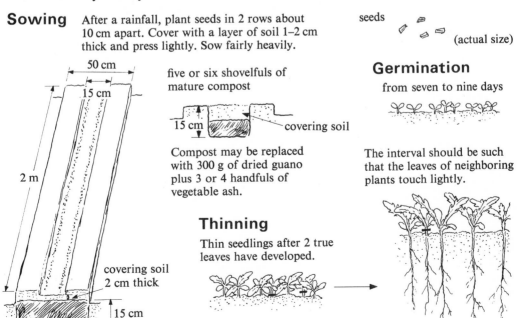

50 cm

15 cm

2 m

covering soil
2 cm thick

15 cm

five or six shovelfuls of mature compost

15 cm   covering soil

Compost may be replaced with 300 g of dried guano plus 3 or 4 handfuls of vegetable ash.

Thinning

Thin seedlings after 2 true leaves have developed.

seeds   (actual size)

Germination

from seven to nine days

The interval should be such that the leaves of neighboring plants touch lightly.

Thinning and harvesting: Thin edible chrysanthemums to an interval of 10–12 cm between plants. At harvest time for seeds sown in the fall, do not pull plants up by the roots. Instead, if they are crowded, pinch of the top three or four sections of the central stalk. In the case of uncrowded conditions, more than four sections may be pinched off. New, lateral buds will emerge from the sections below the place where the first leaves were harvested, providing more leaves for later harvest.

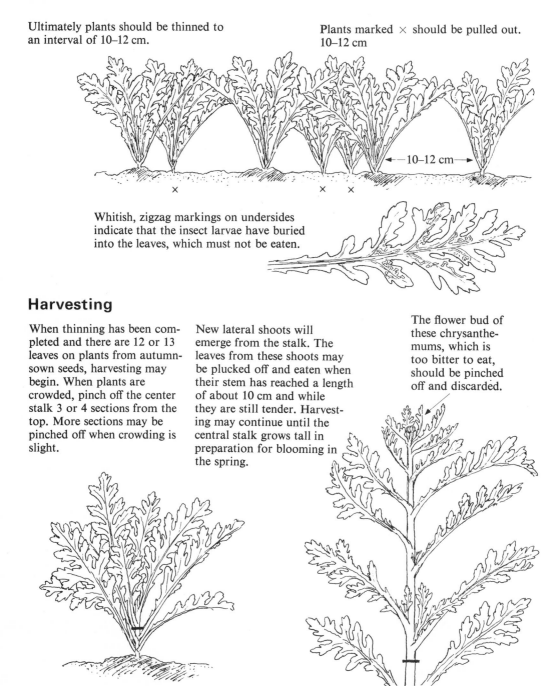

Ultimately plants should be thinned to an interval of 10–12 cm.

Plants marked × should be pulled out. 10–12 cm

←—10–12 cm—→

Whitish, zigzag markings on undersides indicate that the insect larvae have buried into the leaves, which must not be eaten.

Harvesting

When thinning has been completed and there are 12 or 13 leaves on plants from autumn-sown seeds, harvesting may begin. When plants are crowded, pinch off the center stalk 3 or 4 sections from the top. More sections may be pinched off when crowding is slight.

New lateral shoots will emerge from the stalk. The leaves from these shoots may be plucked off and eaten when their stem has reached a length of about 10 cm and while they are still tender. Harvesting may continue until the central stalk grows tall in preparation for blooming in the spring.

The flower bud of these chrysanthemums, which is too bitter to eat, should be pinched off and discarded.

Aburana

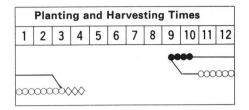

Planting and Harvesting Times											
1	2	3	4	5	6	7	8	9	10	11	12

It is easiest and best to raise vegetables so that they can be consumed at the time of year when they are most delicious and when they manifest their own inherent traits to the fullest. Appearance does not determine quality. It makes no difference if a cucumber is crooked, if a head of cabbage is small, if scallions are short, or if leafy vegetables have holes in them. Taste and safety are the primary considerations. No matter how flawless and beautiful, vegetables permeated with chemical fertilizers and insecticides can scarcely be called excellent. I first discovered the true beauty of vegetables when I began organic agriculture without the use of chemical fertilizers. The glossy leafy vegetables I raise are far lovelier than products offered in most green grocers.

Aburana, like the vegetables discussed on the preceding pages, can be raised with no more fertilizer than what remains in the soil from preceding crops. *Aburana*, *komatsuna*, *taisai*, and *santō-sai* were all once raised by farmers exclusively for their own families' consumption. The leaves of *aburana* are good raw in salads.

Sowing: Since they tolerate low temperatures well, *aburana* seeds may merely be scattered in the autumn, when harmful insects are scarce, in ground where fruiting crops or legumes were grown. There is no need to work the soil if another crop has just been harvested from it. But, if cutworms and *Barathra brassicae* tend to be numerous, dig to a depth of about 5 cm to check for their presence and remove any you find. Left in the ground, these insects will destroy all seedlings. Often apparently low germination rate is actually to be attributed to damage from these insects.

Preparations

These plants grow well without additional fertilizer in ground from which fruiting plants or legumes have recently been harvested. If compost is used, do not work the soil too much. Simply spread the compost on the surface.

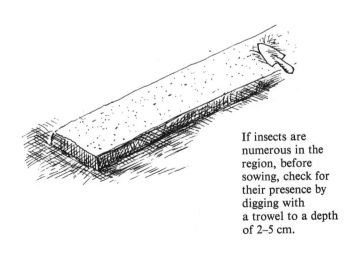

If insects are numerous in the region, before sowing, check for their presence by digging with a trowel to a depth of 2–5 cm.

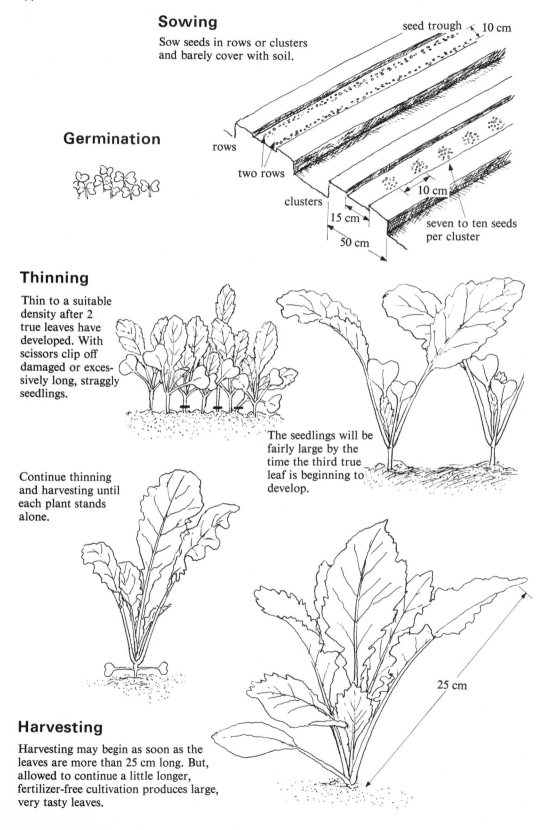

Sowing

Sow seeds in rows or clusters and barely cover with soil.

seed trough
10 cm

Germination

rows

two rows

clusters

15 cm

50 cm

10 cm

seven to ten seeds per cluster

Thinning

Thin to a suitable density after 2 true leaves have developed. With scissors clip off damaged or excessively long, straggly seedlings.

The seedlings will be fairly large by the time the third true leaf is beginning to develop.

Continue thinning and harvesting until each plant stands alone.

25 cm

Harvesting

Harvesting may begin as soon as the leaves are more than 25 cm long. But, allowed to continue a little longer, fertilizer-free cultivation produces large, very tasty leaves.

Chinese Cabbage

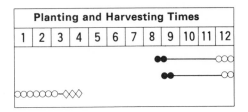

Planting and Harvesting Times

1	2	3	4	5	6	7	8	9	10	11	12

Two or three years ago, I had a mole in my garden. I could tell from the mounds the creature made as it moved about, just under the surface, in my land. No doubt, moles travel in these shallow subterranean areas because of an abundance of grubs and other insects to feed on. About a year ago, I stopped seeing the mole; and in its place appeared a great quantity of earthworms—more than I have ever seen in a field: several can be found in each shovelful of soil dug up. Since it is now very fertile, I no longer use a hoe in the ground where these earthworms live.

More fertilizer is needed to make Chinese cabbage head than is used with other leafy vegetables. But, if the soil is rich, a little mature compost heaped around the base of the plant is enough. Since it is intolerant of high temperatures, Chinese cabbage is usually sown in the early autumn and harvested in the winter.

Preparations

About two or three weeks before sowing, make a furrow 4 m long and 40 cm wide. Dig a trough in the furrow and spread compost in the bottom of it.

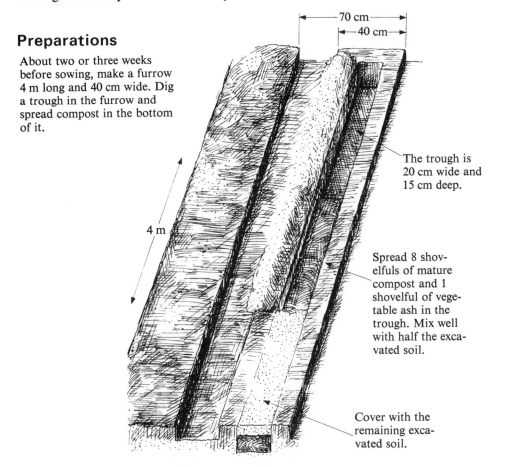

70 cm

40 cm

The trough is 20 cm wide and 15 cm deep.

4 m

Spread 8 shovelfuls of mature compost and 1 shovelful of vegetable ash in the trough. Mix well with half the excavated soil.

Cover with the remaining excavated soil.

Sowing: When seeds are sown in rows, many plants must be thinned out. If the thinning is late, the plants can become long and spindly and difficult to head.

Poor drainage invites illness. Consequently, when the soil drains badly, high furrows of about 10 cm are needed. Sow in clusters and thin crowded zones to prevent the production of spindly plants. It is easy to forget to sow Chinese cabbage because its planting time coincides with busy harvest time for many summer vegetables. Furthermore, timing is very important. Sowing seeds too early invites insect damage, but delaying too long means that growth will be poor and the plants will not head. Chinese cabbage needs plenty of sunlight if it is to form heads.

Harvesting: Press heads of Chinese cabbage with the fingers. If they are firm, they are ready to harvest. It is a bad idea to plant the same land with Chinese cabbage two years running since this increases the danger of insect damage and illness. A two- or three-year rotation cycle is desirable. Avoid planting Chinese cabbage on land where the preceding crop has been cabbage, *komatsuna*, or *santō-sai*.

Sowing

Make holes 5 cm in diameter and 1 cm deep at an interval of 45 cm.

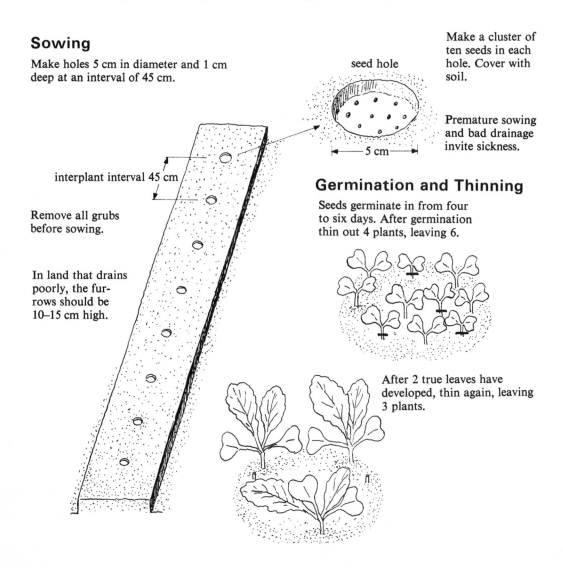

seed hole

Make a cluster of ten seeds in each hole. Cover with soil.

interplant interval 45 cm

Premature sowing and bad drainage invite sickness.

Remove all grubs before sowing.

In land that drains poorly, the furrows should be 10–15 cm high.

―― 5 cm ――

Germination and Thinning

Seeds germinate in from four to six days. After germination thin out 4 plants, leaving 6.

After 2 true leaves have developed, thin again, leaving 3 plants.

Three or four weeks after
sowing, there should be only
1 plant in each location.

Thin and harvest.

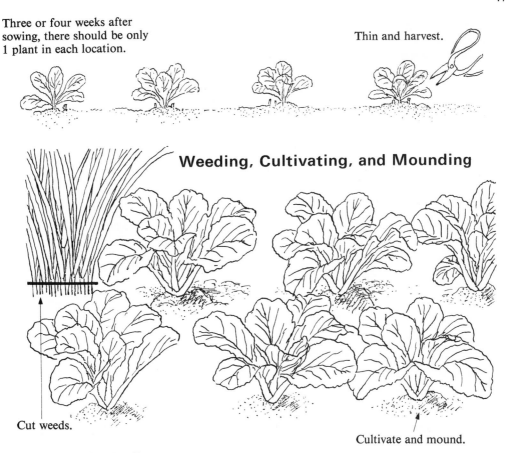

Weeding, Cultivating, and Mounding

Cut weeds.

Cultivate and mound.

Immediately before heading

In the truly natural cultivation system, plants grow slowly. By the time
heading is finished for plants raised from seed sown in early September,
the weather is already getting cold; and leaves will tend to open again.
If temperatures drop below 41°F at night, tie the upper part of the head
with cotton cord. Though the head will be a little loose, the internal
parts of the plant will be protected from cold; and rich-green Chinese
cabbage can be harvested even in winter.

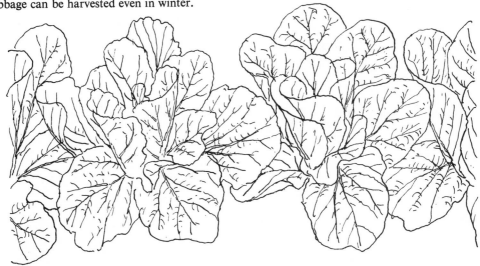

Harvesting

Chinese cabbage may be harvested
when the heads are firm to the
touch.

Tightly headed Chinese
cabbage will not open
again even if exposed to
cold.

Heading has begun.

Cut from the base with
a knife and wrap 2 or 3
outer leaves around the
head while lifting it out.

Santō-sai

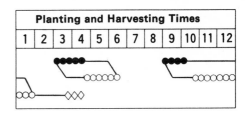

Planting and Harvesting Times											
1	2	3	4	5	6	7	8	9	10	11	12

Weeds, which require no cultivating, perform important roles in the raising of other plants. The virtually countless ramifications of their roots and rootlets loosen and aerate the soil. When weeds wither, their very dense root masses rot, leaving both ventilating cavities in their own shapes and organic matter to serve as nutrition for other plants.

In the process of artificially improving them to serve as food for human beings, vegetables have been weakened through overprotection with the result that, the more they have been tampered with, the more troublesome they are to raise. This is why such vegetables as tomatoes, eggplant, and okra do not produce good crops unless they are fertilized. Some other plants, however—*komatsuna* for example—can be grown without fertilizer and even flourish in the cracks in asphalt pavements. *Santō-sai* too thrives with neither fertilizer nor cultivating.

Preparations

In rich soil, no previous fertilizing is needed. If compost is to be used, however, follow the procedure shown in the drawings. Fertilize two or three weeks before sowing seeds.

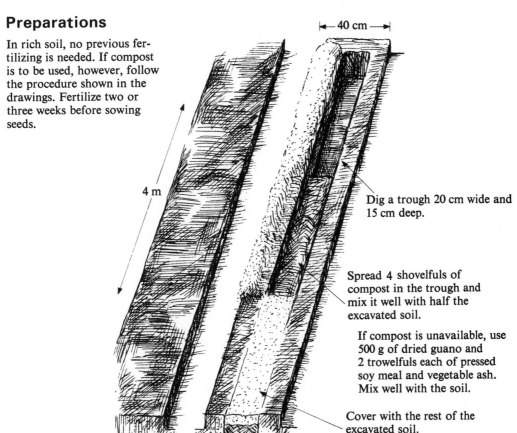

40 cm

4 m

Dig a trough 20 cm wide and 15 cm deep.

Spread 4 shovelfuls of compost in the trough and mix it well with half the excavated soil.

If compost is unavailable, use 500 g of dried guano and 2 trowelfuls each of pressed soy meal and vegetable ash. Mix well with the soil.

Cover with the rest of the excavated soil.

50

Sowing: If the soil is rich in organic matter, has born crops previously, and has never been treated with chemicals, sowing requires no additional fertilizers. Plenty of compost should be added to enrich fields in which chemicals have been used.

Insects: Insect damage arises because unnatural cultivation methods have been used, and the problem can be solved and splendid crops assured if the natural, organic system of avoiding chemical fertilizers and insecticides is followed for two or three years.

Sowing

Sow in rows running east and west.

Germination and Thinning

Seeds germinate in from four to seven days. Thin crowded areas until the leaves of the plants lightly touch each other.

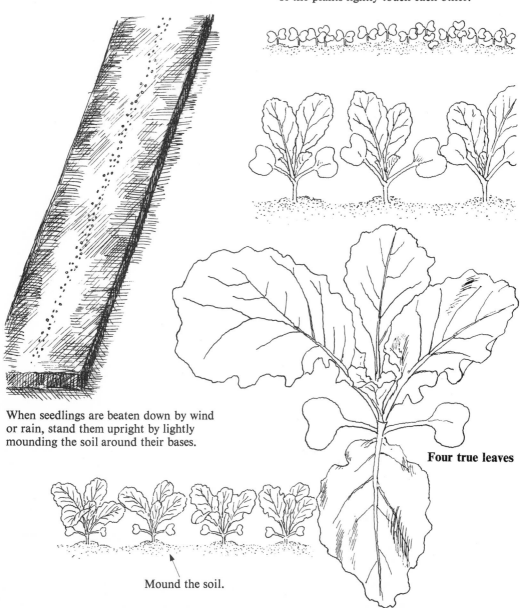

When seedlings are beaten down by wind or rain, stand them upright by lightly mounding the soil around their bases.

Four true leaves

Mound the soil.

Thirty days after germination

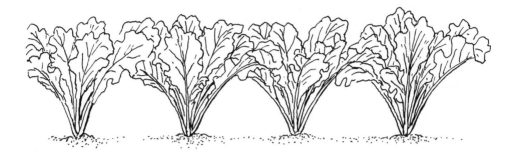

Forty days after germination

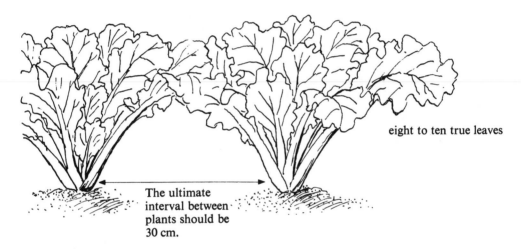

eight to ten true leaves

The ultimate interval between plants should be 30 cm.

Harvesting

Harvest when the plant is thick and has a dense cluster of leaves in the center.

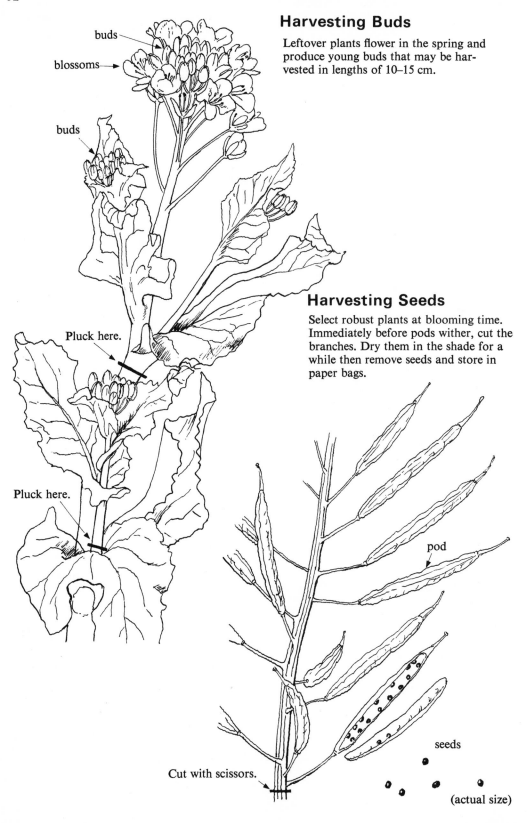

buds

blossoms

buds

Pluck here.

Pluck here.

Cut with scissors.

Harvesting Buds

Leftover plants flower in the spring and produce young buds that may be harvested in lengths of 10–15 cm.

Harvesting Seeds

Select robust plants at blooming time. Immediately before pods wither, cut the branches. Dry them in the shade for a while then remove seeds and store in paper bags.

pod

seeds

(actual size)

Taisai

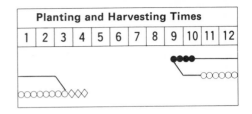
In the lively field that remains unpolluted by chemicals, many creatures busily help in the raising of vegetables. Though it is true that they cause trouble by eating seed —more in spring than in fall—and pecking heads of Chinese cabbage, ripe tomatoes, corn, and other produce, birds are helpful in that they eat the moth larvae, grubs, and other insects that ravage plants. Certain insects too perform a similar function. For instance, the praying mantis and the spider are constantly on the lookout for bugs and worms to eat and in this way assist the farmer in protecting his crops.

Taisai, which is very easy to raise, is sown in the autumn and may be thinned and harvested for a long period.

Preparations: For autumn sowing, no fertilizer is needed if crops were raised on the land in the summer. If the land is being planted for the first time, however, and if homemade, mature compost is unavailable, three or four weeks before sowing, mix dried guano and pressed soy meal thoroughly with the soil.

Preparations

Two or three weeks before sowing, spread compost—2 shovelfuls for each 1 m²— over the soil and mix well.

Sowing and Germination

Sow in rows and cover with a thin layer of soil.

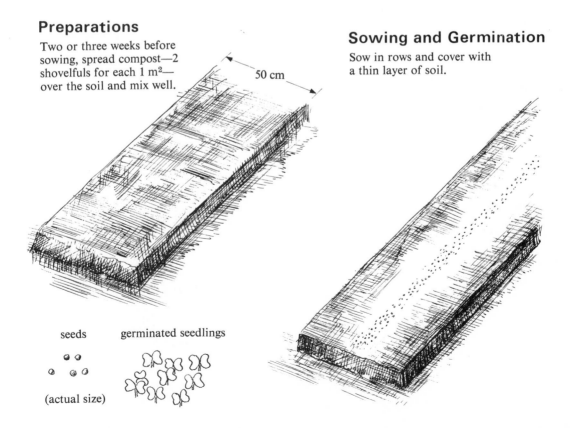

50 cm

seeds   germinated seedlings

(actual size)

Weeds cut from the land should be spread thinly on the ground, dried in the sun, and used in the preparation of compost or vegetable ash. Such tall grasses as pampas may be cut and used as mulch for summer vegetables.

When preparing a weed-field plot for first agricultural use, turn the soil, remove all foreign objects, and fertilize with mature compost. Crops grow slowly in land under fertilizer-free cultivation for the first season. But they pick up speed later; and, if sowing is completed by late September, it is possible to harvest the crop before the cold damages the leaves.

Thinning

Begin thinning and harvesting when two true leaves have developed.

Intervals should be such that the leaves of neighboring plants lightly touch each other.

Harvesting

Harvest when the plants are fully developed.

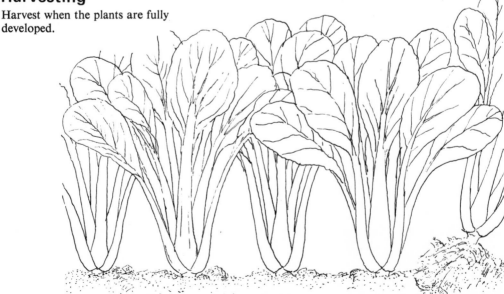

Bitamin-na

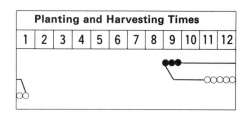
Vegetables are not difficult to raise as long as the method used to cultivate them allows them to manifest their innate characteristics. If crops fail to be satisfactory, there may be a complex of reasons that is not easy to unravel. Human beings frequently do not understand everything they see with their own eyes. And the world of nature is governed by many factors that we cannot even see.

As in human health, so in plants too, unnatural conditions result in illness. The ideal of the organic agricultural system is to borrow nature's strength in raising crops. The use of chemical fertilizers and insecticides, on the other hand, produces unnatural conditions and therefore leads to sickness.

Bitamin-na is hardy and easy to grow. It is cold-tolerant and does not readily bloom or go to seed. If planted in the autumn, it will produce a crop from later that same autumn into spring. This dark-green, glossy, leafy vegetable, the Japanese name of which means vitamin vegetable, is rich in vitamins, including vitamin A.

It will grow well on no more fertilizer than what remains in the soil from the preceding crop. Since it requires no fertilizing, insects are little attracted to it, as they are by the fermentation that takes place in the ground if insufficiently matured compost is used. If it is attacked by *Barathra brassicae*, as sometimes occurs, the problem may be solved by digging carefully at the base of the damaged plant and removing the insect. Cutworms require greater attention, however, because there may be as many as a hundred of these insects, each 1 cm long, in a piece of land 15 cm square.

Like *komatsuna*, *bitamin-na* grown without chemical fertilizer is large and truly delicious.

Sowing

Make a furrow like the one used in planting *komatsuna*. Plant seeds either in rows or clusters and barely cover with soil.

seeds

(actual size)

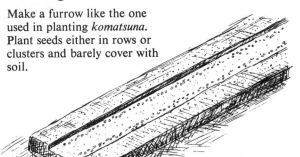

Germination

Seeds germinate in from three to six days. After germination, be on the lookout for damage from *Barathra brassicae*.

Thinning

When 1 or 2 true leaves have
developed, thin by clipping
the tops of unwanted plants
with scissors. Thereafter, thin
and harvest until interplant
interval is 30–40 cm.

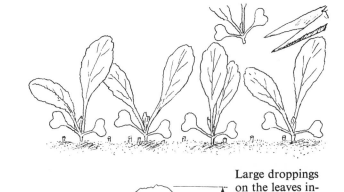

Insects

The natural system of agriculture
avoids pouring chemicals into the
soil or allowing them to penetrate
into the plants themselves. Twenty
or thirty minutes of work a day in
the field is enough to keep down
insects.

Large droppings
on the leaves in-
dicate the presence
of green cater-
pillars.

8 cm

**Fifteen days after
germination**

insect

**Forty days after
germination**

26 cm

Grubs will be found in the ground
almost directly below the scars they
have left near leaf petioles. The size
of the scar indicates the size of the
grub. Using a transplanting trowel,
gently remove the grub, taking care
not to damage the roots.

Harvesting

Plants are ready for harvesting from
sixty to seventy days after germination, by which time they should
have grown large enough to eat.
Large leaves may be harvested
individually.

Fudan-sō

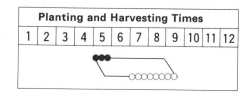
Leafy vegetables tend to be scarce in hot summer weather. But *fudan-sō*, which is tolerant of dryness and temperatures higher than 86°F, fast-growing, and virtually free of both insect damage and illness, is ideal for the hot season.

Sowing: Though any time of the year will do, the period from spring to early autumn is best. But, since many other leafy vegetables may be planted in the autumn, it is advisable to take advantage of this crop's tolerance of summer conditions and sow from spring into summer at times when other harvestable crops of this kind are scarce. In this as in other instances, the natural system of cultivation strives to sow at times making it possible to take maximum advantages of the characteristics of the plant in question.

Fertilizing: Use mature compost. But if it is unavailable, two weeks before sowing, line the planting through with a mixture of dried guano and vegetable ash. Mix well with the soil.

Insects: Although insect pests rarely cause much trouble, small *fudan-sō* seedlings with two true leaves are sometimes ravaged by cutworms or grubs. Guard against this by checking the soil to a depth of 2–3 cm before sowing.

Preparations

The furrow should be 50 cm wide and 2 m long. Spread 4 or 5 shovelfuls of mature compost evenly over the top and mix well.

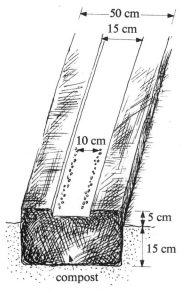

compost

Sowing

In the sowing trough (15 cm wide) sow 2 rows of seeds 10 cm apart.

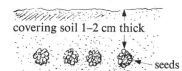

covering soil 1–2 cm thick

seeds

Germination

Seeds germinate in from ten to fifteen days.

The cotyledons grow larger.

After they have grown still larger, the first pair of true leaves begins to emerge.

Harvesting: *Fudan-sō* may be harvested during the thinning process. Ultimately, the remaining plants may be harvested whole; or the plants can be made to last longer by harvesting only the large outer leaves, a few at a time.

Harvesting seed: Allow a robust plant to grow tall, mature fully, and bloom to produce the best possible seeds.

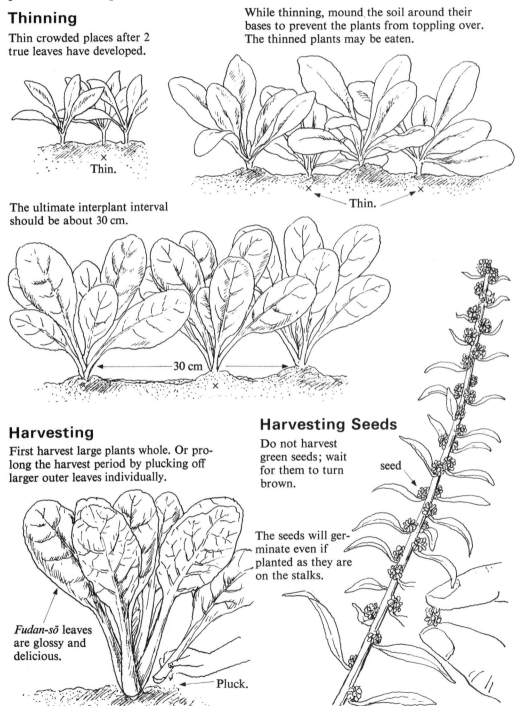

Thinning

Thin crowded places after 2 true leaves have developed.

While thinning, mound the soil around their bases to prevent the plants from toppling over. The thinned plants may be eaten.

Thin.

Thin.

The ultimate interplant interval should be about 30 cm.

30 cm

Harvesting

First harvest large plants whole. Or prolong the harvest period by plucking off larger outer leaves individually.

Fudan-sō leaves are glossy and delicious.

Pluck.

Harvesting Seeds

Do not harvest green seeds; wait for them to turn brown.

seed

The seeds will germinate even if planted as they are on the stalks.

Okahijiki

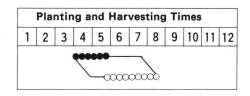

Planting and Harvesting Times

1	2	3	4	5	6	7	8	9	10	11	12

Hijiki is the name of a dark-brown, slender, stalked seaweed frequently enjoyed in Japan cooked in sweetened soy sauce. *Okahijiki* (hill *hijiki*), an annual and a member of the goosefoot family, are so called because, though green instead of brown, they have slender, fleshy, tubular leaves that in texture, appearance, and, oddly enough, flavor resemble the seaweed. To preserve their texture, they should be parboiled no more than sixty seconds and served without being cut or chopped. Topped with soy sauce mixed with *wasabi* horseradish, they are delicious but very unlike most vegetables. They are as rich as flat chives and spinach in carotene and rich in calcium as well.

They probably first grew wild on sandy hills near the seashore and are not in the least finicky about soil. This and their almost total freedom from insect damage make them very easy to raise. New offshoots develop at the axils of leaves. They mature forty days after germination.

Compost should be mixed with soil before sowing. Sow in staggered batches from early April to late May to ensure adequate supplies of tender plants over a long period. *Okahijiki* do well planted in with other crops.

Water is more important than compost in raising these natives of the seashore. Aridity lowers crop quality. To prevent it, encourage a stand of weeds and spread straw on the ground. The straw both retains soil moisture and prevents the plants from being dirtied by sand and soil splashed up by rain.

Harvest as soon as they are 10–15 cm long. Waiting longer permits the plants to age. Their leaves then become short and tough.

Crops may be increased by allowing the plants to remain a little dense and thus to support each other and prevent drooping and falling.

Okahijiki may be used in salads and soups, as an appetizer, and in sautéed foods.

Sowing

Sow in rows 10 cm apart in troughs 10 cm wide.

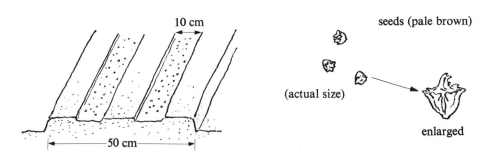

10 cm

50 cm

seeds (pale brown)

(actual size)

enlarged

Germination

Germination takes place in
three or four days.

cotyledons

Fifteen days after germination

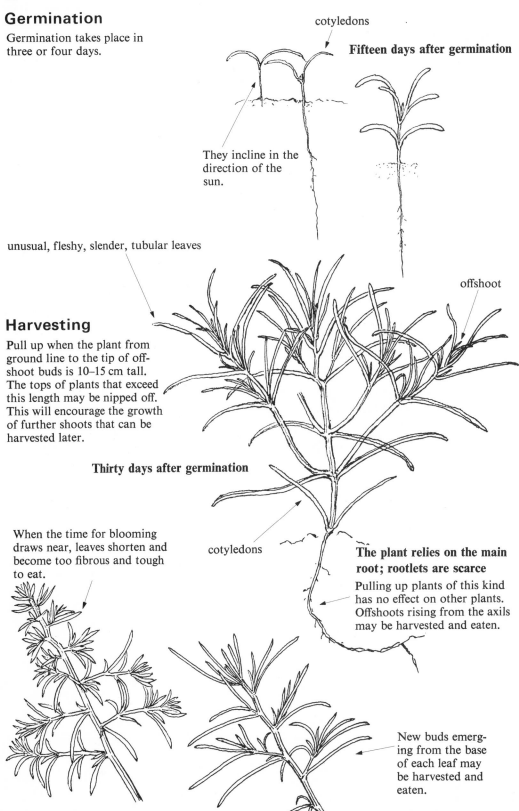

They incline in the
direction of the
sun.

unusual, fleshy, slender, tubular leaves

offshoot

Harvesting

Pull up when the plant from
ground line to the tip of offshoot buds is 10–15 cm tall.
The tops of plants that exceed
this length may be nipped off.
This will encourage the growth
of further shoots that can be
harvested later.

Thirty days after germination

When the time for blooming
draws near, leaves shorten and
become too fibrous and tough
to eat.

cotyledons

**The plant relies on the main
root; rootlets are scarce**

Pulling up plants of this kind
has no effect on other plants.
Offshoots rising from the axils
may be harvested and eaten.

New buds emerg-
ing from the base
of each leaf may
be harvested and
eaten.

Mizuna

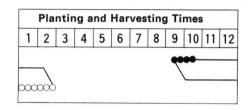

Planting and Harvesting Times											
1	2	3	4	5	6	7	8	9	10	11	12

Developed in the Kyoto region as a kind of fertilizer in water-filled channels between furrows in fields for other crops, *mizuna* (water vegetable), is characterized by serrate, dark-green leaves with whitish petioles. It multiplies with offshoots in early winter and sometimes develops clumps of as many as a hundred plants in what looks like a miniature forest.

Water is more important than soil nutrients in raising *mizuna*, which thrives in moist ground that drains well. Harmful bacteria develop if it is forced to grow in stagnant water. Mature compost—kitchen waste, weeds, guano, rice bran, ground limestone, and so on allowed to ferment completely—provides nutrition, keeps the soil loose, and retains moisture while ensuring good drainage. When it is used, even in dry weather, like that of the winter on the Pacific side of Japan, crops will grow strong.

Spreading dried weeds and leaves on the ground around plants provides additional protection from dryness and gives nutrition to upper levels of plant roots.

Thinning: Since *mizuna* clumps grow large, ensure adequate space for furrows and thin repeatedly to ensure that the tips of leaves of adjacent plants touch lightly. If thinning is late, plants will grow tall and spindly and will fail to tiller and develop characteristic large clumps. Though crowding may protect them to some extent, spindly plants lack the strength to stand on their own and will wither when exposed to cold. It must be repeated, that thinning is essential to the development of large clumps of *mizuna*.

Unfamiliar to the West, *mizuna* is surprisingly versatile. Probably best known in a casserole dish called *harihari-nabe*, served in the Kyoto-Osaka-Kobe region, it may be used in light salt pickle dishes, as an appetizer parboiled and seasoned with soy sauce, as a vegetable side dish, sautéed, or in light broth.

Sowing

Make 1 row if the furrow is 60 cm wide; make 2 rows 30 cm apart if the furrow is 90 cm wide.

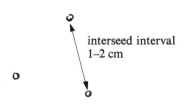

interseed interval 1–2 cm

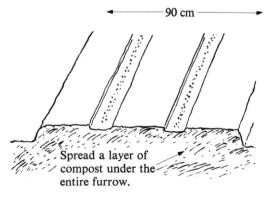

90 cm

Spread a layer of compost under the entire furrow.

62

Seeds sown in
early October will
germinate in from
four to five days.

Eight days after germination

(actual size)

(actual size)

Fifteen to twenty days after germination
Thin periodically as the young true
leaves emerge.

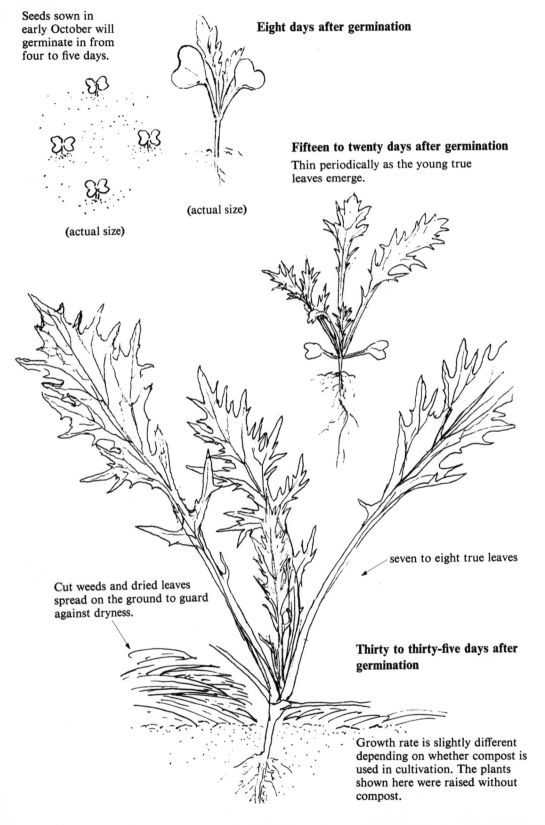

seven to eight true leaves

Cut weeds and dried leaves
spread on the ground to guard
against dryness.

**Thirty to thirty-five days after
germination**

Growth rate is slightly different
depending on whether compost is
used in cultivation. The plants
shown here were raised without
compost.

63

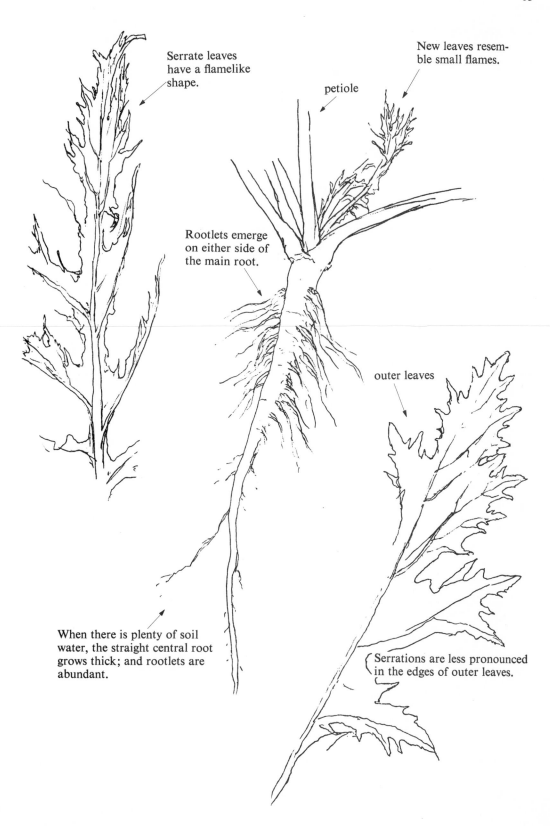

Serrate leaves have a flamelike shape.

New leaves resemble small flames.

petiole

Rootlets emerge on either side of the main root.

outer leaves

When there is plenty of soil water, the straight central root grows thick; and rootlets are abundant.

Serrations are less pronounced in the edges of outer leaves.

Section of the base of the plant

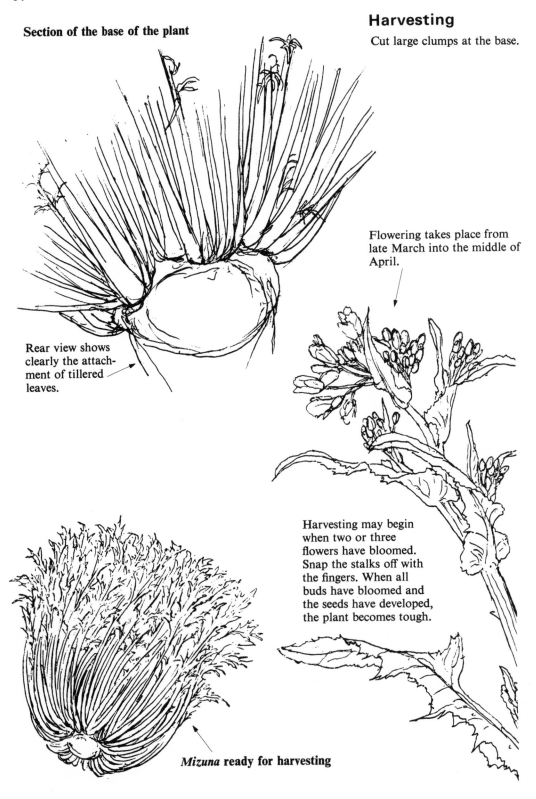

Harvesting
Cut large clumps at the base.

Flowering takes place from late March into the middle of April.

Rear view shows clearly the attachment of tillered leaves.

Harvesting may begin when two or three flowers have bloomed. Snap the stalks off with the fingers. When all buds have bloomed and the seeds have developed, the plant becomes tough.

Mizuna **ready for harvesting**

Yellow Mustard

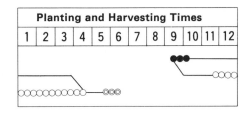

This member of the mustard family has firm leaves and a distinctive pungency that makes it excellent for pickling according to a very simple procedure; quickly parboil the leaves until they are a bright color then sprinkle them with salt and allow them to stand. Their combination of pungency and sweetness makes raw young mustard leaves a delicious garnish or addition to vegetable salads. This is a good way to use plants that are thinned out of the patch. The flower buds, which develop in April, make delicious salt pickles too. The flowers have a useful preservative and antiseptic effect.

The seeds of this, the most piquant of all the mustards, are ground to provide the mustard powder mixed to a paste and used to season sandwiches and many other kinds of food. From the middle of May until early June, when plants reach a height of about 2 m, it is possible to harvest sufficient mustard seeds for ordinary purposes.

Preparations: Tolerant of cold, yellow mustard thrives in most soils and in semishaded places even in severe climates. If the soil is rich in organic matter, no fertilizing is necessary; and insect damage is slight. In the case of lean soil, add four shovelfuls of compost to 1m² and, digging to a depth of 20 cm, mix thoroughly. By the time a stand of chickweed or other weeds has developed, spreading compost on the surface will be sufficient. Avoiding excessive digging and cultivating minimizes insect damage.

Germination

Photophilic, mustard seeds will not germinate unless they sense light. With a thin covering layer of soil, they germinate in from three to four days.

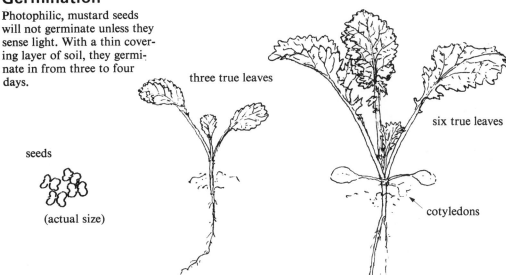

seeds

(actual size)

three true leaves

six true leaves

cotyledons

During the winter, when mustard is in the field, weeds help retain moisture in the soil by remaining low and, either in rosette form or as creepers, covering the surface and reducing evaporation.

Sow in rows and cover with a thin layer of soil. The seeds germinate in three or four days. Thereafter, thin crowded places periodically: the leaf tips of adjacent plants should touch each other lightly.

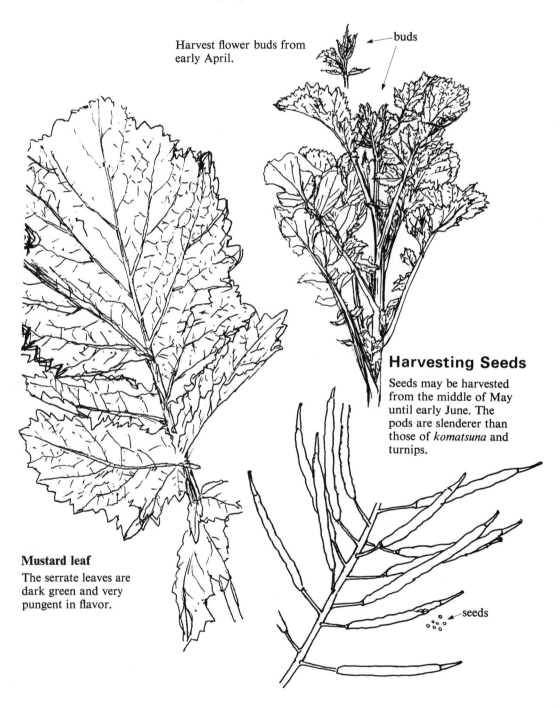

Harvest flower buds from early April.

buds

Harvesting Seeds

Seeds may be harvested from the middle of May until early June. The pods are slenderer than those of *komatsuna* and turnips.

Mustard leaf

The serrate leaves are dark green and very pungent in flavor.

seeds

Leaf Mustard

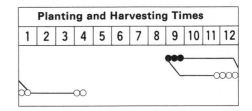
The mustards occur in a great many varieties in India, China, and Japan. This Japanese strain, a great favorite for pickling, has larger leaves than the Chinese strain called *xuelihong* and is closer to another large-leaf Chinese kind called *daye*. Unlike most of the cold-tolerant mustards, it thrives in temperate climates. If tender young leaves are preferred, however, it may be sown late in cold regions and harvested until the weather damages the plants.

The leaves manifest various shapes. Some are crinkly, some head slightly like lettuce, and some are wide with a distinctive excrescence in the center (*kobutakana*).

A versatile vegetable, in Japan, leaf mustard is most familiar in the form of rich, golden-colored pickles. It may also be used in sautées, boiled dishes, and soups and may be steamed together with rice or lightly pickled. It has its own delicious flavor plus the pungency characteristic of the mustard family. Young plants thinned out of the patch to prevent overcrowding are delicious in an instant kind of pickle produced by salting them, allowing them to wilt a while, and then pressing out moisture.

In a fairly temperate climate, if sown in September, leaf mustard may be harvested until the cold of January damages the plants. Even sown from early until middle October, they provide abundant thinning plants, and may be harvested from February until April if planted on the south side of a building where they are protected from severe colds. Like many of the other mustards, this variety is subject to very little insect damage.

Sowing

Fertilize lean soil with compost. Make a trough and sow seeds in rows. Since they like light, the covering layer of soil should be thin.

In the fall weather, soil temperatures do not drop drastically.

Germination

Germinate in three or four days.

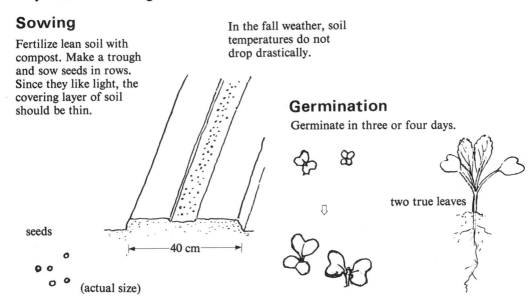

two true leaves

seeds

|← 40 cm →|

(actual size)

Leaf mustard (*kobutakana*) sown in the middle of September and raised without compost

Leaf mustard of the head-forming kind sown in the middle of September and raised without compost

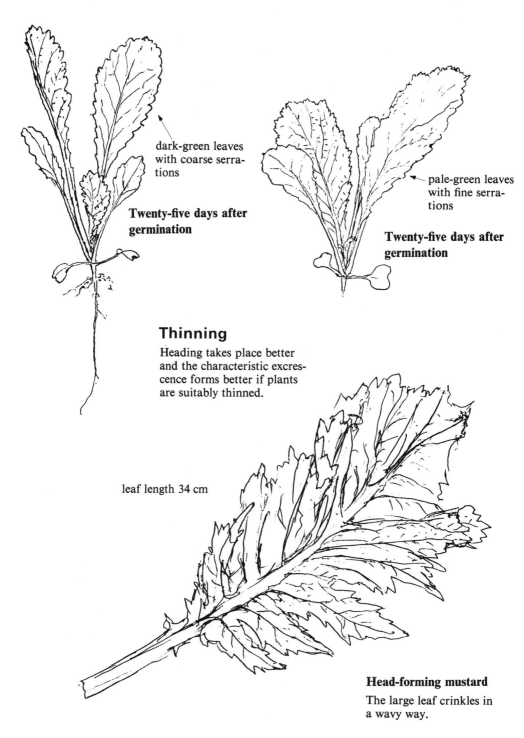

dark-green leaves with coarse serrations

Twenty-five days after germination

pale-green leaves with fine serrations

Twenty-five days after germination

Thinning

Heading takes place better and the characteristic excrescence forms better if plants are suitably thinned.

leaf length 34 cm

Head-forming mustard

The large leaf crinkles in a wavy way.

Formation of the excrescence.

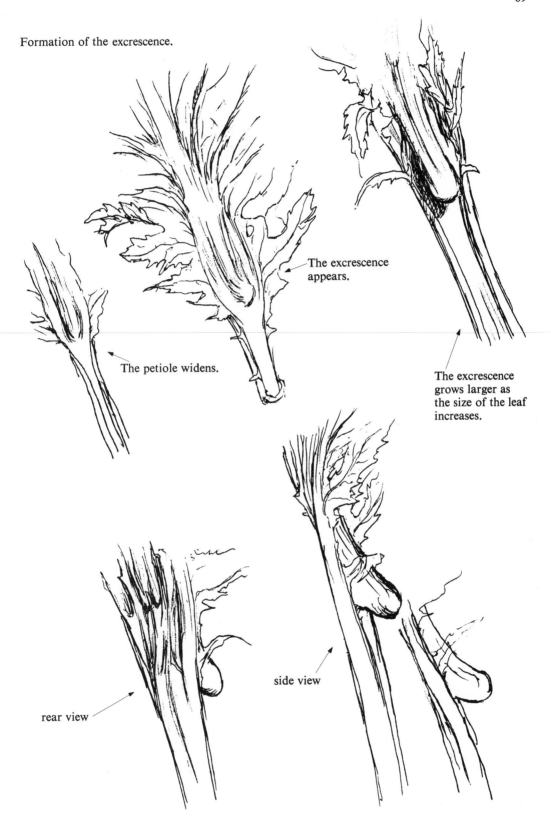

The excrescence appears.

The petiole widens.

The excrescence grows larger as the size of the leaf increases.

rear view

side view

Harvesting flower buds

Occurring in the spring, the flower buds, which may be parboiled and served with soy sauce, are highly nutritious. The heads of buds may be snapped off with the fingers.

The petals are longer and slenderer than those of the blossoms of *komatsuna*, turnips, and *aburana*.

Leaf Mustard (*kobutakana*) in late April

Cabbage

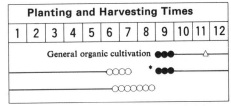

Planting and Harvesting Times

1	2	3	4	5	6	7	8	9	10	11	12

General organic cultivation ●●●—————△

*Seeds sown directly in the ground; plants raised the natural way

Tolerant of cold, cabbage grows well at temperatures of 59°–68°F, but growth drops off sharply when temperatures are higher than 77°F. Though cabbage can be raised at any time, home gardeners do best to sow in the autumn, when cultivation is least troublesome.

Sowing: Fall sowing should be carried out from mid-September until early October. Sowing earlier than this means that the seedlings will grow large before the end of the year. And exposure to the cold at that time causes the flower buds to separate and stimulates the plant to shoot and bloom in the warm days of spring without forming heads.

Germination and thinning: Seeds germinate in from three to five days. Two or three days after germination, first thinning must be performed to prevent cabbage plants from growing long and straggly.

Final planting: Sowing seeds with the ultimate interplant interval in mind eliminates the need for troublesome later transplanting. Indeed, by avoiding damaging roots and decelerating growth, this method results in healthier cabbage. If the crop on the plot in which the cabbage is to be raised has not been harvested, however, it is necessary to sow seeds elsewhere, raise seedlings, and then transplant to the final location. Nonetheless, whenever it is possible, the home gardener will find it easier to plant the seeds in their final plot from the very outset.

Preparing a Seedling Bed

When it is impossible to sow the seeds in their final location from the outset, a seedling bed must be prepared. Seeds are first sown in a sowing bed. After germination, they are transplanted into this seedling bed, which must be fertilized beforehand with 2 or 3 shovelfuls of compost.

When compost is unavailable, fertilize with dried guano and vegetable ash, thoroughly mixed with the soil.

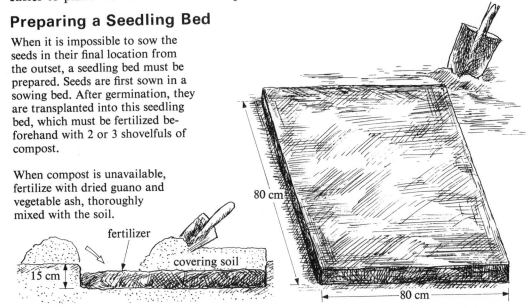

fertilizer

covering soil

15 cm

80 cm

80 cm

Rotation: Cabbage belongs to the mustard family. Because of needs for trace elements in the soil and to prevent formation of root nodules or root rot, crops should be rotated at two- or three-year intervals. Good follow-up crops are snow peas, broad beans, cucumbers, tomatoes, and eggplant, which strengthen the soil. Avoid planting such other members of the mustard family as *komatsuna*, turnips, and *santō-sai* as follow-ups.

Harvesting: Harvest early, as long as the heads are sufficiently large. Leave one or two permanent leaves on the head.

Sowing

First sow the seeds randomly in a worked plot of land separated from the field into which the seedlings will be transplanted. After sowing, barely cover the seeds with soil and top with something like straw to prevent drying.

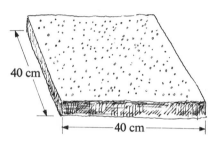

Germination and Thinning

The seeds germinate in from three to five days. Two or three days after germination, thin crowded areas to prevent the seedlings from growing tall and straggly. This is especially important with cabbage.

Use scissors to clip the tops from seedlings requiring thinning.

Transplanting

Water the seedlings two or three hours before transplanting. Lift out of the ground with a fork carefully so as not to damage roots.

Ten or fifteen days after germination, when 1 or 2 true leaves have developed, transplant the seedlings to the prepared seedling bed. The holes for the seedlings should be slightly deep. Keeping an eye on growth, gradually thin.

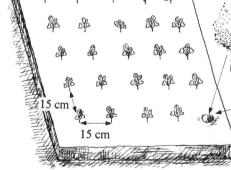

Use a fork in transplanting and avoid breaking the bole of soil around the roots.

hole for planting

Water the seedling bed carefully a day before and a day after transplanting. Watering immediately before transplanting makes the soil muddy and hard to manage because it sticks to fingers and fork.

Bed for Final Planting

Prepare the land for final planting
at about the time when the seedlings
are transplanted to the seedling bed.
This can be the place in which
initial sowing is performed if the
cabbage is to be raised without
transplanting.

Final Planting

For seeds sown in the fall, transplant seedlings to their final location
in the middle of November, when
6 or 7 true leaves should have developed.

Spread 6 or 7 shovelfuls
of mature compost
evenly over the ground.

In the case of direct
planting, sow either in
rows or in clusters of
5 or 6 seeds each.
Thin after the seedlings
appear.

west

east

4 m

25 cm

├─ 50 cm ─┤
furrow width

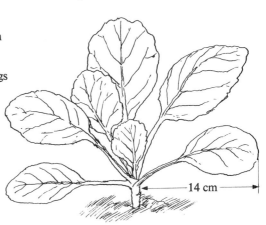

├─ 14 cm ─┤

For fall planting, make the north-
ernmost furrow high to provide
protection from wind.

Water.

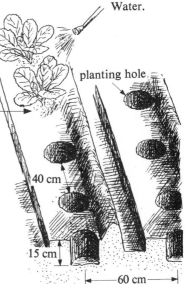

planting hole

40 cm

15 cm

├─ 60 cm ─┤

When final transplanting
is late, plant shallow so
that higher soil tem-
peratures can accelerate
rooting.

Plant to enable the day-
time sun to warm the
soil, and it will be un-
necessary to spread
straw on the ground.

covering soil

When compost is un-
available, at the time of
transplanting thoroughly
mix dried guano, pressed
soy meal, and vegetable
ash with the soil and
cover with additional
soil.

When 2 furrows are
prepared, there should
be an interval of 60 cm
between them.

Allow pressed soy meal
to rot in 10 times its
own volume of water.
Dilute this further, 1
part to 10 of fresh
water, and use the liquid
as additional fertilizer.

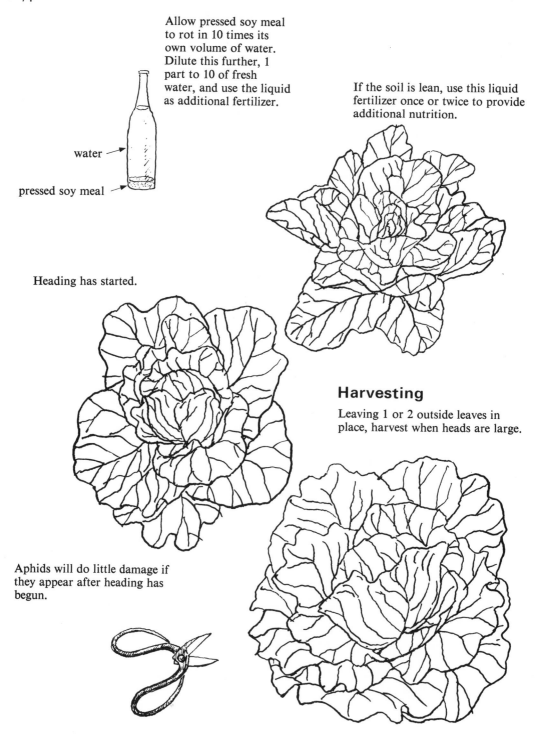

water

pressed soy meal

If the soil is lean, use this liquid
fertilizer once or twice to provide
additional nutrition.

Heading has started.

Harvesting

Leaving 1 or 2 outside leaves in
place, harvest when heads are large.

Aphids will do little damage if
they appear after heading has
begun.

Cut thick stalks with shears or
a knife.

Kale

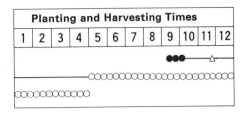

A kind of cabbage that does not head, kale is easier to raise than ordinary cabbage. Cooked or parboiled and used in salads, it is nourishing and especially rich in vitamins A, B₂, and C. Since leaves are plucked a few at a time from the lower parts of the stalk, the harvesting period is long. Kale is excellent for the home vegetable garden.

Sowing: Like cabbage, it thrives in most soils. But it is strong enough to tolerate the heat of summer and to put out fresh leaves one after another. Do not sow too soon: as for cabbage, the best time is from the middle of September to early October. If sowing is earlier than this, the stalks will grow large before the end of the year; and the plants will flower in the spring.

Germination and thinning: Germination takes place from three to five days after sowing. Two or three days after germination, thin dense areas. The leaves of neighboring plants should not touch. At thinning time, carefully check for damage from grubs or cutworms. If any is apparent, dig around the roots and remove the pests to prevent the seedlings from being destroyed. Continue thinning crowded places until permanent planting.

Permanent planting: Five or six true leaves will have developed about forty-five days after germination. If space is available, plants may be grown to maturity in the ground in which the seeds were sown, without transplanting. This system reduces the danger of disease.

Sowing

Rid the soil of grubs and cutworms and level it before sowing. Cover lightly with soil.

seeds

—80 cm—

80 cm

Three or four weeks before sowing, mix 2 shovelfuls of compost well with the soil. This is unnecessary if the soil is rich in organic matter.

Germination and Thinning

Germination takes place two or three days after sowing. Thinning begins at this time and should continue thereafter in accordance with the growth of the plants. The leaves of neighboring plants should not touch each other.

Seedlings are small at germination but soon grow larger.

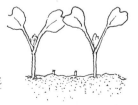

76

Fertilizing: If the soil is rich in organic matter, kale will grow well without fertilizer until permanent planting, if this is to be carried out.

Rotation: To prevent disease, to the greatest extent possible, avoid following kale on the same plot with such members of the mustard family as *komatsuna*, *santō-sai*, and turnips.

Harvesting: In spring the plants will become startlingly large. At this time, harvest, beginning with the leaves farthest down on the stalk.

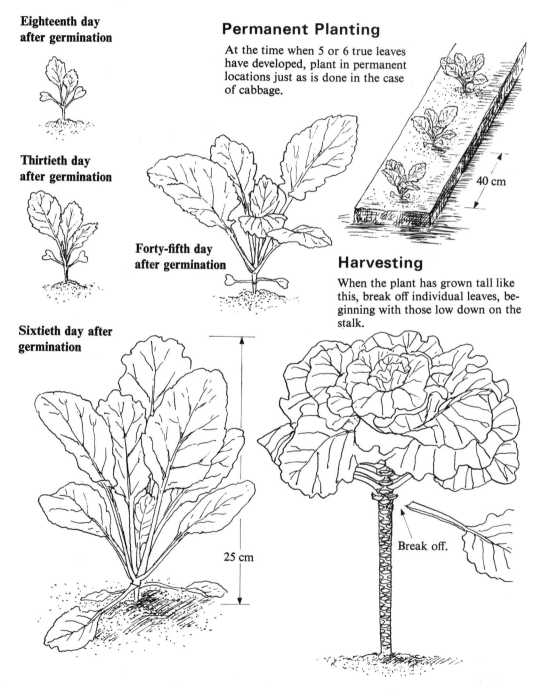

Eighteenth day after germination

Thirtieth day after germination

Forty-fifth day after germination

Sixtieth day after germination

25 cm

Permanent Planting

At the time when 5 or 6 true leaves have developed, plant in permanent locations just as is done in the case of cabbage.

40 cm

Harvesting

When the plant has grown tall like this, break off individual leaves, beginning with those low down on the stalk.

Break off.

Kohlrabi

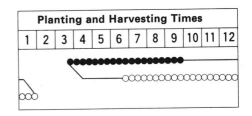

Planting and Harvesting Times

1	2	3	4	5	6	7	8	9	10	11	12

The edible part of the kohlrabi, which is a member of the mustard family related to cabbage, Brussels sprouts, cauliflower, broccoli, and kale, is a swelling of the stem immediately above ground line. Unlike other relatives of cabbage, which are considered difficult to raise because of insect damage, kohlrabi is troubled little by grubs and caterpillars. Since they mature quickly they are easy to raise and may virtually be left alone, as long as care is taken to prevent overcrowding and to remove whatever insects appear.

This is why I was once perplexed to see that some of these plants in my garden had lost their leaves while neighboring plants were flourishing. Close examination revealed wild-rabbit droppings near the kohlrabi in a small patch of ground where weeds remained and on which no agricultural chemicals of any kind had been used.

At full maturity the stem swellings reach diameters of 10–12 cm, but they are tenderer and tastier when only 4–5 cm across. They must be peeled; and the fleshy, juicy inner parts may be boiled, sautéed, used in salads, or pickled.

Preparations: Kohlrabi grows well in moist, well-drained soil that is rich in organic matter. Further enrich the soil with compost beforehand since the stem bulbs of plants raised from seed sown in late September may not have time to mature in lean soil.

Sowing: Sow in rows about 20 cm apart. Begin thinning when four or five true leaves have emerged and continue until plants stand alone at an interval of 15 cm. If thinning is delayed, plants will get insufficient sunlight because of overcrowding. As a result, the stem swellings will not enlarge properly.

Harvesting: Harvest early, as soon as the swellings are 4–5 cm in diameter. Exposure to frost increases kohlrabi's sweetness, which is still further intensified by cooking. Leaves too are edible.

Cotyledons three to four days after germination

Seeds are maroonish black.

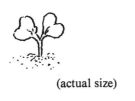

(actual size)

view from above

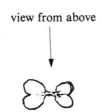

(actual size)

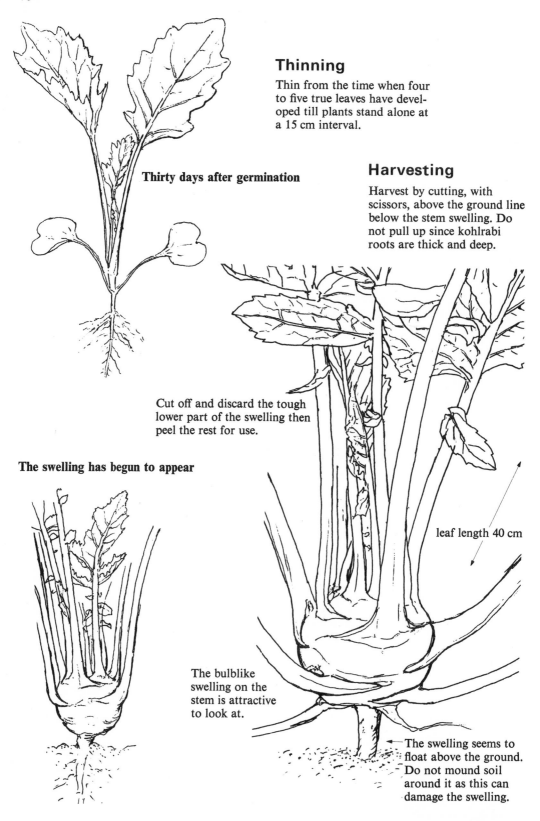

Thirty days after germination

Thinning

Thin from the time when four to five true leaves have developed till plants stand alone at a 15 cm interval.

Harvesting

Harvest by cutting, with scissors, above the ground line below the stem swelling. Do not pull up since kohlrabi roots are thick and deep.

Cut off and discard the tough lower part of the swelling then peel the rest for use.

The swelling has begun to appear

leaf length 40 cm

The bulblike swelling on the stem is attractive to look at.

The swelling seems to float above the ground. Do not mound soil around it as this can damage the swelling.

Boston Lettuce

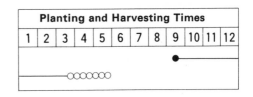
Artificial tampering with strains for the sake of what is called improvement has made vegetables difficult to raise. In the past, when people raised these plants for their own consumption and used no chemicals, vegetables manifested their own characteristics and grew well with little damage from disease or insects. And people did not think about various strains of the same kind of vegetable. Like chemical fertilizers and pesticides, strain improvement runs counter to natural agriculture and only came into being to satisfy the needs of a commercial vegetable market.

I pay little attention to strain but sow seeds and then attempt to harvest further seeds from those plants that demonstrate best results.

For easy cultivation, seeds for Boston lettuce, which does not form as tight a head as iceberg lettuce does, are best planted in the autumn. These plants are relatively cold-tolerant.

Weeds: Weeds allowed to grow around the base of each plant will provide coverage, prevent evaporation, and help keep the soil moist.

Preparations

Either spread 3 or 4 shovels of compost on each 1 m² of soil or make use of organic matter remaining from the preceding crop.

If compost is unavailable, mix dried guano with the soil.

Sowing

Sow in 2 rows of clusters.

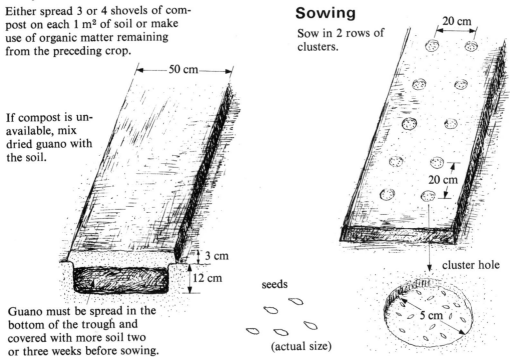

50 cm

3 cm

12 cm

Guano must be spread in the bottom of the trough and covered with more soil two or three weeks before sowing.

seeds

(actual size)

20 cm

20 cm

cluster hole

5 cm

80

Insect damage: After germination, the early growth period takes a little time. This is when the seedlings are often damaged by grubs or snails. Dig around the roots of seedlings that have been attacked and remove the insects. Once the plants have attained some size, they are less susceptible to these pests.

Rotation: To minimize insect danger, rotate Boston lettuce with other vegetables at a two- or three-year interval.

Germination

Germination occurs from five to eight days after sowing. At this time, keep a careful eye out for insect damage.

Thinning

Thin until the leaves of neighboring plants touch each other lightly.

Twentieth day after germination

Thirtieth day after germination

By the time 4 or 5 true leaves have formed, plants should be well separated from each other.

If the soil is lean, fertilize with pressed soy meal allowed to ferment in water and diluted 1 part to 100 as seems necessary from the rate of growth.

A stand of weeds around the plants keeps Boston lettuce healthy. In addition it protects from disease and keeps sand and dirt from splashing onto the leaves.

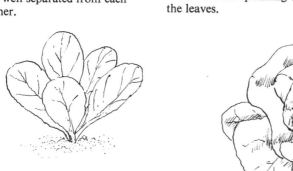

Harvesting

Plants are ready to harvest when about 10 true leaves have formed.

Sunny Lettuce

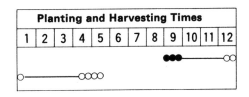

Planting and Harvesting Times											
1	2	3	4	5	6	7	8	9	10	11	12

Of the many kinds of lettuce, all of which are annual or biennial members of the composite family, some form firm, tight heads, like the familiar iceberg lettuce, and some do not, like Boston lettuce or this currently popular, crinkly lettuce with red-edged leaves, which goes under the name of sunny lettuce. With its refreshing taste and pleasing texture, it is a welcome addition to salads. Like chicory and Boston lettuce, it is hardy and much more disease-resistant than iceberg lettuce. Under reasonable environmental conditions, it can be grown with practically no care at all.

The quality of lettuces drops if the soil is dry. On the other hand, excess moisture can lead to disease. The use of immature compost or of such nitrogen fertilizers as ground limestone invites aphids and leads to plant sickness.

Preparations: Choose soil that retains moisture and drains well. Places with good stands of such weeds as chickweed, which dislikes acid, are good for this kind of lettuce.

Weeds that emerge in autumn gently cover the ground and protect crops from cold and dryness in winter. Sunny lettuce raised together with weeds thrives and is handsome, since the surrounding plants prevent soil and sand from splashing up and damaging its leaves.

Sowing

If soil is lean, mix compost with it 2 or 3 shovelfuls for each 1 m².

seeds

(actual size)

Sow 5 or 6 seeds to a cluster and cover with a thin layer of soil.

20 cm

Germination

Sown at the proper time, seeds germinate in three days.

Cotyledons are small immediately after germination.

(actual size)

True leaves begin to emerge on the fifth day.

Five days after germination

Cotyledons close at night.

Cotyledons are slenderer than those of the other lettuces.

Sowing: Like those of Boston lettuce, seedlings of sunny lettuce tolerate transplanting. Sow in rows in a starting bed and then, when three or four true leaves have emerged, plant permanently in rows at an interval of 20 cm. Water the ground well beforehand and plant in the evening to protect the transplanted seedlings from damage caused by the hot sun.

If they are sown directly in the field, make clusters 20 cm apart or sow in rows 30 cm long. In the latter case, thin early to prevent overcrowding. Though sunny lettuce is usually harvested by the entire plant, it is possible to pluck the large, lower leaves a few at a time.

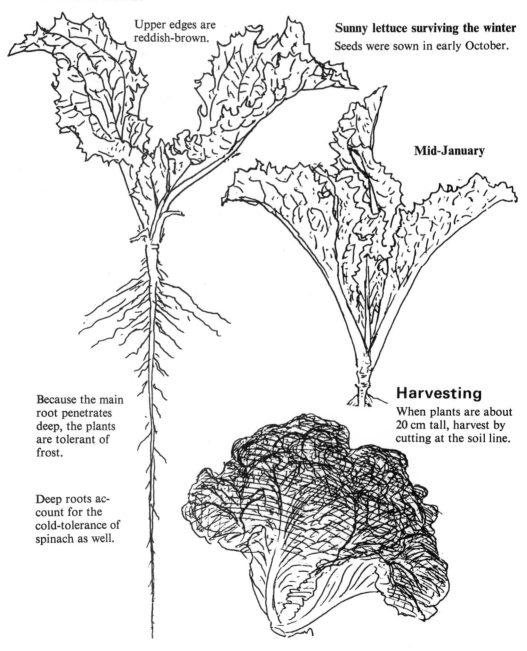

Upper edges are reddish-brown.

Sunny lettuce surviving the winter
Seeds were sown in early October.

Mid-January

Because the main root penetrates deep, the plants are tolerant of frost.

Deep roots account for the cold-tolerance of spinach as well.

Harvesting
When plants are about 20 cm tall, harvest by cutting at the soil line.

Endive

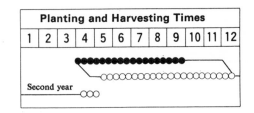

Planting and Harvesting Times

1	2	3	4	5	6	7	8	9	10	11	12

Second year

Another member of the composite family used for salads, endive is crisp and slightly bitter. The bitterness may be decreased by tying the upper parts of the large outer leaves together and blocking out sunlight for a week. This has the additional effect of blanching the leaves. But this seems a pity, since it is the distinctive bitterness of the fresh, young, green leaves that sets endive apart from the other leafy vegetables. A thick layer of those leaves makes a delicious and unusual sandwich on bread coated with margarine free of additives.

Seeds may be sown from April till August, or even into September, if the aim is to harvest small, young leaves. Endive, which grows faster than lettuce or Boston lettuce, reaches a height of about 18 cm in a month. Free of insect damage, it is one of the few vegetables that may be sown in summertime and is welcome in the autumn, when fresh vegetables are in short supply.

No additional fertilizer is needed if the soil is rich in organic matter. Endive may be conveniently and efficiently grown among rows of other vegetables. The plants can thus protect each other's environments and help each other grow. Weeds are important to endive, which tends to open outward as it grows, because they hold the plants up and protect them from splashing mud.

Sowing: Since seedlings tolerate transplanting, endive may be first sown in planter boxes and moved to the field when three or four true leaves have developed. If they are to be sown directly in the field, set the seeds 1 cm apart in rows 20 cm long and barely cover them with soil.

Thinning: If the aim is to raise large plants, thin regularly to prevent them from becoming spindly. The tips of the leaves of neighboring plants should just touch. Thin out crowded spaces until the ultimate interplant interval is 25 cm. If thinned after they have been allowed to become tall and straggly, the plants will be unable to stand alone and will topple over. Though stronger and more firmly fleshed than lettuce, endive will not stand driving rains. In case of storm, cover the plants with a protective layer of cut weeds.

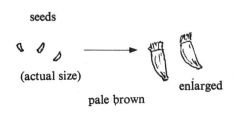

seeds

(actual size)

pale brown

enlarged

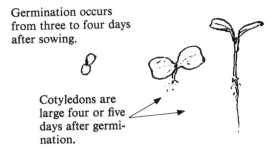

Germination occurs from three to four days after sowing.

Cotyledons are large four or five days after germination.

Ten to fourteen days after germination

Plants thinned
from the garden
àre good in salads.
The central root
will grow to 2 or
3 times the height
of the leaves.

Thirty days after germination

Crinkly leaves have
sharply serrated edges.

Twenty days after germination

There will be large
quantities of plants to
thin. The pale green
leaves have a much
crisper texture than
those of iceberg lettuce.

Harvest by cutting the
plant off at the soil line
with scissors.

Tomatoes

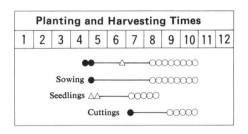
Although considered difficult, among vegetables of the kind, tomatoes are actually surprisingly easy to grow. They will bear satisfactorily if planted in a sunny place, if nitrogen fertilizers (including pressed soy meal) are used no more than moderately, and if side shoots are carefully removed. Raised in the shade, they bloom and bear poorly. If too much nitrogen fertilizer is used, the stalks and leaves will flourish at the expense of the blooms. Too many side shoots with their blossoms and buds rob nourishment from the stalks from which tomatoes are expected. As long as these points are kept in mind and natural, organic cultivation methods are used, you may expect a good crop and little trouble with insects.

Tomatoes may be raised from seedlings, usually marketed in May, or from seeds. Seedlings, which generally have been submitted to treatment with agricultural fertilizers and pesticides, are susceptible to diseases. Though it is a little more troublesome, raising from seed results in healthier plants and better harvests.

Sowing: Tomato seeds may be sown in pots or directly in the ground in about May, when temperatures begin to rise. Seedlings raised in pots must be transplanted to the field or garden plot later. Weed and thin seedlings early until there is only one plant in each location. Ensure plenty of sunlight to prevent the growth of long, straggly plants.

Preparations (Middle of March)

Only if the soil is being cultivated for the first time, dig down to a depth of about 30 cm and remove whatever rubbish or stones you find.

About two or three weeks before permanent planting, spread 3 kg (2 shovelfuls) of mature compost on each 1 m² of ground. For direct sowing, make furrows at this time and plant seeds in 8 clusters of 4 or 5. Good composts for tomatoes may be made from guano, dried leaves, bone meal, or rice bran.

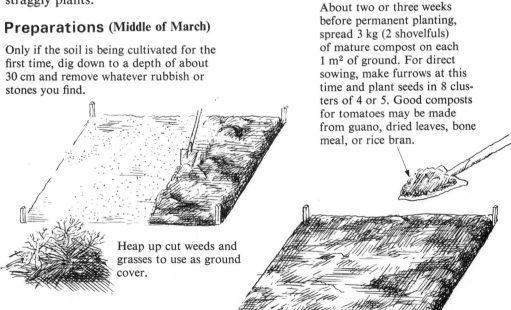

Heap up cut weeds and grasses to use as ground cover.

Cuttings: Numbers of plants may be increased by taking cuttings and setting them in the ground, though plants produced in this way do not bear large crops.

Fertilizing: Use ample compost, although tomatoes require less than eggplant. Tomatoes that have been raised with plenty of compost are sweet, whereas those raised with too little are sourish. Tomatoes grown with chemical fertilizers have no taste at all. Thirty years ago, our family raised tomatoes without fertilizers and chemicals and in soil that resembled river sand. They were sour, but sound and disease-free.

Make holes for fertilizing. In the bottom of each, place 1 kg (about 2 shovelfuls) of compost. Mix with soil. Return the soil to the holes.

Two places in every 1 m²

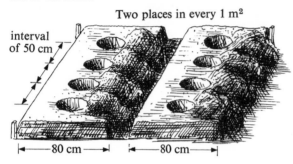

interval of 50 cm

80 cm   80 cm

Mix soil and compost together well.

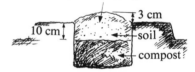

soil

25 cm

35 cm

Return remaining soil.

3 cm

10 cm

soil

compost

Preparing beds when homemade compost is unavailable

Clear the earth of rubbish and stones as on the preceding page.

Make planting holes 25 cm deep. To each planting hole add 500 g of dried guano and 200 g of pressed soy meal (about 2 trowelfuls), 1 trowelful of vegetable ash, and 2 handfuls of fish meal. Fill within 10 cm of the rim with soil. Mix well and top with remaining soil.

About one month before permanent planting, spread 5 kg of dried guano and 1 kg of pressed soy meal on the soil. Digging to a depth of 20–30 cm, mix soil and fertilizer together carefully. Make 2 furrows.

Instead of covering the ground with it, you may mix fertilizer with soil in holes.

Permanently planted plants will be in this position.

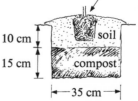

10 cm   soil

15 cm   compost

35 cm

Sowing

low-sided, unglazed ceramic
pot about 18 cm in diameter

screen

Fill to about 80% of
capacity.

Carefully level the top
of the soil and water
with the fine head of
a sprinkling can.

Cover with 3–5 mm of
soil and press lightly
with the palms.

Soil

Thoroughly mix 6 parts homemade
compost, 3 parts soil, and 1 part
river sand.

Sift through a 3–5 mm-mesh sifter.

soil 3

river sand 1

compost 6

If the soil has many
coarse particles, sift
again through a 1 mm-
mesh sifter.

fine soil on top
coarse soil in the bottom

Plant 13 seeds at
3.5 mm intervals.

Planting directly in the pots where seedlings will be raised until final planting

Sow 3 to 5 seeds to a pot.
Allow the seedlings to grow
until 3 or 4 true leaves have
developed. Thin out under-
developed seedlings until
there is only one hardy one
left in the pot. Allow it to
grow in this same pot until
time for permanent planting.

pot diameter 11 cm

Germination

Seeds sown in May will germinate
in about ten days. Germination is
retarded by low temperatures.

seed case

Growth is good if
daytime tempera-
tures are 70°–75°F
and nighttime
temperatures
55°–59°F.

Leaves of plants grown at the
right temperatures are a good
green. Those of plants grown
at low temperatures are
purplish.

Weed carefully until 5 or 6
true leaves have formed.
Cut all weeds down within
a radius of 10–15 cm from
the base of the plant to ensure
plenty of sunlight.

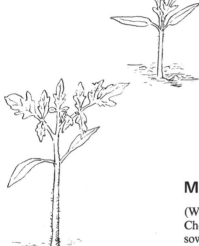

Moving to Transplanting Pots

(When 2 to 3 true leaves have developed)
Choose a warm day. Sift soil as was done at
sowing time. Transplanting pots should be
11 cm in diameter.

Watering before
transplanting
prevents soil from
dropping away
from roots.

Use a fork.

After transplanting,
water moderately. Too
much water inhibits the
formation of blooms.
Until permanent plant-
ing, ensure proper
warmth and ventilation.

Pot with soil

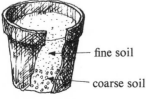

— fine soil

— coarse soil

Make a hole for the plant.

A Plant Ready for Permanent Planting

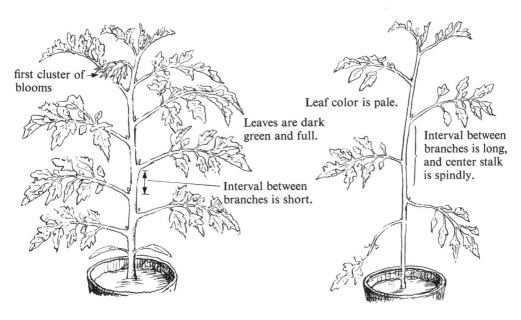

A healthy plant

first cluster of blooms

Leaves are dark green and full.

Interval between branches is short.

A straggly plant

Leaf color is pale.

Interval between branches is long, and center stalk is spindly.

Permanent Planting

Remove the pot by pressing the soil through the hole in the pot bottom.

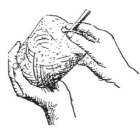

Choose a fair, warm day.

Take care that soil does not fall away from roots.

Planting shallow is good since, at that range, higher soil temperatures invigorate roots.

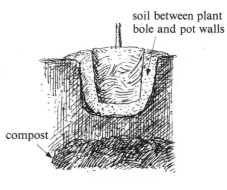

soil between plant bole and pot walls

compost

Supports

Obtain bamboo poles about 2 m
and 10 cm long and 1.5–2 cm in
diameter. You will need nine poles
for eight tomato plants. Thrust them
into the soil and assemble them with
twine as shown in the drawing.

The supports must be
stable and steady.

Bind at a height of
1.5 m.

All subsequent clusters
of blooms will be orien-
ted in the same direction
as the first one. For
tomatoes that have been
planted permanently
before late May, arrange
the support poles so
that the flower clusters
are directed outward.

For tomatoes grown
from seed sown in May
and permanently planted
by July, arrange sup-
port poles so that the
flower clusters are
directed inward to pro-
vide protection from
the burning heat of the
midsummer sun.

Tie the tomato plants to the poles
with soft, tough twine. The knot
should be made immediately above
a segment in the bamboo and immediately below the base of a leaf
on the tomato plant.

Prevent drying by
spreading cut
grass or weeds
over the ground.

The poles should be thrust into the
soil to a depth of about 30 cm at
a location about 10 cm outside of
the base of the plant and should
rise on a slant.

Single-stalk Plant

All lateral buds are removed
so that 5 or 6 clusters of
blooms develop on the single
main stalk.

Nipping Growing End

Leaving 2 or 3 leaves,
nip off the growing end
above the fifth cluster of
blooms to stop growth
and thus to allow the
tomatoes in the 6 clusters
to mature well.

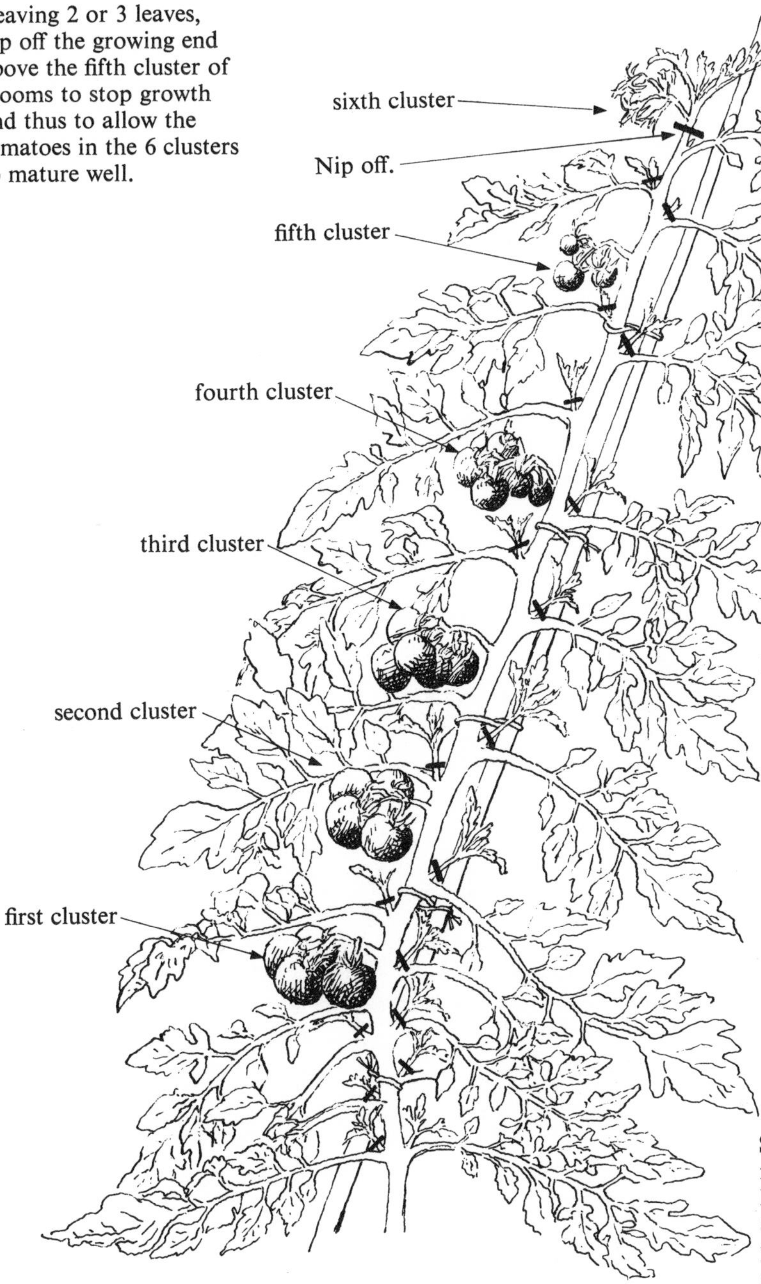

sixth cluster

Nip off.

fifth cluster

fourth cluster

third cluster

second cluster

first cluster

Removing lateral buds
Before they are large,
with your fingertips,
remove lateral buds by
bending them in the
horizontal direction.

Since harmful bacteria
may enter the wounds
left when lateral buds
are removed, never use
your fingernails or scis-
sors. Remove buds on
a sunny day.

Diagnosing Nutritional Condition from Bud Tips

Properly nourished   **Overnourished**   **Undernourished**

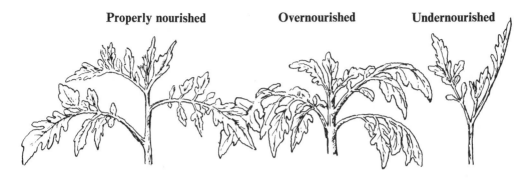

The leaves are fresh, spread well laterally, and dark in color.

The leaves are thick and tend to bend downward. They are dark in color.

The leaves are turned upward and inward, have pale color, and are puny and small. Give such plants a dose of diluted pressed soy meal fermented in water.

Dealing with Diseases

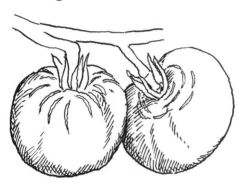

Splitting

This seems to occur when rains fall after a period of dry, hot weather. The heat hardens the outer skin, which splits when the tomatoes swell from a sudden intake of water. The best way to prevent splitting is to maintain a steady level of moisture and nutrition in the soil. Spreading straw on the ground around the bases of the plants is effective. Furthermore, it is a good idea to encourage roots to sink as deeply as possible.

Bottom Rot

Black spots on the bottoms of the tomatoes indicate possible lime insufficiency, high temperatures, and dryness.

Deformation

In the late harvest period, potassium deficiency frequently retards development. To deal with this situation, use vegetable ash in basic and supplemental fertilizing.

Curled Leaves

Nitrogen deficiency causes lower leaves to curl inward. The malady gradually moves upward.

Early Picking

Attempting to raise to maturity all the blossoms in a cluster—which may number as many as from 7 to 10—results in small, undernourished tomatoes. To prevent this, pluck buds early, saving only 4 or 5 tomatoes, all of which are at a similar stage of development.

After preliminary plucking, remaining tomatoes grow large

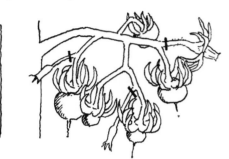

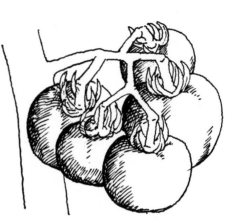

Taking Cuttings

When more plants are desired, increase the number by planting the picked lateral shoots as cuttings.

cuttings planted first in pots and later transferred to the ground

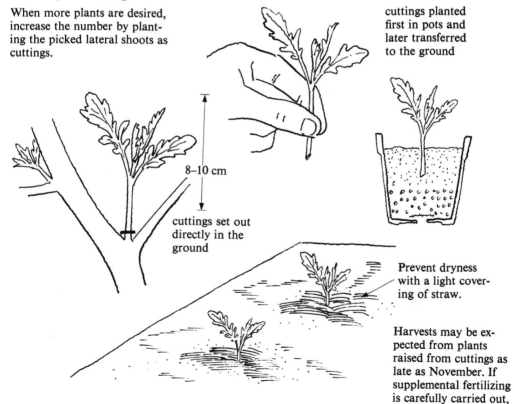

8–10 cm

cuttings set out directly in the ground

Prevent dryness with a light covering of straw.

Harvests may be expected from plants raised from cuttings as late as November. If supplemental fertilizing is carefully carried out, crops will be large.

Harvesting

Harvest when tomatoes are mature and red. Do not use scissors. Instead, putting the thumb at the joint as shown in the drawing, lightly pull the tomato upward and free.

Press the ball of the thumb against the stem joint.

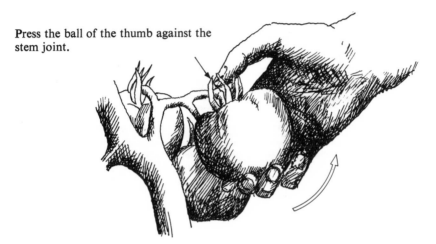

Allow lateral buds in the upper parts of the plant to grow.

When the tomatoes of the 5 or 6 basic clusters have developed to a certain point, summer heats will be above 86°F; and the plant may weaken. At this stage, allow lateral buds in the upper parts of the plant to grow freely. This will invigorate the roots and prevent fatigue. These buds will bear some tomatoes.

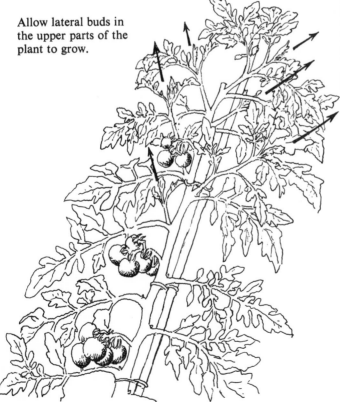

Miniature Tomatoes

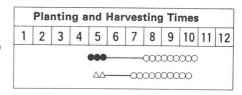

The place of origin of the tomato is variously given over a range extending from the Galapagos Islands to the Andes; but it was in Mexico that strains were improved and fixed. The Spaniards took the tomato to Europe, where, because thought to be poisonous, it remained only an ornamental plant until the nineteenth century. It was introduced into Japan in the late nineteenth century but was not eaten widely until the twentieth century.

There are several varieties of miniature, sometimes called cherry, tomatoes including *Toy Boy*, *Tiny Tim*, *Petit*, *Otohime*, and *Piko*, all of which are easy to raise. There is no need to pluck lateral buds from *Tiny Tim* and *Otohime*. Moreover, most of them can be virtually left to grow by themselves since *Toy Boy* and *Tiny Tim* are only 20–40 cm tall and since none of the others except *Piko* grows as high as 70 cm and therefore need no support props.

They require little fertilizer and will thrive if seeds are merely sprinkled in the location of last year's compost heap.

In May, after there is no longer danger of late frosts, sow tomato seeds in clusters of three or four at an interval of 50 cm. Thin periodically until, by the time four or five true leaves have developed, there is only one plant in each location. Crowding will cause plants to grow straggly.

Plant commercially marketed seedlings too in May, after the weather begins to grow warm. Since setting them deep robs them of moisture and exposes them to low soil temperatures, plant seedlings shallow and during the daytime. It is important to remember that in the spring underground temperatures may be about 39°F lower than the temperatures of the air.

Sowing

Plant in clusters of 4 or 5 seeds at a 50 cm interval.

seeds

Otohime

Germinate in six or seven days

Toy Boy

Five days after germination

Seed cases remain attached to seedlings too weak to shake them off.

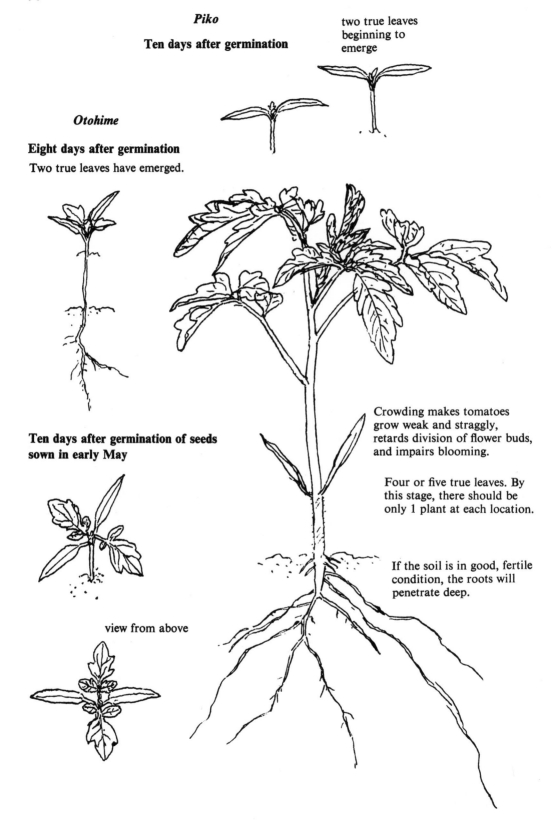

Piko

Ten days after germination

two true leaves
beginning to
emerge

Otohime

Eight days after germination

Two true leaves have emerged.

**Ten days after germination of seeds
sown in early May**

Crowding makes tomatoes
grow weak and straggly,
retards division of flower buds,
and impairs blooming.

Four or five true leaves. By
this stage, there should be
only 1 plant at each location.

If the soil is in good, fertile
condition, the roots will
penetrate deep.

view from above

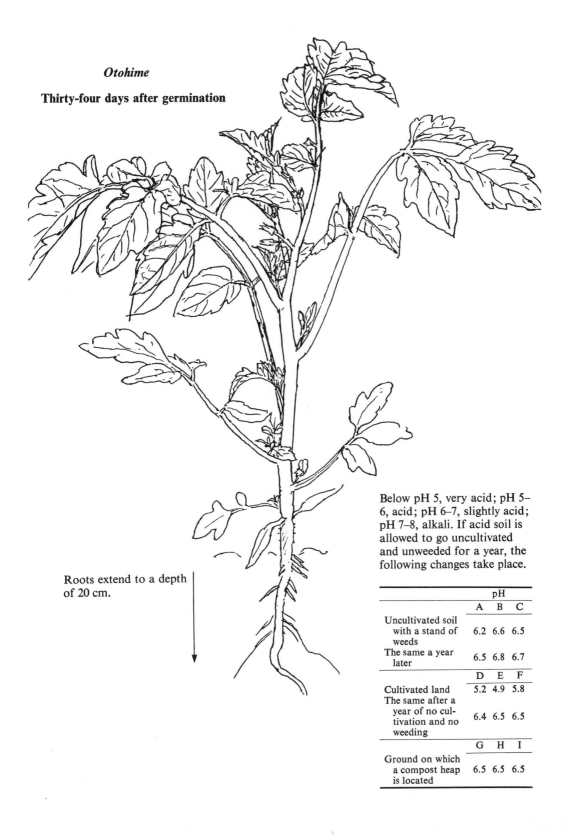

Otohime

Thirty-four days after germination

Roots extend to a depth
of 20 cm.

Below pH 5, very acid; pH 5–
6, acid; pH 6–7, slightly acid;
pH 7–8, alkali. If acid soil is
allowed to go uncultivated
and unweeded for a year, the
following changes take place.

	pH		
	A	B	C
Uncultivated soil with a stand of weeds	6.2	6.6	6.5
The same a year later	6.5	6.8	6.7
	D	E	F
Cultivated land	5.2	4.9	5.8
The same after a year of no cultivation and no weeding	6.4	6.5	6.5
	G	H	I
Ground on which a compost heap is located	6.5	6.5	6.5

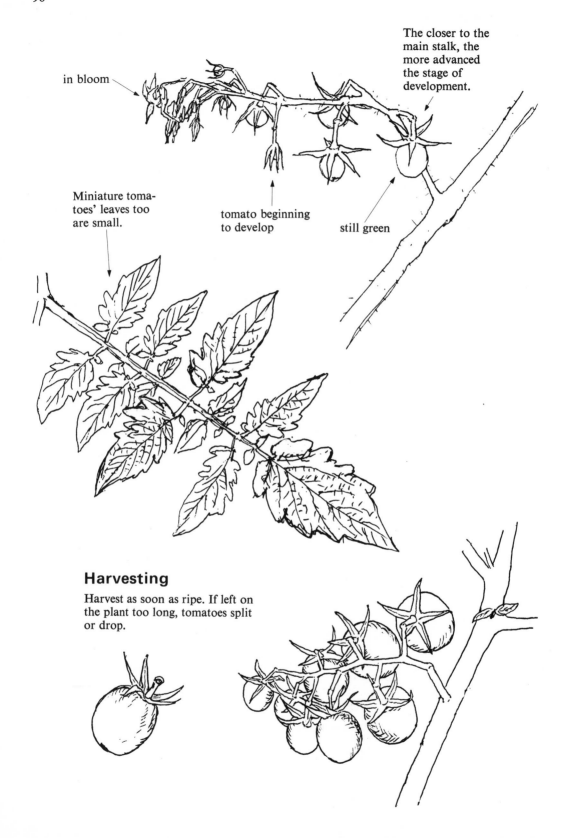

in bloom

The closer to the main stalk, the more advanced the stage of development.

Miniature tomatoes' leaves too are small.

tomato beginning to develop

still green

Harvesting

Harvest as soon as ripe. If left on the plant too long, tomatoes split or drop.

Eggplant

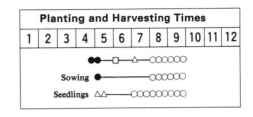

Planting and Harvesting Times											
1	2	3	4	5	6	7	8	9	10	11	12

In the days before toothpaste, the stem end of this very popular summer vegetable was burned black and used as a dentifrice. Of course, its most important uses, in Japan and in the West, are as foods. In Japan it is served in many different ways, including tempura, sautées, soups, grills, and steamed dishes and foods simmered in miso bean paste. In addition it is popular pickled.

Home gardeners generally raise eggplant from seedlings marketed in April and May. But it is important to purchase from a reliable dealer since these seedlings have usually been pampered in hot houses and doctored with chemical fertilizers and pesticides. Such plants are highly susceptible to insect damage. Seedlings are often preferred since it takes a hundred days to raise eggplant from seed. Nonetheless growing from seed is more interesting and makes the harvest all the more thrilling.

Sowing: For natural, unforced cultivation sow seeds, either in pots or directly in the ground, in May when temperatures begin to rise. Under natural conditions, transplantation and permanent planting may be avoided by sowing directly in the field.

Fertilizing: If you have not prepared compost, in the first year, use pressed soy meal or dried guano. In the second year, use only compost. And, after the soil becomes rich in organic matter, gradually stop using fertilizer altogether.

Insects: The insect known as *Epilachna sparsa orientalis* is the greatest menace to eggplant, although plants raised the organic, natural way are very little damaged. Use of chemical fertilizers or too much immature compost invites insects. This is why it is an excellent idea to spread compost in about November, when insects are inactive.

Rotation: Avoid growing such other members of the nightshade family as green bell peppers and tomatoes for four or five years in ground in which eggplant was the preceding crop.

Direct Sowing
(In early May)

Plant in clusters of from 4 to 5 seeds.

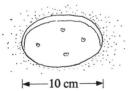

|←—10 cm—→|

Germination

Germination takes about two weeks. Seeds germinate at temperatures of 59°–86°F.

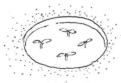

Thinning

Judging the degree of crowding, thin until, by the time 5 or 6 true leaves have formed and the plants are 10 cm tall, there is only 1 to each location.

10 cm

Pot Planting

When the preceding crop, still remaining in the plot, makes direct sowing impossible, eggplant may be raised as seedlings in pots.

After watering well, sow in clusters of 4 or 5.

seed

(actual size)

six parts of compost to four of soil

coarse soil

an unglazed earthenware pot with a diameter of 12 cm

Sow 29 seeds at intervals of 2.25 cm.

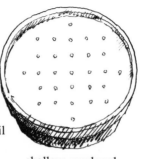

shallow, unglazed pot with a diameter of 18 cm

Barely cover the seeds with soil and press it lightly with the fingertips. Keep the pot in a sunny, windowside location till germination. Or protect it under plastic out of doors and guard against dryness and low soil temperatures.

Germination

Germination takes place in about two weeks, at soil temperatures of 59°–86°F.

Transplanting

When 1 or 2 true leaves have opened, select undamaged, hardy plants. Remove each gently, allowing soil to remain in place and taking care not to break the roots. Transplant each one into an individual pot about 11 cm in diameter.

Transplant with a fork.

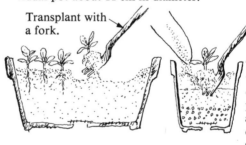

The potting mixture should consist of 6 parts compost, 4 parts soil, and a handful of ground limestone and should be sifted.

At the time for permanent planting, commercially sold seedlings usually have 6 to 8 true leaves. Those raised from seeds sown in May have four or five.

Keeping an eye out for straggly or undernourished stock, thin seedlings in a 12 cm pot early until there is only 1 left.

pressed soy meal allowed to ferment in water and then diluted one part to a hundred of water

Raising seedlings after transplantation protects roots.

Keeping the pots in a wooden tray or on a board facilitates moving them later.

The plant at the proper time for permanent setting

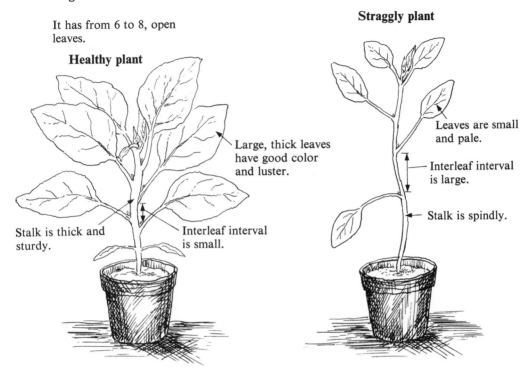

It has from 6 to 8, open leaves.

Healthy plant

Large, thick leaves have good color and luster.

Stalk is thick and sturdy.

Interleaf interval is small.

Straggly plant

Leaves are small and pale.

Interleaf interval is large.

Stalk is spindly.

Bed for Planting or Sowing

Fifteen days before permanent planting

On 3.3 m² of ground (enough for 6 plants) spread more than 20 shovelfuls of compost. Since eggplant is very intolerant of soil acidity, sprinkle 400 g of ground limestone on the soil. Mix well.

Prepare 2 furrows about 80 cm wide and 10–12 cm high. Though relatively immune to airborne diseases, eggplant is frequently attacked by illnesses transported through the soil. Making the furrow somewhat high protects plants from splashing mud in rainy weather. For direct sowing, make holes for seed clusters in the furrow at a suitable interval.

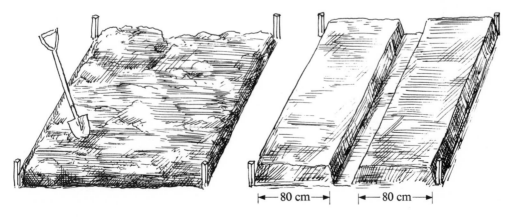

|← 80 cm →| |← 80 cm →|

Preparing a Bed When Mature Compost Is Unavailable

On 3.3 m² of spaded soil spread 5 kg of dried guano and 1 kg of pressed soy meal. Digging down 30 cm, mix well.

In the middle of March, at sowing time, prepare liquid fertilizer by mixing 1 part of pressed soy meal and 0.5 part of fish meal with 8.5 parts of water. Put this in a bottle, seal, and store in a warm place until ready for use in late June.

Allow room in the bottle for gases given off in fermentation.

water 8.5

fish meal 0.5

pressed soy meal 1

Thirty days before permanent planting

Make furrows 10–12 cm high. Estimating the sizes of plants themselves, dig holes in the furrow at intervals of 60 cm. Pile the excavated soil on one side of the hole.

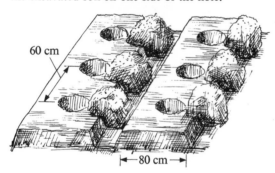

60 cm

80 cm

20–25 cm

35 cm

In the bottom of each hole, for 1 plant, add 1 kg (1 shovelful) of dried guano, and a handful of vegetable ash. Add soil till it is 10 cm from the rim of the hole. Mix carefully.

Return the remainder of the soil and mound it to a height of 5 cm.

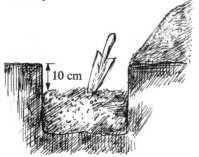

10 cm

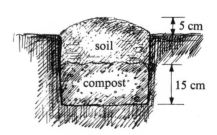

5 cm

soil

compost

15 cm

Permanent Planting

Choose the middle of a sunny, windless day. Dig a hole large enough to accommodate the roots of the seedling. Before planting, water the ground well with a sprinkling can. Plant permanently when temperatures are above 64°F. At lower temperatures, rooting is slow; and plants are susceptible to disease.

At the same time, water the soil in the seedling pot to facilitate clean, easy removal.

Remove the seedling and its soil bole by pulling gently from the top and pushing with a finger through the hole in the bottom.

Hold the plant by the stalk at the soil line and slide the pot away.

As you plant, cradle the bole in the right hand to prevent the soil from dropping away.

Spread with compost to prevent drying.

vegetable ash

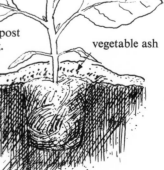

Set shallow and mound vegetable ash around the base of the plant to protect from disease and insect damage.

For the sake of growth, leave the lateral buds immediately below the first blossom and the one below that shoot. Remove all the others, leaving 3 stalks, including the main central one.

Spread straw around the base of the plant to prevent diseases that rise from the soil.

In hot, dry weather, cover the whole furrow with straw to keep soil temperatures down and prevent aridity.

At the appearance of the first eggplant, prop the plant on poles.

pole

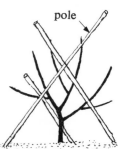

Cuttings

Set the plucked lower lateral shoots in the ground as cuttings at any time before late July.

Harvesting from three-branch plants

Remove the first eggplant as soon as it begins to fill out in order to improve the quality of the ones that will appear later.

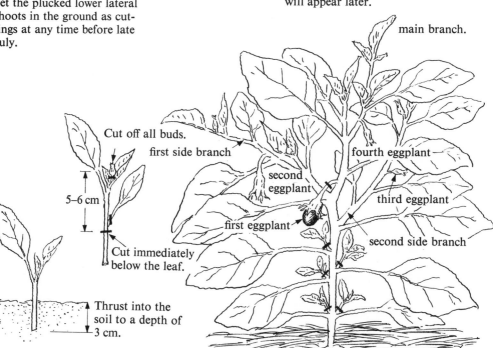

Cut off all buds.

5–6 cm

Cut immediately below the leaf.

Thrust into the soil to a depth of 3 cm.

main branch.

first side branch

second eggplant

first eggplant

fourth eggplant

third eggplant

second side branch

Evaluating Plant Condition

Good
four or five open
leaves beyond the
blossom

Borderline
one or two open
leaves beyond the
blossom

Poor
no open leaves be-
yond the blossom

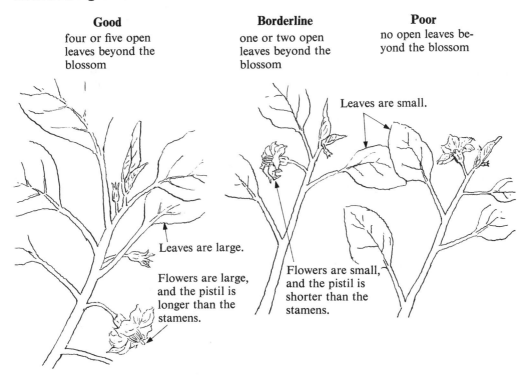

Leaves are small.

Leaves are large.

Flowers are large,
and the pistil is
longer than the
stamens.

Flowers are small,
and the pistil is
shorter than the
stamens.

Additional Fertilizing

Fertilize borderline plants with
fermented pressed soy meal diluted
with water until the mixture is clear.

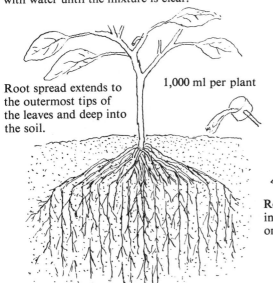

Root spread extends to
the outermost tips of
the leaves and deep into
the soil.

1,000 ml per plant

Insects and Diseases

Eggplant is susceptible to damage from
ticks, aphids, and beetles and to mildew
and the wilting disease; but thorough-
going organic cultivation methods lessen
the damage year by year. Wilted plants
should be pulled out, but refraining from
the use of agricultural chemicals is enough
to deal with all other sicknesses and pests.

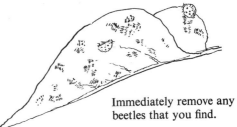

Immediately remove any
beetles that you find.

Remove the yellow
insect eggs you may find
on leaf undersides.

insect eggs

Harvesting

To strengthen the plant and promote better blooming, eggplants are harvested before they grow very large. They are fresher and better if cut in the morning or evening.

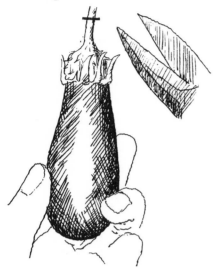

Pruning

A certain degree of foliage density makes for stronger plants. But overcrowding impedes good ventilation. Trim away damaged leaves and a minimum of other foliage.

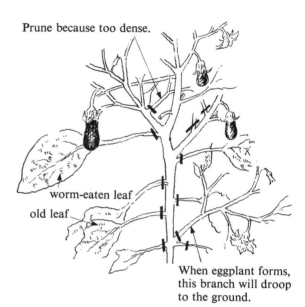

Prune because too dense.

worm-eaten leaf

old leaf

When eggplant forms, this branch will droop to the ground.

Pruning to Invigorate
(Middle to late July)

Harvests usually may begin in the middle of June. But plants weaken as summer temperatures rise. Vigorous plants may be pruned only slightly at this time. But those that have been attacked by ticks or other insects and are blooming poorly should be given a rest. Prune them as shown to allow them to recover and grow strong.

New buds should appear about a week after pruning, and autumn eggplants may be harvested about a month later.

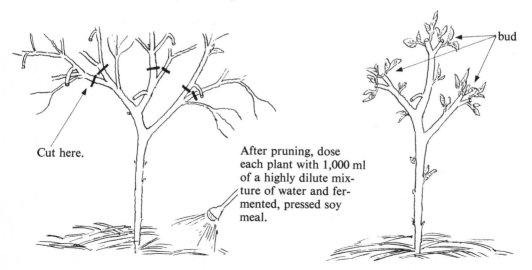

Cut here.

After pruning, dose each plant with 1,000 ml of a highly dilute mixture of water and fermented, pressed soy meal.

bud

Cucumbers

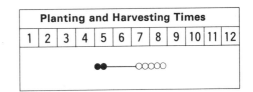

Cucumbers occur in spring and summer varieties. In the spring variety, which prefers cool weather, female flowers develop on the main stalk. In the summer variety, there are few female flowers on the parent vine. Instead they occur in the first and second sections of the first and second branchings; and the plants therefore tolerate hot weather. The summer variety is better suited to home gardens.

Preparations: Fertilization must be shallow and over a considerable area since cucumber roots spread wide and shallow. The soil should be suitably moist, and the location protected from strong winds, which damage cucumber vines badly. Use pressed soy meal moderately since fertilizers high in nitrogen make for straggly plants and inhibit blooming.

Sowing: Since cucumbers are especially prone to mildew, avoid commercially available seedlings and raise healthier plants from seeds. Cucumbers grow faster than eggplant and tomatoes.

Ground covering and support poles: Because their roots spread shallow, cucumbers require a ground cover of straw to protect them from high soil temperatures caused by direct sunlight. Hot soil can destroy cucumber vines. Furthermore, a

Preparations

Two or three weeks before sowing, dig holes at an interval of 40 cm. Add 1 shovelful of compost to each hole and mix well with the soil.

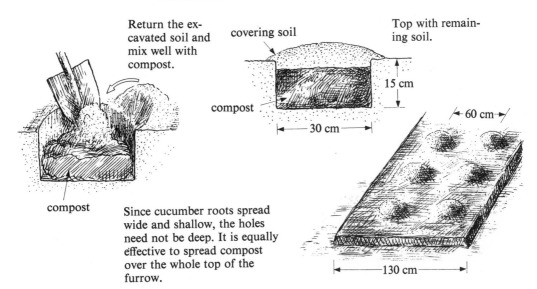

Return the excavated soil and mix well with compost.

covering soil

Top with remaining soil.

compost

15 cm

30 cm

60 cm

130 cm

compost

Since cucumber roots spread wide and shallow, the holes need not be deep. It is equally effective to spread compost over the whole top of the furrow.

covering of straw prevents soil dryness. This is a vitally important consideration in the case of ground-trailing summer cucumbers. A covering of straw or cut weeds minimizes the transmission of soil-carried diseases.

For climbing varieties provide pole frames as soon as vines begin to grow long and train the tendrils on them.

Nipping Growth Ends: Since, in the summer variety, female flowers are not produced on it, nip off the growth end of the main stalk at the seventh segment. This will stimulate production of female flowers on the first and second branchings. Though troublesome, this nipping process is essential.

Rotation: To minimize the diseases to which cucumbers are prone do not plant them on the same land in successive years but rotate at a cycle of two or three years.

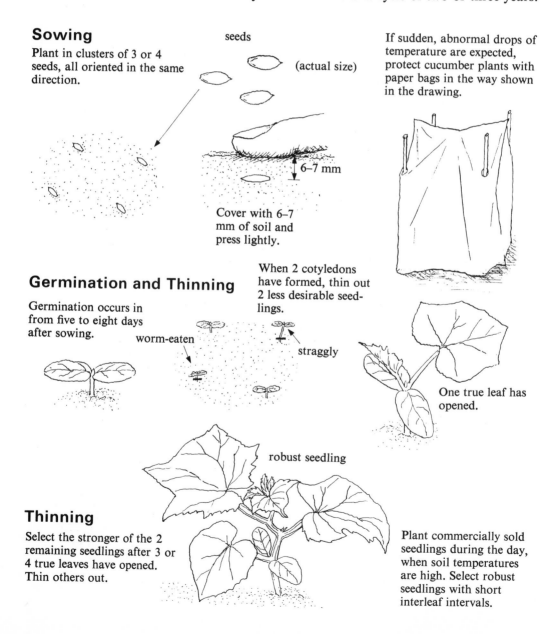

Sowing

Plant in clusters of 3 or 4 seeds, all oriented in the same direction.

seeds

(actual size)

6–7 mm

Cover with 6–7 mm of soil and press lightly.

If sudden, abnormal drops of temperature are expected, protect cucumber plants with paper bags in the way shown in the drawing.

Germination and Thinning

Germination occurs in from five to eight days after sowing.

worm-eaten

When 2 cotyledons have formed, thin out 2 less desirable seedlings.

straggly

One true leaf has opened.

robust seedling

Thinning

Select the stronger of the 2 remaining seedlings after 3 or 4 true leaves have opened. Thin others out.

Plant commercially sold seedlings during the day, when soil temperatures are high. Select robust seedlings with short interleaf intervals.

Spring cucumbers

After the first female flower develops, others emerge at virtually each segment.

female flower →

Nip off lateral buds as far as the seventh segment.

Single-stalk cultivation

Summer cucumbers

Few female flowers emerge on the main stalk. But there are always female flowers at the first and second segments of the first and second branchings.

Nip off the lateral buds as far as the fifth or sixth segment.

Single-stalk cultivation

Three-stalk cultivation of summer cucumbers

Nip the growth end of the main stalk after it has reached the seventh segment. Allow 3 first branchings, emerging from the fourth through the sixth segments of the main stalk, to grow to the tips of the support poles. Then nip their growth ends.

Nipping growth ends is important in raising cucumbers. Once the ends of the first branchings have been nipped, however, the plants may be allowed to grow freely.

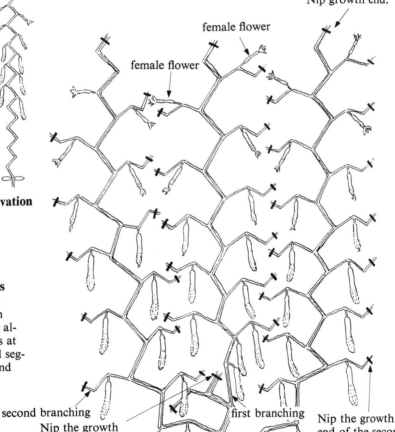

Nip growth end.

female flower

female flower

second branching

Nip the growth end of the main stalk at the seventh segment.

first branching

first branching

Nip the growth end of the second branching at the second segment.

first branching

parent vine

Three-stalk cultivation

Ground-trailing cultivation

If poles are unavailable, allow the cucumbers to crawl over the ground. In this instance, nip the first-stalk growth end at the seventh segment, the growth end of the first branchings at the eighth segment, and that of the second branchings at the fifth segment.

110

When the vine begins to grow, train it on a support pole and spread a thick layer of cut weeds or straw on the ground around the base of the plant.

Wind causes great damage
Tendrils act as springs absorbing wind shock and reducing the trembling of stalks and leaves. In this way they contribute to good growth. To assist them, plant cucumbers at a somewhat small interplant interval and put support poles where tendrils can reach them easily. A ground cover of cut weeds is essential in the cultivation of ground-trailing cucumbers.

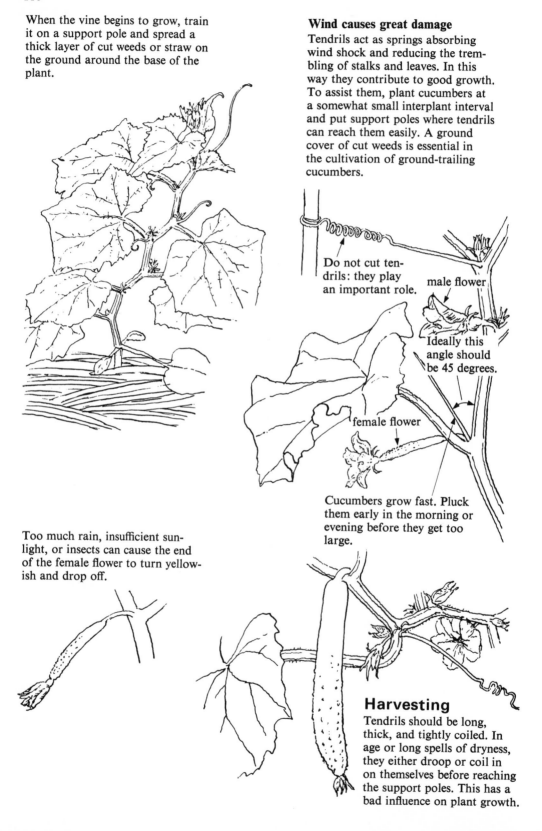

Do not cut tendrils: they play an important role.

male flower

Ideally this angle should be 45 degrees.

female flower

Cucumbers grow fast. Pluck them early in the morning or evening before they get too large.

Too much rain, insufficient sunlight, or insects can cause the end of the female flower to turn yellowish and drop off.

Harvesting
Tendrils should be long, thick, and tightly coiled. In age or long spells of dryness, they either droop or coil in on themselves before reaching the support poles. This has a bad influence on plant growth.

Bitter Melon

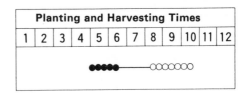

Planting and Harvesting Times											
1	2	3	4	5	6	7	8	9	10	11	12

This melon, native to India and tropical Asia, is an annual and produces gourdlike melons of the so-called litchi variety. Unripe, it is bitter. It grows well in such warm regions as Okinawa and Kyūshū and is easy to raise in the hot summertime.

In general, the melons are 10–15 cm long—though one variety reaches lengths of 40–50 cm—and are green or yellow till ripe, when they turn orange. Allowed to ripen further, they split lengthwise to reveal seeds surrounded by bright red flesh.

The vine, which looks somehow pitiably slender for the fruit, is sometimes planted by windows so that the plants may double as leafy, green awnings.

For food, the melon is picked before ripe, peeled, and sliced thin for use in sautéed foods, pickles, and vinegar-seasoned appetizers. Soaking in salted water reduces the bitterness. Sometime it is roasted whole with miso. The flesh of the ripe melon is sweetish.

Use mature compost consisting of cut weeds or of kitchen scraps that are completely free of any of the detergents or soaps used in the sink. If compost is unavailable, three to four weeks before sowing, add one handful of ground limestone for each plant and mix well with soil to a depth of 20 cm.

Sow in clusters of three or four seeds at an interval of 30 cm. Thin periodically until, by the time three or four true leaves have emerged there is only one plant in each location. After one or two additional true leaves have developed, nip the growing bud. Set up poles of a convenient height and arrange several horizontal cords on which tendrils can wrap themselves.

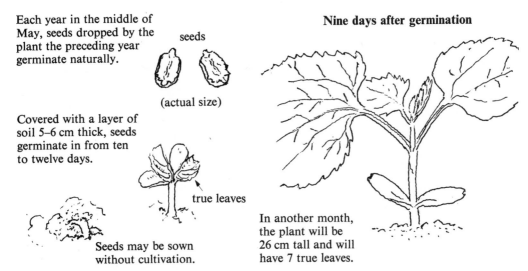

Each year in the middle of May, seeds dropped by the plant the preceding year germinate naturally.

seeds

(actual size)

Covered with a layer of soil 5–6 cm thick, seeds germinate in from ten to twelve days.

true leaves

Seeds may be sown without cultivation.

Nine days after germination

In another month, the plant will be 26 cm tall and will have 7 true leaves.

112

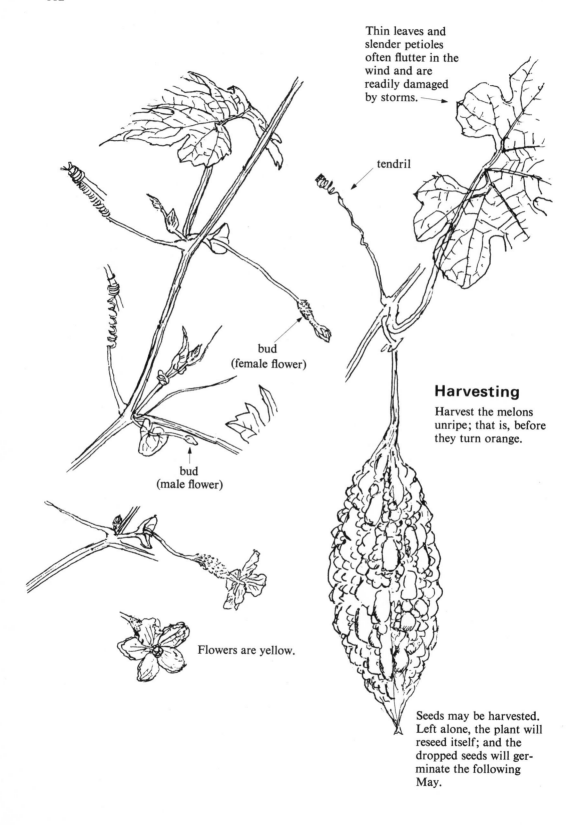

Thin leaves and slender petioles often flutter in the wind and are readily damaged by storms. →

tendril

bud (female flower)

bud (male flower)

Flowers are yellow.

Harvesting

Harvest the melons unripe; that is, before they turn orange.

Seeds may be harvested. Left alone, the plant will reseed itself; and the dropped seeds will germinate the following May.

White Melon

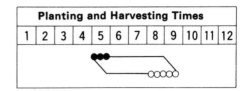

Planting and Harvesting Times											
1	2	3	4	5	6	7	8	9	10	11	12

Native to tropical Asia, this annual melon, widely raised in several varieties through-out the country, is said to have been known in Japan since the reign of the Emperor Daigo (897–930). The long, oval fruit is used mostly in a pickle prepared by seeding the melon; filling its cavity with kelp, hot red pepper, and leaves of the beefsteak plant; salting it; and allowing it to stand weighted. It thrives in the hot summertime.

White melon likes soil that drains well, retains a suitable degree of moisture, and is rich in organic matter. Use mature compost to enrich land with few weeds and free of all chemical fertilizers. As long as such toxic agricultural products are not used, there will be no need of lime to adjust soil acidity.

Since female flowers do not develop readily on the main stalk, nip the growing bud when the plant is five segments long to stimulate first branching. Leave four branches in place until they have grown to eight or nine segments in length and then nip their growing buds to induce second branching. Then, leaving two or three leaves on each, nip the growing buds of the second set of branches. Female flowers will develop on the first segment of each of the second-stage branches.

Sow seeds directly in the plots where they are to be raised since melons are intolerant of transplanting. Because they run long, prepare a furrow 150 cm wide and plant seeds in clusters of three to five at an interval of 90 cm. Cover with a layer of soil 7–8 mm thick.

Thin periodically until by the time two true leaves have emerged there is only one plant at each location. Permit a suitable stand of weeds to grow and allow the melon vines to run along their tops. Weak seeds lack the strength to shake off seed covers as they germinate.

Select the strain of melon that suits the location and local climate.

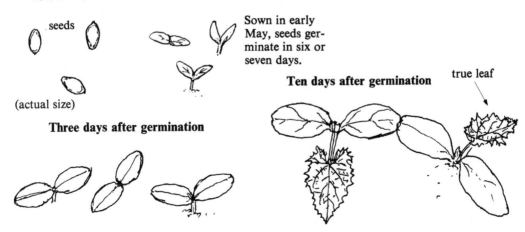

seeds

(actual size)

Three days after germination

Sown in early May, seeds ger-minate in six or seven days.

Ten days after germination

true leaf

Vine trimmed to produce four branches

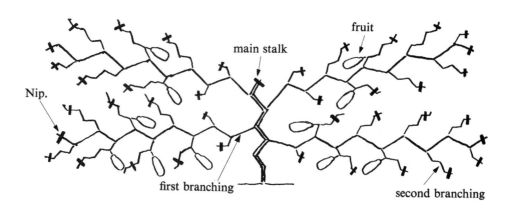

fruit

main stalk

Nip.

first branching

second branching

Twenty-seven days after germination

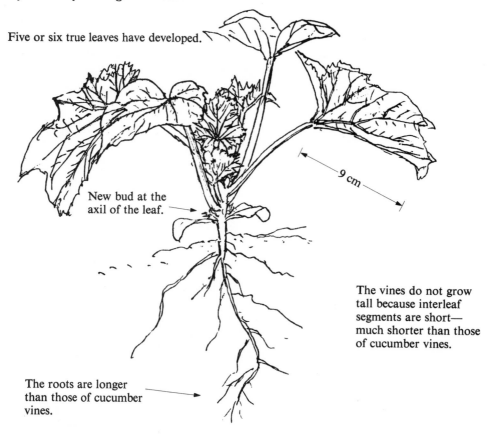

Five or six true leaves have developed.

New bud at the axil of the leaf.

9 cm

The vines do not grow tall because interleaf segments are short— much shorter than those of cucumber vines.

The roots are longer than those of cucumber vines.

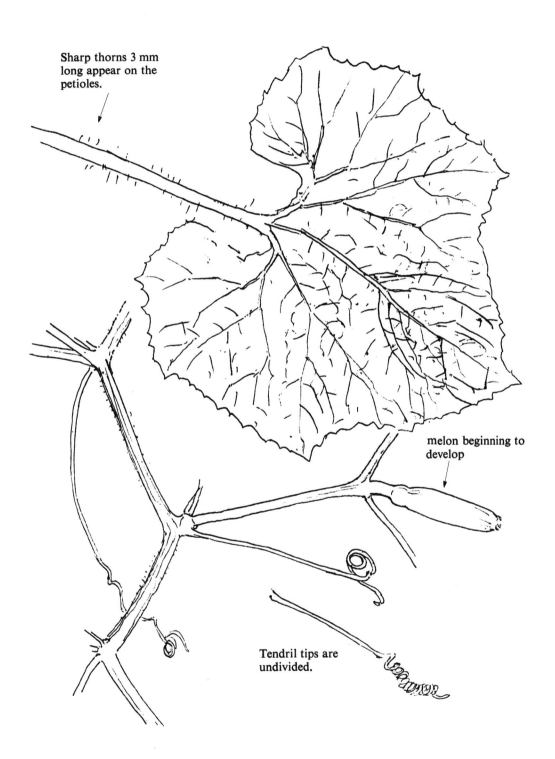

Sharp thorns 3 mm long appear on the petioles.

melon beginning to develop

Tendril tips are undivided.

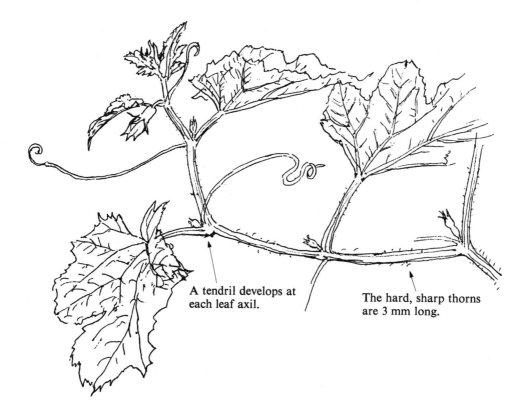

A tendril develops at
each leaf axil.

The hard, sharp thorns
are 3 mm long.

Harvesting

Melons may be harvested twenty days
after flowering. If they grow too large,
their taste becomes inferior.

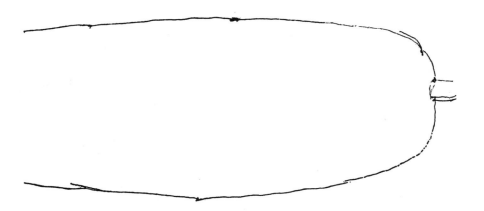

Snow Peas

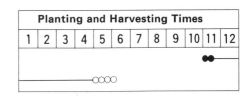
Since they tolerate low, but not high, temperatures, in temperate climates (like that of Tokyo) snow peas may be sown in the late autumn and harvested in early summer of the following year.

Soil: Snow peas are said to dislike soil acidity. But this is not a problem with the natural, organic agricultural system, in which weeds are not pulled out and the soil is not tilled. Under such conditions, the soil will not become acid; and there is no need to use lime to neutralize it.

Sowing: The sowing season must be selected on the basis of the weather of the year and of the location. If sown too soon, the plants will suffer from the cold and frosts of winter. If seed is sown too late, on the other hand, the roots will not have developed enough when cold weather sets in. In Tokyo, snow peas may be sown from early to mid-November.

Usually seeds are sown directly in the fields. But if the preceding crop on the land has not been harvested, they may be temporarily sown in pots. This system eliminates the danger of the root damage that occurs at permanent planting time if seeds are sown in a seedling bed and then transplanted. Snow pea roots are easily damaged and cannot stand rough treatment.

Preparations

When the soil is very acid, three or four weeks before sowing, sprinkle 150 g of ground limestone on every 1 m² of soil and mix well.

Avoid planting snow peas in soil high in volcanic ash.

One or two weeks before sowing, make 2 troughs about 20 cm wide in the bed and into them sprinkle compost or a mixture of dried guano and vegetable ash.

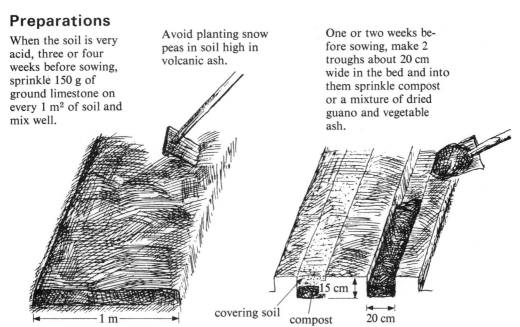

1 m

covering soil   compost   15 cm   20 cm

Protection from cold: Do not overprotect but allow the beans to encounter cold in a natural way. Plants from seeds sown at the proper time survive the winter when surrounded by withered grasses and a stand of weeds that sprout in autumn. In other words, dried grasses and weeds guard the new life of the seedlings from frost and northern wind.

Support poles: Set up slender bamboo poles in spring when the vines begin to grow· Plastic or other smooth substances to which tendrils cling with difficulty should be avoided or wrapped with something like straw. Poles should be positioned to assist tendrils in holding fast.

Rotation: Leave four or five years between crops of snow peas on the same piece of land. Furthermore, do not plant them as a follow-up on land on which green beans have just been raised.

Sowing

Make sowing troughs in the furrow and plant seeds in clusters of 3 or 4.

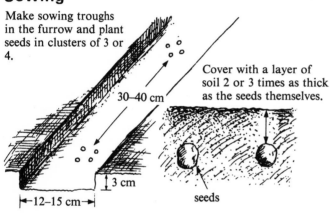

Cover with a layer of soil 2 or 3 times as thick as the seeds themselves.

30–40 cm

3 cm

12–15 cm

seeds

When the plot scheduled for use is not yet free, plant snow pea seeds in pots. Cultivate them in the pots for a month before transplanting to the permanent beds. Sowing them in different beds for later transplantation is a bad idea since it results in too much root damage.

Sow 2 or 3 seeds in a pot.

Germination

Germination takes place in from six to seven days.

Snow pea seedlings are lovely.

Eight days after germination

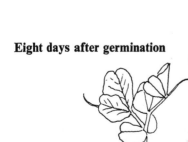

Protection from Cold

Such low plants as bamboo
grass may be planted north of
the snow peas for protection
in especially windy places.

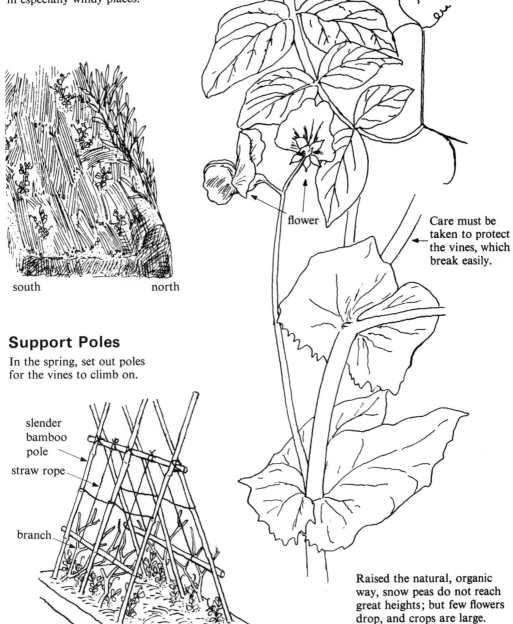

south   north

flower

Care must be
taken to protect
the vines, which
break easily.

Support Poles

In the spring, set out poles
for the vines to climb on.

slender
bamboo
pole

straw rope

branch

Raised the natural, organic
way, snow peas do not reach
great heights; but few flowers
drop, and crops are large.

When setting out the poles,
thin the plants so that there
are 2 poles for each plant.

Harvesting

Pods may be harvested about twenty days
after the flowers have wilted and fallen.
Plucked this early, the immature pods are
tender and delicious.

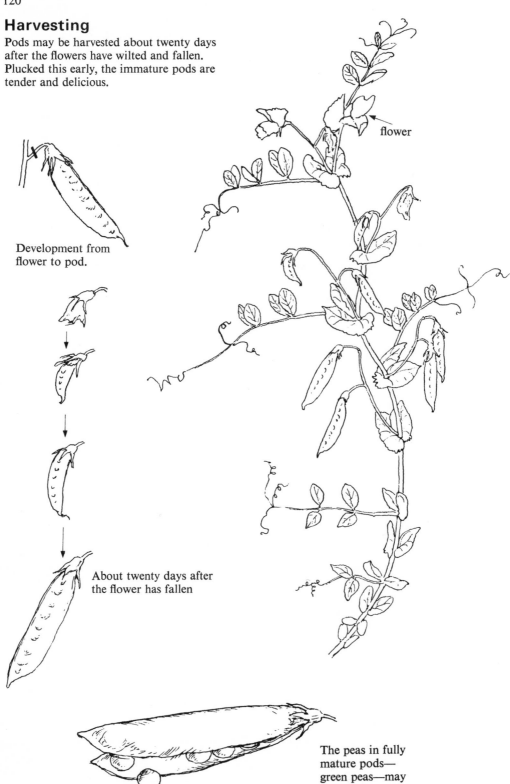

Development from
flower to pod.

flower

About twenty days after
the flower has fallen

The peas in fully
mature pods—
green peas—may
be eaten.

Green Beans (String Beans)

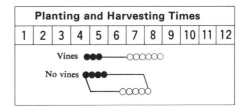
This legume does not require a great deal of fertilizer and is one of the varieties that are raised for the pod, which does not become tough as it does in the case of such other beans as green peas or navy beans. Green beans and green soybeans, which like moderate temperatures, are sown in the spring and harvested in the summer. Such other legumes as snow peas and broad beans tolerate cold and are sown in autumn and harvested the following spring or early summer.

Some green beans form vines and some do not. In cultivating the climbing, vine-producing variety, poles are necessary. The vines grow as flowers bloom, first in the lower and then gradually upward to the higher parts of the plant. Though it takes longer for vine green beans to reach the harvest stage, the harvest period is correspondingly long. The bush variety reaches maturity more quickly, bears beans all at once, and therefore has a short harvest period. Intolerant of temperature extremes, both are suited to mild weather. Their flowers drop if they are exposed to high temperatures and wither if hit by frost.

Preparations

Two or three weeks before sowing, dig a trough and mix 4 shovelfuls of compost with the soil.

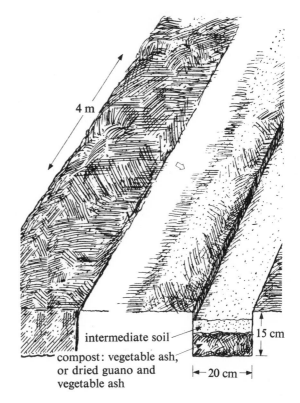

4 m

intermediate soil

compost: vegetable ash, or dried guano and vegetable ash

15 cm

20 cm

122

Preparations: Choose a sunny place to encourage large crops. These legumes tend to be intolerant of soil acidity. Rely mainly on mature compost and use such nitrogen fertilizers as immature compost and pressed soy meal sparingly as they can cause flowers to drop, reduce crop sizes, and attract aphids. Plants tend to fall victim to disease less and to produce bigger crops when raised in land that has not been used for agricultural purpose before. Rotate at a cycle of from three to four years.

Insects: Ants sometimes chew into stalks of newly germinated buds. When damage is great, resow immediately, using robust seed. When summer weather sets in, aphids become numerous.

Weeding: Cut weeds at ground line and spread them on the soil as a cover preventing aridity. Harvest while pods are still tender.

Sowing

Plant in clusters of 3 or 4 seeds with 30 cm between clusters.

30 cm

interseed interval 4–6 cm

Cover the seeds with a layer of soil 1 cm thick and press with the fingers.

1 cm

Germination

Germination generally occurs from five to seven days after sowing. Ants sometimes attack the stalks of newly germinated plants.

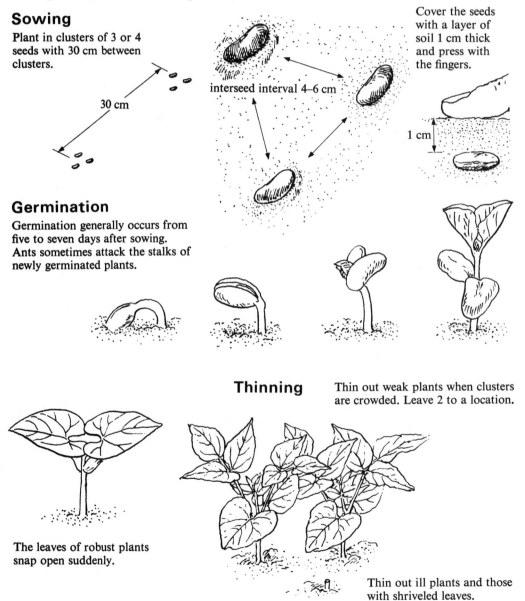

Thinning

Thin out weak plants when clusters are crowded. Leave 2 to a location.

The leaves of robust plants snap open suddenly.

Thin out ill plants and those with shriveled leaves.

Poles

Set up poles for the vines to climb on when they start developing. The poles should be only about 180 cm tall. If taller, they permit vines to grow too high and make harvesting inconvenient.

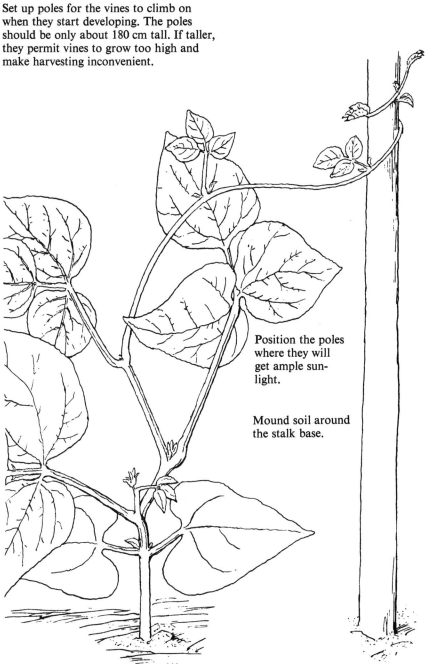

Position the poles where they will get ample sunlight.

Mound soil around the stalk base.

Spread straw on the ground to prevent both splashing with mud in rainy weather and infection of leaf undersides.

Ground Cover

Begin with a thin cover of chopped straw around the base of the plant. As temperatures rise, gradually increase the area and thickness until a full, heavy layer has been formed.

Harvest

Harvest before pods grow too large,
usually from sixty to seventy days after
sowing.

Green Soybeans

Planting and Harvesting Times											
1	2	3	4	5	6	7	8	9	10	11	12

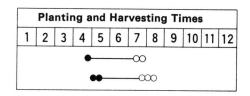

One of the easiest and most productive of the legumes, green soybeans will grow well in almost any soil as long as they get plenty of sunlight.

Sowing: It is, of course, possible to sow directly in the fields; but the danger is great that crows or pigeons will eat the seeds before germination. Consequently, it is safest to sow in pots first and transplant the seedlings to the field when they are about 10 cm tall. If they are sown in the field, protect seeds from birds with a covering of leaves.

The size of the bowlike depression left in the ground after the damage has been done reveals whether the seeds were stolen by crows or pigeons. If you see a crow in the vicinity on sowing day, wait a day or so.

Fertilizer: Green soybeans require practically no fertilizers. Since bacteria in nodules on their roots fix nitrogen in the air and impregnate the ground with nitrates, which nourish the plant, nitrogen fertilizers are unnecessary. Indeed an over-abundance of such fertilizer causes the plant to put out too many leaves and too few beans. A little vegetable ash is all that is required.

Green soybeans are comparatively tolerant of both high and low temperatures; but soil aridity, especially after blooming, drastically reduces crop sizes. Water well to prevent this. Do not overwater, however, as this causes the plants to grow tall and spindly and to lose their blossoms.

Rotation: It is possible to raise green soybeans on the same land in successive years, but it is a good idea to avoid planting them in ground on which green beans were the preceding crop. When the pods are mature, cut stalks with scissors at ground line. Harvest as early as possible to minimize insect damage.

Sowing

Plant at three separate times (A, B, and C) about fifteen days apart.

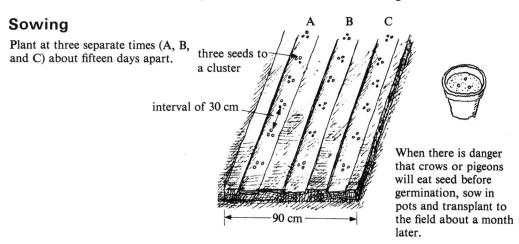

three seeds to a cluster

interval of 30 cm

90 cm

When there is danger that crows or pigeons will eat seed before germination, sow in pots and transplant to the field about a month later.

Germination
After germination do not allow the ground to dry out.

About two weeks after germination, thin one of the three seedlings, leaving two at each location.

Green soy beans are intolerant of aridity. To prevent it, allow weeds to grow around the plants.

Harvesting
Cut stalks with scissors slightly above ground line as soon as pods are mature and before insects can do much damage.

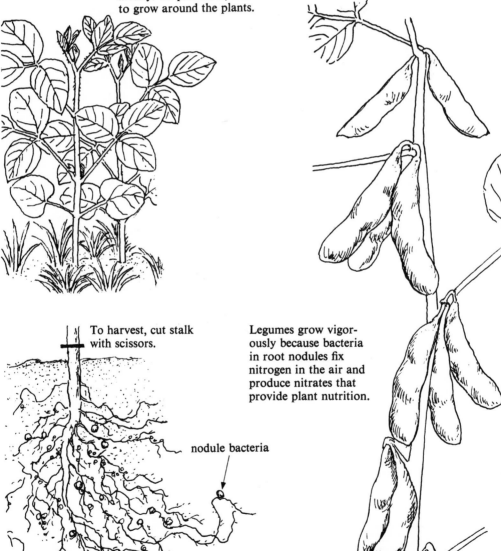

To harvest, cut stalk with scissors.

nodule bacteria

Legumes grow vigorously because bacteria in root nodules fix nitrogen in the air and produce nitrates that provide plant nutrition.

Broad Beans

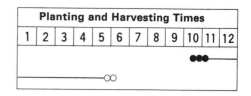
Native to the Mediterranean region, the broad bean was introduced into Japan by way of China in the Edo period (1600–1867). In early spring, spotted white or lavender blossoms appear at the base of each petiole. When the flower withers, the large pod develops in this crotch and seems to rise skyward. This accounts for the bean's Japanese name *soramame* (sky bean).

Since they are fairly tolerant of cold, broad beans grow well in cool climates. They are sown in the autumn and harvested in the early summer of the following year. Insects do little damage, and the beans are in general easy to raise. They grow very well when springtime is rainy.

Preparations: Choose a sunny spot. Broad beans are intolerant of high soil acidity. Plant in soil in which broad beans have not been raised for four or five years. Use mature compost, which keeps the soil moist and protects from frost.

Sowing: Broad beans are fairly tolerant of cold, although less so than other legumes such as navy beans. If sowing is too early, the plants will be large and easily harmed by cold when winter sets in. If it is too late, on the other hand, they will be too small and will grow poorly when the weather turns cold. In temperate climates they may be sown in the middle to late October. But sowing should be gauged to local weather conditions.

Preparations

Two or three weeks before sowing, dig a trough and mix 2 or 3 shovelfuls of compost with the soil.

If soil is highly acid, spread 200 g of lime on it three or four weeks before sowing.

50 cm
15 cm
2 m
intermediate soil
compost
15 cm
5 cm

Sowing

Sow 3 seeds to a cluster at an intercluster interval of 30 cm.

30 cm

1 cm

This is the correct way to plant.

This is an incorrect way of planting.

Four days after sowing
Germination has begun.

128

Protection from cold: To protect from the severe cold of winter nights, raise mounds of soil or plant such things as bamboo grass on the north side of the furrow. Spread compost on the ground to protect from cold wind and frost. Another good way to protect the plants by minimizing freezing of the ground is to allow stands of fall weeds to grow up around them. This will prevent evaporation of ground water and protect from frost and freezing.

Mounding: In March, the plants will begin to grow vigorously. Mound soil around them early to prevent their falling over.

Harvesting: When the formerly sky-pointing pods turn downward, fill out, and become glossy green, harvest by cutting them from the plant, one by one, with scissors. Delaying will allow the pods to turn black and the beans to become tough.

Germination and Thinning

Germination takes place from six to ten days after sowing. Thin out the weakest seedling, leaving two at each location.

Fourteen days after germination

Trim all but four or five of the lateral shoots.

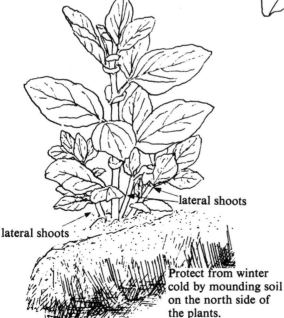

lateral shoots

lateral shoots

Protect from winter cold by mounding soil on the north side of the plants.

Harvesting

Harvest while the pods are full and glossy green.

It is time to harvest when the pods, which originally pointed upward, begin to point down.

Peanuts

Peanuts grow well in dry places (in volcanic ash or sandy soil) and in strong sunlight. They thrive in most parts of Japan, except Hokkaido, in the north, although Kanagawa and Chiba prefectures are especially noted for their production. They are an excellent and very welcome crop for a small corner of a garden and are easy to raise.

As is true of the other legumes, in raising peanuts, nitrogen fertilizers must be used sparingly since the plants have the characteristic legume root nodules, in which bacteria fix nitrogen in the air, thus producing nitrates for nutrition. Peanuts require fertilizing only when grown in completely new ground.

Rotation: Though easy to raise, peanuts are intolerant of acid soil and series planting on the same land. Rotate at one-year intervals.

Sowing: Peanuts may be sown directly in the field. But, when there is danger of marauding by birds or field mice, to which, like green soybeans, they often fall victim, plant in pots first and later transplant the germinated seedlings to the open ground.

Sowing

Peanuts may be sown directly in the ground, but when there is danger of damage from birds or mice, sow in pots first.

seed

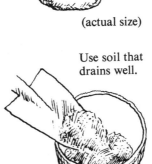

(actual size)

Plant 1 seed per pot.

pot diameter about 10 cm

Use soil that drains well.

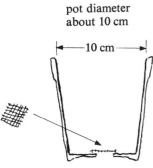

piece of screen to keep out insects

Until germination, the soil must not be allowed to dry out. Excess moisture, however, must be avoided.

Cover with a layer of soil 3 cm thick and press lightly with the fingers.

3 cm

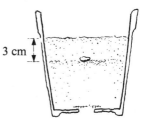

Weeding and mounding: Both of these processes are essential to good peanut crops. After flowering, ovules in the ovaries are fertilized. The lower parts of the ovaries develop into long runners, the tips of which burrow underground, where eventually pods form and ripen. Crop size, therefore, depends on ensuring that the tips of all of the ovaries are enabled to reach a subterranean level. For this reason, weeding and mounding are essential.

The mounds must be flat, and sowing must be at a level still lower. If mounds are high, ovaries have difficulty reaching the ground; and mounding is difficult.

Harvesting: In October, when leaves begin to turn yellow, pull the plants up, roots and all, and hang them upside down to dry.

Preparation

Furrows must be level, and planting troughs must be low.

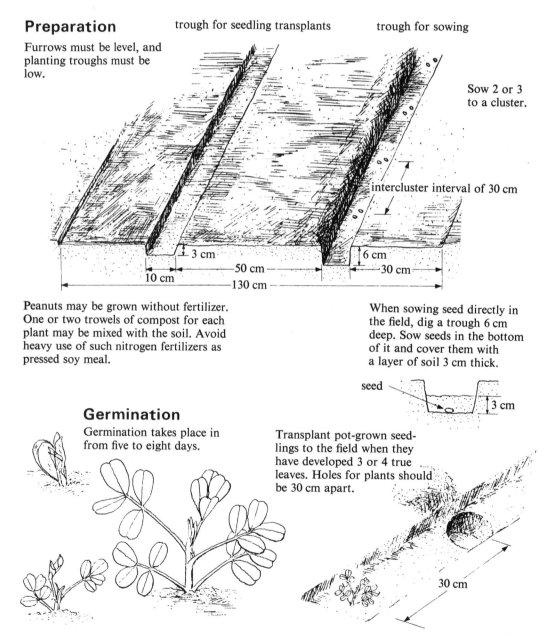

trough for seedling transplants

trough for sowing

Sow 2 or 3 to a cluster.

intercluster interval of 30 cm

3 cm
50 cm
6 cm
10 cm
30 cm
130 cm

Peanuts may be grown without fertilizer. One or two trowels of compost for each plant may be mixed with the soil. Avoid heavy use of such nitrogen fertilizers as pressed soy meal.

When sowing seed directly in the field, dig a trough 6 cm deep. Sow seeds in the bottom of it and cover them with a layer of soil 3 cm thick.

seed

3 cm

Germination

Germination takes place in from five to eight days.

Transplant pot-grown seedlings to the field when they have developed 3 or 4 true leaves. Holes for plants should be 30 cm apart.

30 cm

After blooming, the ovaries lengthen and burrow underground. Their ends ultimately thicken to form pods.

Sprinkle vegetable ash around the base of the plant.

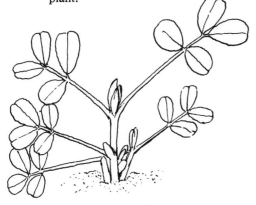

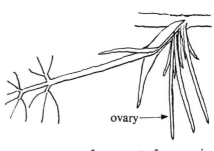

ovary⟶

from one to four ovaries

Weeding

To facilitate ovaries' burrowing underground, remove weeds early. Loosen the soil carefully and mound it around the base of the plant.

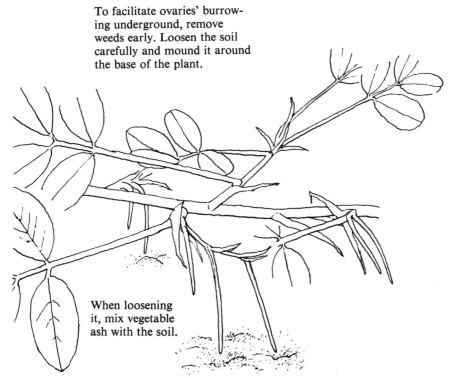

When loosening it, mix vegetable ash with the soil.

Crush and loosen hard soil to enable ovaries to burrow into it readily.

When preparing furrows, make it easy for ovaries to burrow by preparing troughs well below the ground line for both sowing of seeds or transplanting of seedlings.

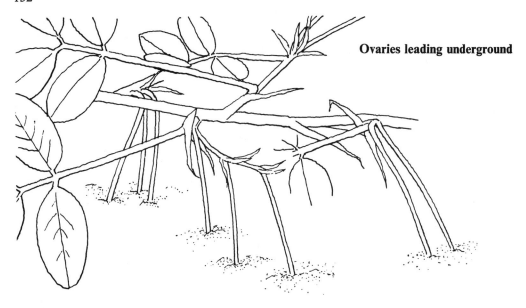

Ovaries leading underground

Harvesting

When the leaves begin to yellow, pull the plants, roots and all, from the soil. Hang them upside down to dry for two or three days. Then cut the peanuts from the ovaries and spread them on straw mats to dry thoroughly.

Returned to the soil, roots with their nitrogen-fixing bacteria nodules become natural fertilizer.

Pods develop on the ends of ovaries.

Cut.

Sanjaku Cowpeas

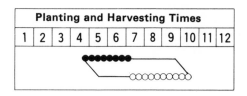

Planting and Harvesting Times											
1	2	3	4	5	6	7	8	9	10	11	12

Of the several varieties of cowpeas, all of which are annual legumes, *Sanjaku* cowpeas have the longest (60–80 cm) pods, in which they bear maroon beans resembling, though longer than, *azuki*. They should be picked and eaten while still green, as they grow tough with maturity.

Since they thrive in hot weather, their seeds are sown from early May till early July. With their cascading long green pods, they make a startling visual impression.

Choose a sunny spot since insufficient light causes their flowers to drop. They may be planted at the edge of the garden, beside fences, or by windows where their foliage provides a natural awning. As is true in the cases of all other legumes, use no nitrogen fertilizers, which have various bad effects, including making the vines straggly, lowering productivity, and inviting aphids and disease. All legumes satisfy their own nitrogen needs by means of root nodules that fix nitrogen in the air to produce nitrates. Artificially dosing them with more causes a superfluity, which collects at growth points and in young leaves to attract aphids, which are fond of nitrogen. A casual examination of growth points and leaves clearly reveals accumulations of nitrogen.

Germination

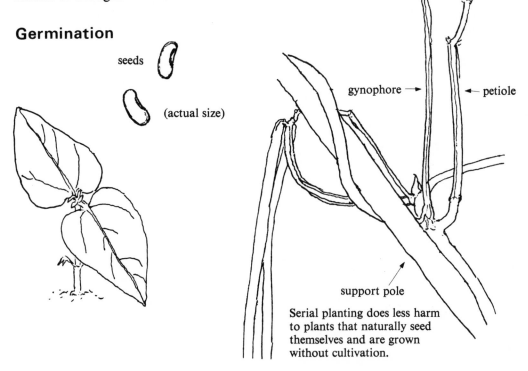

seeds

(actual size)

gynophore → ← petiole

support pole

Serial planting does less harm to plants that naturally seed themselves and are grown without cultivation.

If the soil is rich in organic matter, no further fertilizer except a ground covering of cut weeds is needed. Cultivation with only fertilizers of this kind prevents excess foliage, stimulates productivity, and promotes absorption of natural nutrients to improve flavors.

Sow in clusters of three or four seeds at an interval of 30 cm and cover with a layer of soil two or three times as thick as the seeds themselves. After two or three true leaves have developed, thin until only two plants remain in each location. When the plants are 15 cm tall, provide a 2 m pole for each to climb on. Nip growth buds when the vines have climbed to the tops of the poles.

An unbroken, longer harvest is ensured by sowing two or three times at twenty-day intervals.

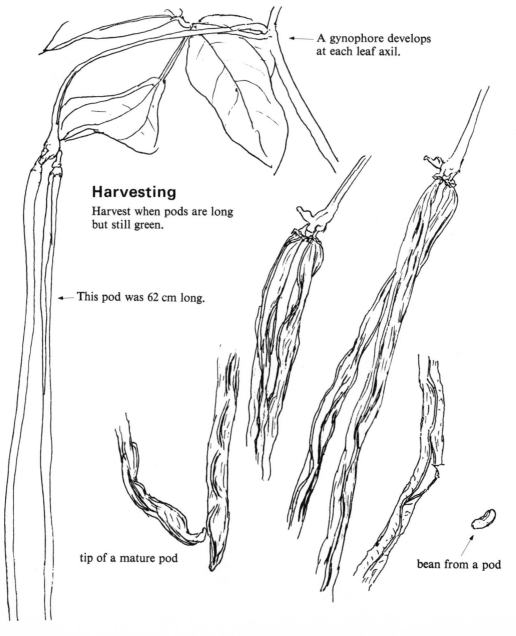

A gynophore develops at each leaf axil.

Harvesting

Harvest when pods are long but still green.

This pod was 62 cm long.

tip of a mature pod

bean from a pod

Sprouts

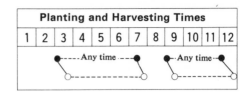
For from two to five days after germination, sprouted seeds are even richer than the seeds themselves in such important nutrients as vitamins, proteins, calcium, and iron. Thereafter, however, they consume their nutrients in the growth process. Soybean sprouts are extremely popular; and in recent years sprouts of such other seeds as watercress, alfalfa, and mustard have been increasingly widely used. In addition, it is possible to produce domestic, highly flavorsome sprouts from the Japanese red bean known as *azuki*, green beans, peas, *daikon* radish, turnips, yellow mustard, sesame, radishes, fennel, dill, and onions, all of which are distinctively fragrant, spicy, and refreshing.

Since sprouts are eaten as soon as possible after germination, neither soil nor fertilizer is needed. All that is required is water and a container. Though for growth, a room temperature of about 68°F is needed, for sprouts, while warmth prolongs the growing period, lower temperatures are satisfactory. Frequent changes of fresh, clear water—four or five times a day in warm weather and two or three times a day in cool weather—are essential. This is especially true of soybeans and *azuki*, which, sprouted in summer, tend to damage and spoil easily.

Flowerpot cultivation
Wash a shallow, unglazed flowerpot (9–12 cm in diameter) well in hot water. Spread a double layer of cheesecloth or gauze in the bottom. Allow the cloth to project slightly above the walls of the pot.

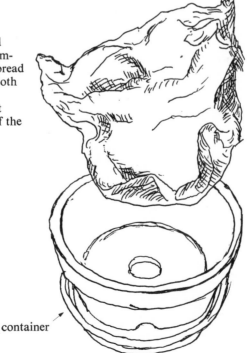

Wash the cloth well with soap and hot water and rinse thoroughly.

container

You will require either a large, wide-mounted glass container, like the kinds of jars used for jam and honey, or a shallow, unglazed flower pot (9–12 cm in diameter). The kind used for miniature bonsai is convenient. Cultivated in the dark for about a week, the white sprouts will grow till they fill the container. After a two-hour exposure to sunlight, the cotyledons will turn bright green.

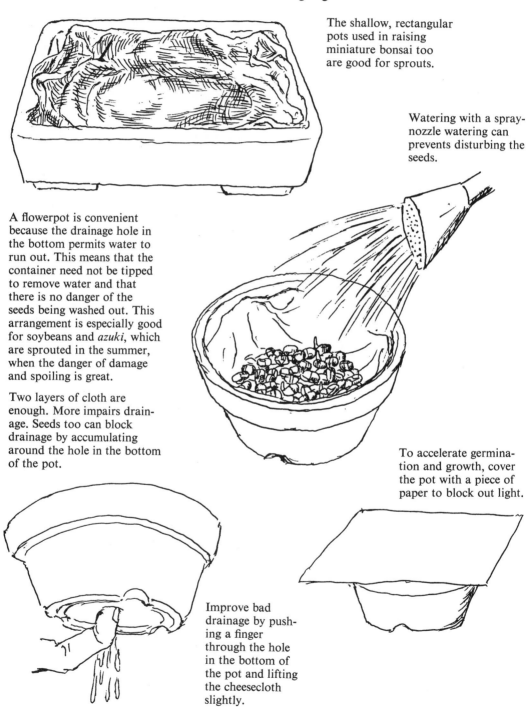

The shallow, rectangular pots used in raising miniature bonsai too are good for sprouts.

Watering with a spray-nozzle watering can prevents disturbing the seeds.

A flowerpot is convenient because the drainage hole in the bottom permits water to run out. This means that the container need not be tipped to remove water and that there is no danger of the seeds being washed out. This arrangement is especially good for soybeans and *azuki*, which are sprouted in the summer, when the danger of damage and spoiling is great.

Two layers of cloth are enough. More impairs drainage. Seeds too can block drainage by accumulating around the hole in the bottom of the pot.

To accelerate germination and growth, cover the pot with a piece of paper to block out light.

Improve bad drainage by pushing a finger through the hole in the bottom of the pot and lifting the cheesecloth slightly.

Cultivation in a glass jar

Select a wide-mouthed jam or honey jar.

Incline the bottle and fill it gently with water.

The larger the jar, the greater the crop. Jars are suitable for raising many kinds of sprouts, including alfalfa, watercress, *daikon*-radish, soybean, green bean, and *azuki*. But because addition of water disturbs the seeds considerably, during the hot weather, soybeans, green beans, and *azuki* are likely to be damaged and to spoil.

gauze

Drain well and store in a dark place. The jar may be stood upright or laid on its side. It should be set in another container.

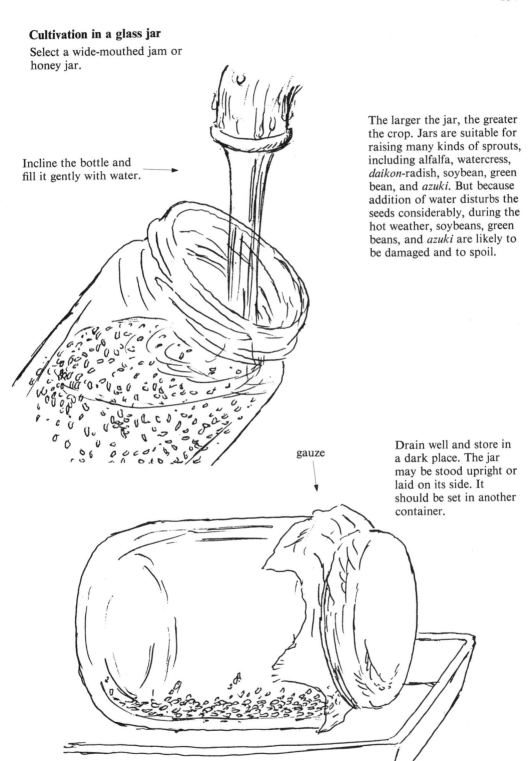

Alfalfa

Native to the shores of the Mediterranean, alfalfa produces threadlike, crunchy sprouts, that can be produced in large quantities in a glass jar. Do not overcrowd, as alfalfa sprouts are 10 times the original seeds in bulk. Sprouts may be harvested in from 3 to 10 days if kept at a temperature of about 68°F.

seeds

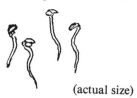

(actual size)

Wash seeds well. Cover the mouth of the jar with gauze held in place with a rubber band. Water may be added and drained out through the gauze, which need not be removed.

Three days after sowing

Raised at a temperature of 68°F.

(actual size)

long, thin sprouts

Be certain to use new seeds.

Ten days after sowing

Their cases may be removed by washing the seeds in a colander before using.

About two hours' exposure to sunlight will turn cotyledons on developed sprouts green.

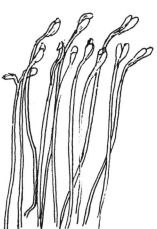

(actual size)

Green Beans

Green beans produce roughly four times their own volume in sprouts. (Most of the bean sprouts currently marketed in Japan are made from black beans.) The sprouts should be eaten within the first four days after germination, when they are most nutritious.

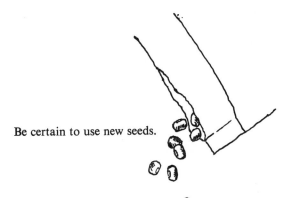

Be certain to use new seeds.

Two days after germination

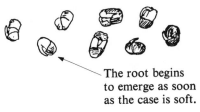

The root begins to emerge as soon as the case is soft.

Ten days after germination

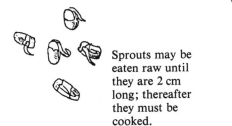

Sprouts may be eaten raw until they are 2 cm long; thereafter they must be cooked.

Three days after germination

When the cotyledons begin to emerge, the sprouts produce a vaguely cranelike impression.

The beaklike projection is the true leaf.

cotyledons

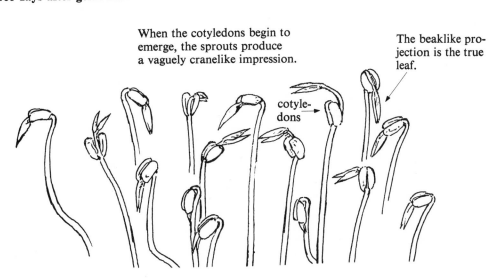

Daikon-radish Sprouts

Piquancy accounts for the major charm
of the flavor of *daikon*-radish sprouts. In
summertime, when the cotyledons of
sprouts grown in jars are easily bruised,
it is best to eat them as soon as possible.

Exposure to the sun-
light turns the white
cotyledons a beautiful
green.

Four days after sowing

Use when the white
sprouts are 5–6 cm long.

In the early stage of
cultivation, the sprouts
move considerably each
time they are washed.
Movement ceases as
they grow.

Seven days after sowing

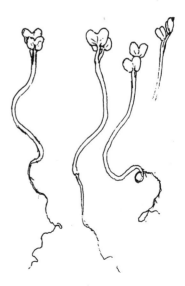

Always use new seeds.

Corn (Maize)

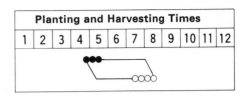
Plants, insects, other animals, microorganisms, and all other creatures contribute to the system that maintains life on earth. None can be eliminated. Man is not the sole lord of the planet. Essentially, from the universal viewpoint, all forms of life are the same and intimately interrelated. Consequently the ecological system suffers by the loss of even one microorganism species. The insect who eats plant leaves performs some functions that assist plant growth. This is why the presence of insects is only natural; insects are a part of the harmonious whole of the world of nature.

Insects proliferate in abnormal numbers when that harmony has been disrupted by such human action as the use of chemical fertilizers and pesticides that destroy useful microorganisms and natural insect enemies. It would seem that, when the operations of the natural world become apparent, human beings would stop resorting to such harmful substances.

Corn is subject to few diseases and little insect damage. It is true that the larvae of the *Pyrausta nulibalis* moth do some damage, but the harm can be minimized by

Preparations

Two or three weeks before sowing, dig a trough, add 4 or 5 shovelfuls of compost to it, and mix well with the soil.

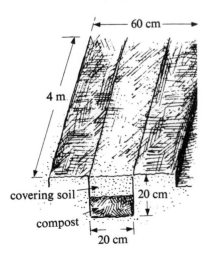

Sowing

Plant 3 or 4 seeds in each cluster.

Clusters should occupy a space 5 cm wide and should be 30 cm apart.

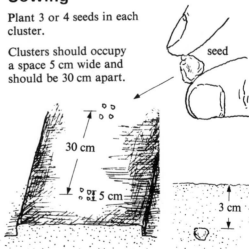

Cover with a fairly thick (3 cm) layer of soil to keep pigeons, crows, and other birds from eating the seed.

harvesting ears early. Corn grows well in sunny places where the soil is suitably moist; dryness is a frequent cause of poor crops. Owing to great root-absorption powers, corn grows well even in fairly lean soil. While developing rapidly even in the early stages, the plants grow with much greater vigor after they pass about 30 cm in height. At about this time, a number of lateral buds will develop at ground line. They must be removed quickly. Corn is naturally wind-pollinated.

Germination and Thinning

Germination occurs in from six to nine days. Thereafter, thin out weak plants until, when they are about 10 cm tall, there are only 2 in each sowing location.

Removing Lateral Buds

Remove lateral buds as soon as they emerge at ground line.

Pollination

Pollination occurs when pollen from tassels fertilizes the ears.

Harvesting

Harvest ears as soon as the silk turns brown. If harvesting is late, worms will eat the ears, which will harden and be plucked by birds.

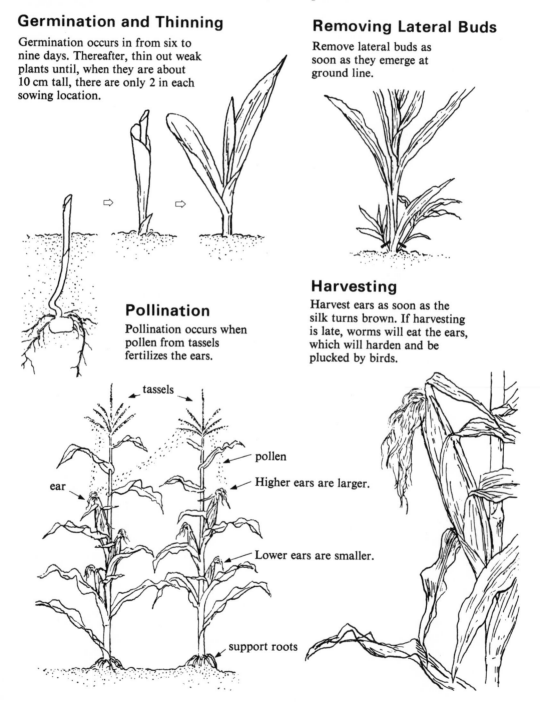

tassels

pollen

Higher ears are larger.

ear

Lower ears are smaller.

support roots

Squash

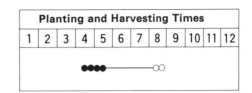
In autumn fields from which all summer crops have been harvested, it is not un-common to find tomato, green-bean, and corn plants grown from seeds dropped naturally. Similarly, in spring, squash seeds dropped in the autumn often germinate and begin growing. Cutting weeds in summer, I have been surprised to see how many squash seeds have fallen to the ground.

Most members of this family are easy to raise. In general squash may be divided into the summer and winter varieties. In this book, I deal with the winter squash, which requires virtually no care and thrives even at low temperatures.

Preparations: Squash vines run for considerable distances. This can be com-pensated for by twining them on poles; but, if space is available, letting them run is better. Some varieties that do not produce vines may be grown one plant to 1 m². Provide adequate space because crowding impedes ventilation and reduces sunlight with the result that blossoms drop. Squash, which are not finicky about soil, grow well even under dry conditions and may be raised successively on the same plot.

Since they absorb nutrients well, squash should be fertilized moderately. Too much fertilizer, especially nitrogen, causes blossoms to drop.

Sowing Bed

Make a furrow 1.5 m wide three or four weeks before sowing time. In it make holes 1.5 m apart.

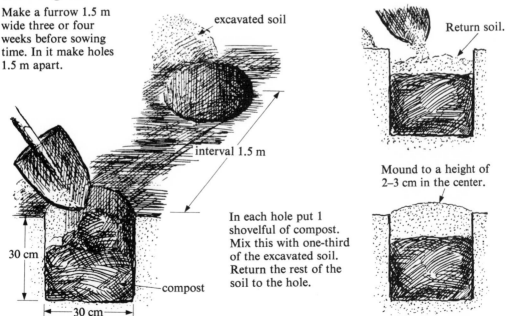

excavated soil

interval 1.5 m

30 cm

30 cm

compost

In each hole put 1 shovelful of compost. Mix this with one-third of the excavated soil. Return the rest of the soil to the hole.

Return soil.

Mound to a height of 2–3 cm in the center.

Secondary vines develop from the primary one, but there is no need to nip growth buds. Allow the vines to grow freely. As soon as they begin to lengthen, spread straw or cut weeds on the ground around the plants. Allow the tendrils to coil. In the later phase of growth, leave weeds uncut to protect vines and tendrils.

Diseases: Squash are prone to mildew. Do not use chemical insecticides and do not remove the mildewy leaves. Loss of leaves does the plant more harm than the disease.

Sowing

Winter squash

Laying them flat, plant 4 seeds to a hole. Cover with a layer of soil 2 or 3 times as deep as the seeds are thick. Water well.

Erect poles and tie plants to them if there is danger that cats or other animals may do damage.

slender bamboo poles

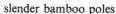

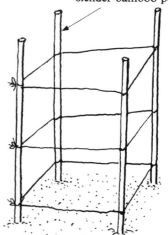

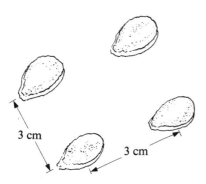

3 cm

3 cm

If the ground is moist, there is no need to water after sowing. Press lightly with the hands to ensure soil adheres to seeds.

Germination and Thinning

Germination takes place in from six to ten days.

Leaving the 2 better ones, thin out 2 seedlings from each sowing location.

In the warm weather of May, remove the plastic bag. After 2 or 3 true leaves have developed, thin out one plant, leaving the healthier one in place.

leaf

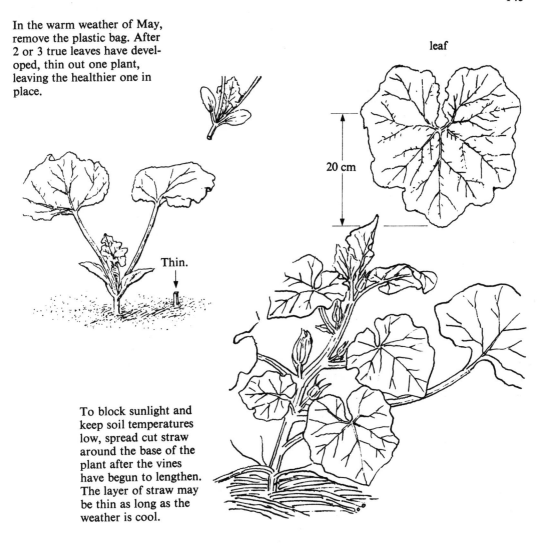

20 cm

Thin.

To block sunlight and keep soil temperatures low, spread cut straw around the base of the plant after the vines have begun to lengthen. The layer of straw may be thin as long as the weather is cool.

Winter squash requires no training and may be allowed to run freely.

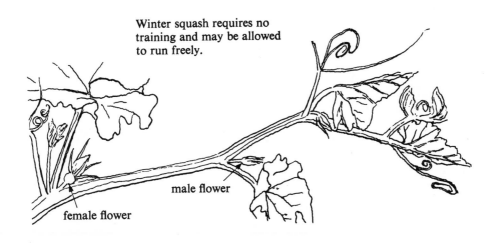

female flower

male flower

Artificial Pollination

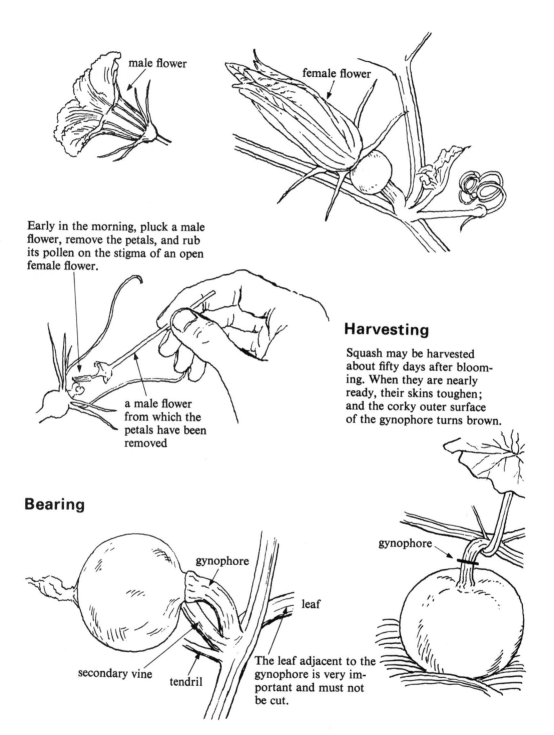

male flower

female flower

Early in the morning, pluck a male flower, remove the petals, and rub its pollen on the stigma of an open female flower.

a male flower from which the petals have been removed

Harvesting

Squash may be harvested about fifty days after blooming. When they are nearly ready, their skins toughen; and the corky outer surface of the gynophore turns brown.

Bearing

gynophore

leaf

secondary vine

tendril

The leaf adjacent to the gynophore is very important and must not be cut.

gynophore

Okra

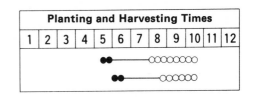

A member of the Hibiscus family, okra, which is native to northern Africa, has lovely yellow blossoms. An important vegetable in subtropical zones, it is intolerant of severe cold. But, if sown directly in the field when the weather is warm and if given plenty of compost, it is relatively easy to grow.

Preparation: Though the nature of the soil is comparatively unimportant, okra should be planted in a spot that is sunny all day in ground that drains well and is rich in organic matter.

Fertilizing: The okra harvesting season is long. Since it bears poorly in lean soil, use plenty of mature compost. If organic matter and soil moisture are insufficient, the plants will not bear well; and the individual pods will be fibrous and tough.

Sowing: Since it is sensitive to cold, sow in late May. Because it has a simple straight-root system making transplanting difficult, sow directly in the growing bed or field. If this is impossible, sow in pots and transfer to the field or bed after germination.

The seedlings grow slowly as long as the weather is cool but develop more rapidly

Preparations

Two or three weeks before sowing, spread from 10 to 15 shovelfuls of compost over the ground. Digging to a depth of 20 cm, mix the compost well with the soil.

Sowing

Taking advantage of a rainfall, at a time when the soil is thoroughly moist, sow 4 or 5 seeds in clusters 45 cm apart and cover with a layer of soil 1 cm thick.

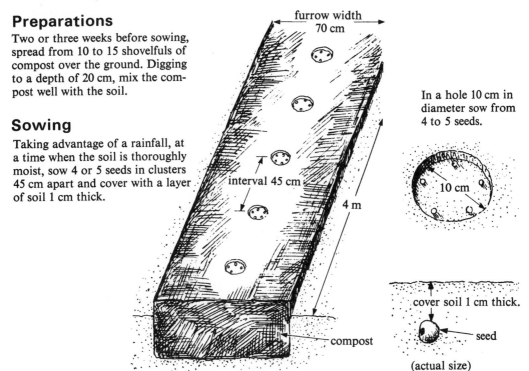

furrow width
70 cm

interval 45 cm

4 m

compost

In a hole 10 cm in diameter sow from 4 to 5 seeds.

10 cm

cover soil 1 cm thick.

seed

(actual size)

when it warms up. Insects cause so little trouble that okra can usually be allowed to grow untended. Nonetheless, young plants are sometimes attacked by cutworms and grubs.

Harvesting: Harvesting for plants raised from seed sown in late May begins in August. The flowers bloom in the morning and wilt before afternoon. Tender, young pods may be harvested in from four to six days after blooming. It is important to pick them as soon as possible from strong plants to stimulate further blooming.

Insufficient fertilizer and tardy harvesting produce tough, inedible pods. Wear long-sleeve shirts when harvesting as the juice on okra leaves can cause itching and skin eruptions.

Harvesting seed: Leave two or three pods on a robust plant. Cut them from the plant before they shrivel. Dry them in the sun, remove the seeds, put them in a paper envelope, and store them in a can.

Germination

Germination takes place at 77°F.

Okra will not germinate in the cold. In temperate climates (like that of Tokyo), late May is a suitable sowing time.

After germination, seedlings grow very slowly but develop with much greater speed when the hot weather of July sets in.

Thinning

Thin out plants that seem retarded or that insects have damaged until, by the time 4 or 5 true leaves have developed, only 1 plant remains at each sowing location.

Though a simple, straight-root system makes transplanting difficult, okra plants that have been sown and raised for a while in pots may be transplanted without incurring root damage.

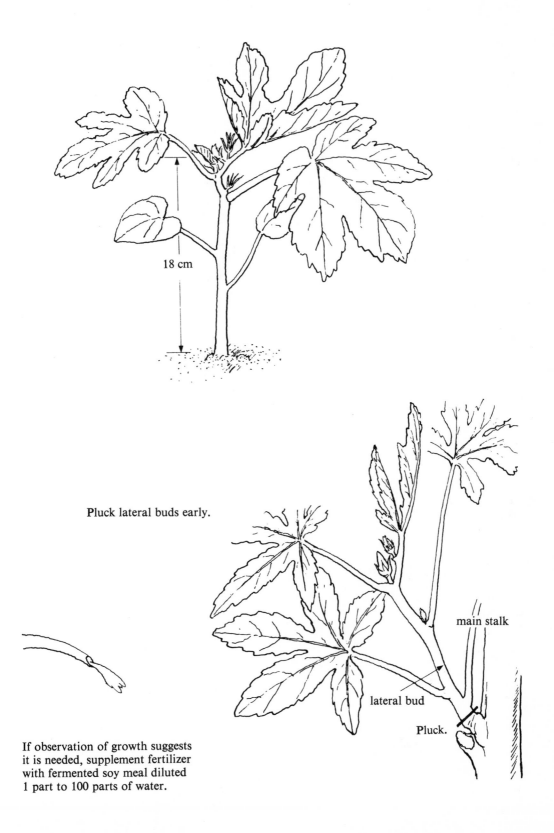

18 cm

Pluck lateral buds early.

main stalk

lateral bud

Pluck.

If observation of growth suggests
it is needed, supplement fertilizer
with fermented soy meal diluted
1 part to 100 parts of water.

Harvesting

Harvest young pods that have reached a length of 7–10 cm. Without forgetting, harvest early in the morning, daily. Pods harvested late are tough and inedible.

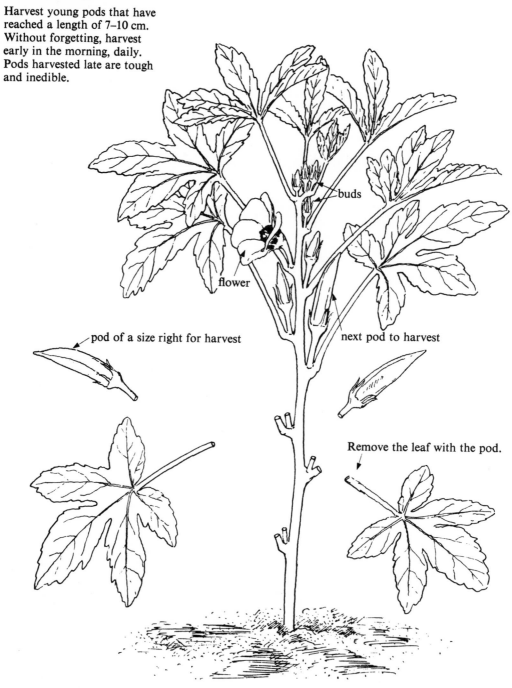

buds

flower

pod of a size right for harvest

next pod to harvest

Remove the leaf with the pod.

Because the juice found on the edges of okra leaves causes itching, always wear gloves and a long-sleeve shirt when harvesting.

Strawberries

Planting and Harvesting Times											
1	2	3	4	5	6	7	8	9	10	11	12

Later than second year

Two furrows 60 cm wide and 4 m long will probably produce enough berries to fill five or six of the kinds of transparent-plastic boxes in which they are usually sold. But just a few plants are enough to enrich the family table with the bright red of early summer.

Seedlings: It is best to raise strawberries from commercially supplied seedlings. But it is unnecessary to purchase a large number of them since each plant puts out runners on which new plants appear. Seedlings are generally available at suppliers in about September. Plants obtained from friends may be safely planted at any time from late May until late October.

Temporary planting: New plants obtained from runners of older ones are temporarily planted from the middle until the end of August and permanently planted from the middle to the end of October. For planting in the temporary bed, select new plants that are second or third along the runner from the old plant. The first plant is already too large and will age too quickly. The temporary bed must be adequately fertilized with mature compost. Although some people use dried guano or pressed soy meal, this can retard growth by scorching strawberry roots, which are very sensitive to fertilizer. Work quickly so as not to allow the roots to dry out. Water after planting and remember that strawberries are intolerant of dryness.

Seedling in Ideal Condition for Temporary Planting

Select plants that are robust and free of insect damage and have 3 or 4 true leaves.

Two or three weeks before temporary planting, spread 3 kg of mature compost on each 1 m² of the bed and mix well with the soil.

Do not use immature compost, which can scorch strawberry roots.

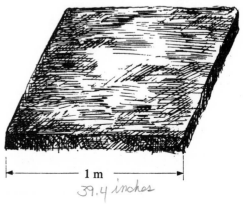

1 m
39.4 inches

Permanent planting: Weed and cultivate for about two months and plant in permanent beds from the middle to the end of October. Before transplanting, remove all old or dead leaves and all lateral buds. Once again, work quickly to prevent root drying. To stimulate good root growth, water well after planting to enable the plant to withstand winter cold. Keep the soil moist until the middle of December and then stop watering and cover the ground with straw to prevent damage from frost.

Harvesting: Begin harvesting ripe, red berries from about the middle of May. Insects will spoil fruit left on plants too long.

Weeding: After harvest, weed carefully and remove all rubbish from the soil to enable runners to spread freely in all directions.

Selecting New Plants from Runners
(Middle to late August)

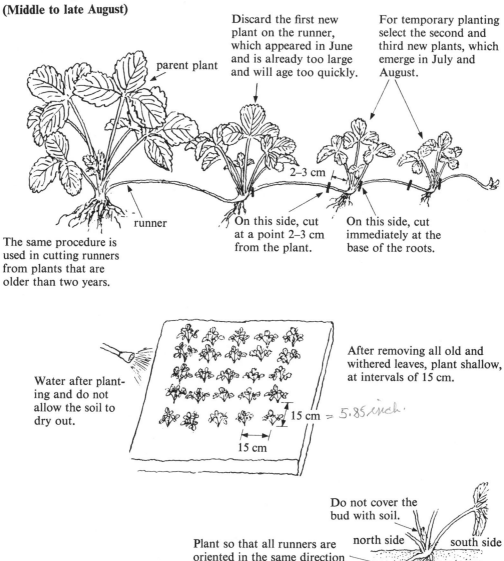

parent plant

Discard the first new plant on the runner, which appeared in June and is already too large and will age too quickly.

For temporary planting select the second and third new plants, which emerge in July and August.

2–3 cm

runner

The same procedure is used in cutting runners from plants that are older than two years.

On this side, cut at a point 2–3 cm from the plant.

On this side, cut immediately at the base of the roots.

Water after planting and do not allow the soil to dry out.

After removing all old and withered leaves, plant shallow, at intervals of 15 cm.

15 cm = 5.85 inch.

15 cm

Plant so that all runners are oriented in the same direction and underground, where they can grow further.

Do not cover the bud with soil.

north side   south side

Care after Plants Are Well-rooted

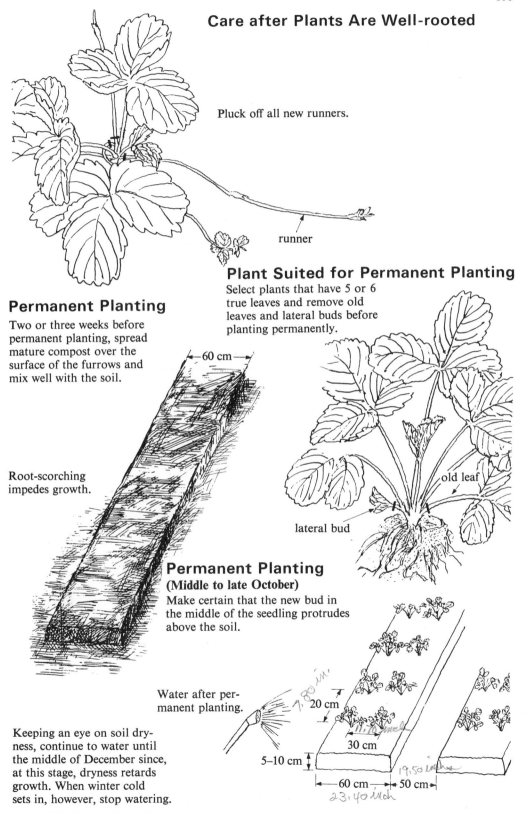

Pluck off all new runners.

runner

Plant Suited for Permanent Planting

Select plants that have 5 or 6 true leaves and remove old leaves and lateral buds before planting permanently.

Permanent Planting

Two or three weeks before permanent planting, spread mature compost over the surface of the furrows and mix well with the soil.

Root-scorching impedes growth.

60 cm

old leaf

lateral bud

Permanent Planting
(Middle to late October)

Make certain that the new bud in the middle of the seedling protrudes above the soil.

Water after permanent planting.

Keeping an eye on soil dryness, continue to water until the middle of December since, at this stage, dryness retards growth. When winter cold sets in, however, stop watering.

20 cm

30 cm

5–10 cm

60 cm   50 cm

154

Harvesting

In the middle of May, using scissors, begin harvesting ripe, red berries.

Post-harvest Care

After harvest, plants will begin putting out new runners.

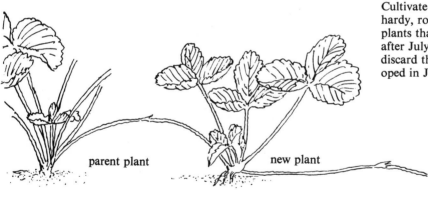

parent plant   new plant

Cultivate runners of hardy, robust parent plants that emerged after July. Pluck off and discard those that developed in June.

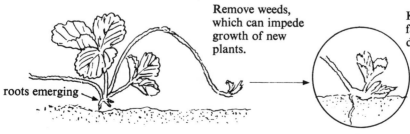

roots emerging

Remove weeds, which can impede growth of new plants.

Keep soil loose to facilitate root development.

Daikon Radishes

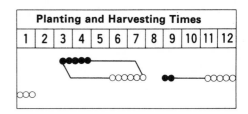
A member of the mustard family, *daikon* radishes bear cruciate, white or lavender blossoms in the spring. Raised the organic, no-chemical way, they grow large and are relatively free of the insects that are said to have become a problem in Japan in recent years. There are several varieties of *daikon* radish, some of which are sown in the spring, some in the summer, and some in the fall.

Daikon radishes require little fertilizer. A little vegetable ash suffices generally; and, if there is a good stand of weeds, no fertilizer at all is needed. Nutrients from compost applied for the preceding crop are enough to grow fine *daikon* radishes.

When raised with nitrogen fertilizers they seem to grow robust and quickly at first but soon develop internal hollows and have a short harvest period. Raised without fertilizer, however, though they develop slowly in the early stage, they are sound, have few internal splits, and may be harvested over a long time.

I have experimented with three methods of raising *daikon* radishes: (1) tilling the soil and adding compost, (2) adding compost but not tilling the soil, and (3) neither tilling the soil nor adding compost. And, contrary to the general belief that deep tilling is needed, I have found that methods (2) and (3) produce large vegetables as consistently as method (1).

Preparation

After tilling the soil carefully, make a flat furrow and dig a trench about the width of a hoe in it. Sow the seeds in a line along one side of the trough. Sowing seeds directly on top of compost causes the radishes to fork. Consequently, make a line of compost on the opposite side of the trough. Cover with a layer of soil 2–5 cm thick and press lightly.

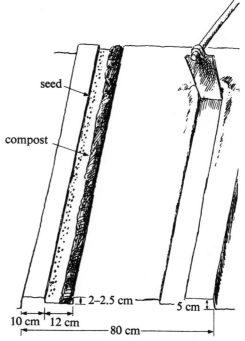

Sowing: In Japan, it is often said that *daikon* seeds should be sown in the fall when the great masses of summer cumulonimbus clouds have passed and the high, feathery clouds of autumn have arrived; that is, when air currents and atmospheric pressure are high. This is thought to be the season in which radishes grow long, straight, and vigorous. They do not grow straight, however, if submitted to heavy rains or high moisture immediately after seeds have been sown. They should be sown on a sunny day and should have a period of fine weather during the germination period.

No Tilling and No Compost

When using land that has not been put to agricultural purposes before, it is necessary to dig up the soil and remove all stones and foreign matter. There must be weeds, however, since if they will not grow, neither will vegetables.

Add 200 g of ground limestone for each 1 m² of soil and mix thoroughly.

Before sowing, inspect the soil to a depth of 2–3 cm and remove all grubs and cutworms, which damage seedlings.

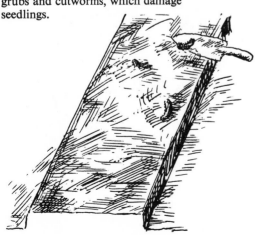

Daikon can be raised without tilling and without fertilizer on land from which summer vegetables or legumes have just been harvested. With the exception of some such plants as pampas, cut weeds at ground line and leave the roots in the soil.

Make a trough 2–5 cm deep, sow the seeds in a line, cover with soil, and press lightly.

Germination and Thinning

Germination begins from three
to five days after sowing. Thin
enough that cotyledons of
adjacent plants do not overlap.

Seventh day after germination

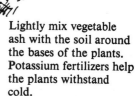

Lightly mix vegetable
ash with the soil around
the bases of the plants.
Potassium fertilizers help
the plants withstand
cold.

Thinning

Thinning must be gradual. One by one,
remove all weak, bug-eaten, spindly, or
bent seedlings till the cotyledons of adjacent plants do not overlap.

Mound soil after thinning.

Leaves of thinned plants are edible.

One month after germination

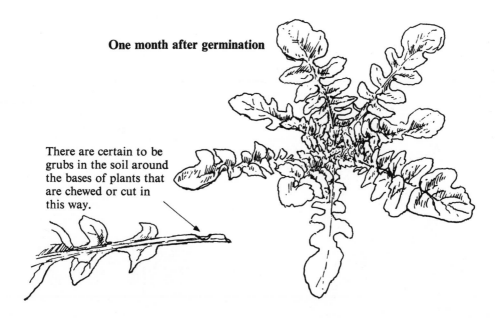

There are certain to be
grubs in the soil around
the bases of plants that
are chewed or cut in
this way.

158

Thinning and Harvesting

Allowing plants to be equally spaced and
dense enough that the tips of their leaves
touch protects roots from direct sun and
high temperatures and prevents the
emergence of insect pests. But when they
are more crowded than this, young radishes
should be pulled up. They may be eaten.

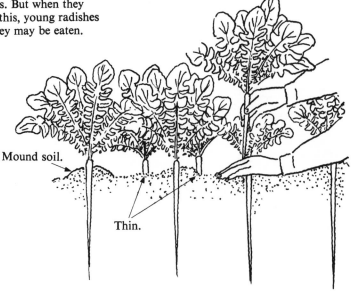

Mound soil.

Thin.

Seeds sown in early September
produce plants that may be
harvested before severe cold
weather sets in.

Harvesting

The growing period for plants raised with
compost or with no fertilizer at all is
slightly long. Radishes produced by seeds
sown in the fall may be harvested after
about seventy days. They are more delicious and have fewer internal splits if
allowed to mature slowly.

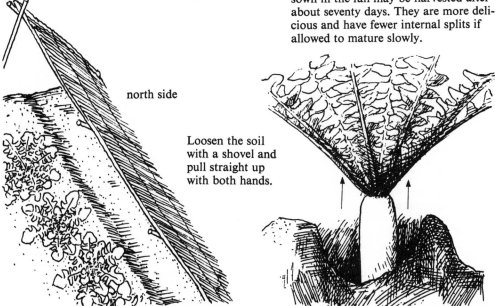

north side

Loosen the soil
with a shovel and
pull straight up
with both hands.

Daikon-radish Sprouts (*Kaiware Daikon*)

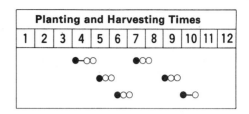

Planting and Harvesting Times

1	2	3	4	5	6	7	8	9	10	11	12

Dense stands of weeds naturally thin themselves. Some plants are sacrificed to enable others to grow strong and reach full maturity. A similar phenomenon is observed in the case of some vegetables. Edible chrysanthemums, for instance, if sown very dense will naturally thin themselves. Many other plants, however, will not do this successfully. For instance, unless they are artificially thinned, tomato plants grow long and straggling and fail to develop normally.

In the case of radish sprouts, seeds of the *daikon*-radish are sown as dense as possible; and the plants are forced to develop long, white sprouts before true leaves emerge. Sprouts and cotyledons are harvested together to be eaten in soups, pickles, and salads. Most of the several varieties of *daikon*-radish seeds may be raised this way, though the ones with large cotyledons are best. Recently dealers have begun selling seeds expressly for the cultivation of sprouts.

Sowing: Since the aim is to produce long, white sprouts topped by green cotyledons, work the soil as fine as possible. Sow seeds to maximum density and cover with soil two or three times as deep as the seeds are thick. Water gently.

The amount of seeds in a commercial packet is small. Do not attempt to sow a wide space with them. It is important to sow as dense as possible so that the seedlings will be crowded.

Sowing

Though they may be sown in the ground, sprouts are easier to raise in pots. No fertilizer is needed.

Select an unglazed pot with a diameter of 18 cm. Sift the soil and mix it with sand.

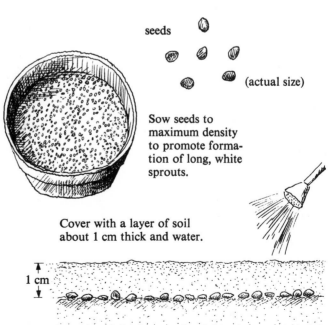

seeds

(actual size)

Sow seeds to maximum density to promote formation of long, white sprouts.

Cover with a layer of soil about 1 cm thick and water.

1 cm

Germination: After germination, the white sprouts will naturally begin to lengthen. Mounding soil around them is unnecessary if they are sufficiently crowded. If mounding is to be performed, however, the soil should do no more than lightly surround the sprouts. Keep the soil moist.

Harvesting: Though it depends on the time of the year and the richness of the soil, sprouts may generally be harvested in from ten to thirty days. Before true leaves appear, either cut the sprouts at the bases or pull them from the ground, roots and all.

Harvesting seed: In a corner of the garden, in the autumn, sow seeds from which to raise two or three plants that will be allowed to bloom in the spring and reach full maturity. Take seeds from them.

Germination

Germination occurs five or six days after sowing.

If the seeds are sparsely sown, the seedlings will fail to send out long shoots. To rectify this situation, mound soil around them.

Harvesting

Harvest before true leaves appear and when the sprouts are 5–6 cm long.

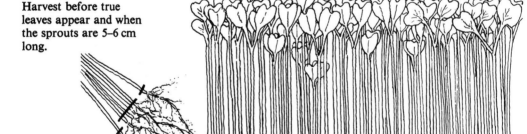

Harvesting Seeds

Allow seeds sown directly in the earth in a corner of the garden to reach full maturity and go to seed.

Take plenty of pods since there are never many seeds in a single one.

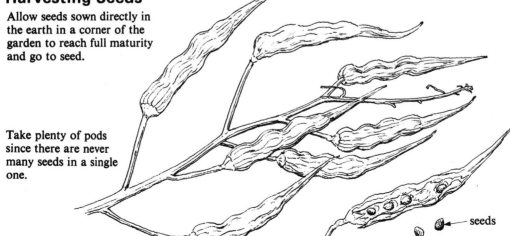

seeds

Radishes

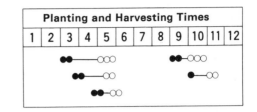

Because they are easy and trouble-free to raise and mature in a short time, radishes are an excellent plant for inexperienced vegetable-gardeners. They may be grown at any time except the dead of winter and midsummer. But they are most delicious grown from seeds sown in the autumn.

In addition to being good eaten alone, bright red radishes are an excellent addition to vegetable salads.

Sowing: Large crops are ensured by scattering seeds over the entire surface of the furrow. When plenty of space is available, lengthen the harvest period and increase crops by sowing at two or three different times.

Thinning: Thin spindly or damaged seedlings from crowded zones. The leaves of neighboring plants should just touch.

Insect pests: Without hysterically resorting to chemical pesticides, it is safest to remove by hand the various insects that attack radishes. Avoiding the possibly lethal effects of such pesticides is much more important than increasing crop sizes. Minimize damage by avoiding those times of year when insects are most prevalent. By all means refrain from poisoning the soil and yourself with chemicals. If sensible procedures are followed, easy-to-raise radishes will not suffer from extensive insect damage.

Harvesting: Like turnips and *daikon* radishes, the radish emerges from the ground, making its state of development perfectly apparent. Harvest when the radishes are about 1.5 cm in diameter. Quality decreases if harvesting is late.

Sowing

Either scatter or sow in rows. Cover with a layer of soil two to three times as thick as the seeds themselves and press lightly with the hands.

Water well before sowing.

For spring sowing, mix mature compost well with soil. For fall sowing, the nutrients remaining in the soil from the summer crop suffice.

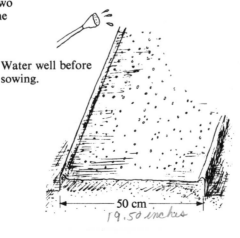

50 cm
19.50 inches

Germination and Thinning

Germination takes place from three
to five days after sowing. Thereafter,
using scissors, thin out spindly or
damaged seedlings from crowded
places.

After thinning, mound
soil around the bases
of the plants.

Cut with scissors.

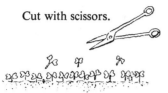

As growth proceeds, in the densest
areas, the leaves of adjacent plants
should just touch.

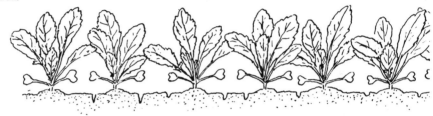

Harvesting

Harvest when the radishes are
1.5–2 cm in diameter. If harvesting is late, the quality and
freshness of the radishes
decrease.

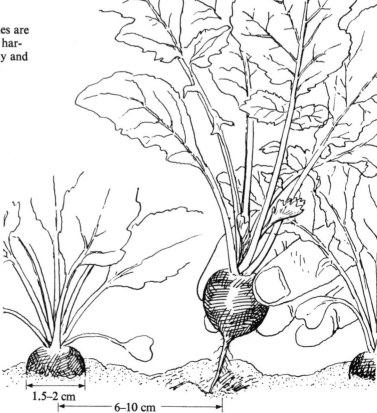

The ultimate interval
between adjacent plants
should be 6–10 cm.

1.5–2 cm

6–10 cm

Icicle Radishes

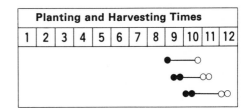

Planting and Harvesting Times

1	2	3	4	5	6	7	8	9	10	11	12

Though they taste very much like the familiar, small, round, red radishes, icicle radishes—pure white or red on the outside and translucent white on the inside—are an interesting variation for salads and a piquant, refreshing, and easy-to-eat snack. Radish leaves too may be eaten. The red variety is somewhat slenderer than the white one. They may be pickled in salt overnight. Or they may be vinegared for a few hours, after which the white part turns red. If left in vinegar for two or three days, the entire radish turns pink.

Though they may be sown in the spring, the best time is during the fall—in Japan before the autumn rains set in. Sow in rows 20 cm apart. Thin regularly until, by the time the roots thicken, the plants are about 5 cm apart. A good red and ample root thickness depend on plenty of sunlight. The use of immature compost can damage skins. Dry soil increases fiber content and makes the radishes tough. Late harvesting allows rootlets to develop, but radishes raised without chemical fertilizers on natural nutrients grow large without internal hollows and splits.

Since they are photophobic, the seeds should be covered by a layer of soil about 1 cm thick. If the layer is thinner, rain water can wash them up and damage them.

Sowing

Prepare a furrow about 60 cm wide. In it sow seeds in 2 rows 20 cm apart and cover with 1 cm of soil. If the soil is rich in organic matter, no additional fertilizing is necessary. But if compost is available, it may be spread on the soil. If it unavailable and fertilizing is required, three to four weeks before sowing, mix pressed soy meal with the soil, avoiding the bottoms of the sowing troughs.

|← 20 cm →|

Do not put compost immediately below the sowing troughs.

Red icicle radish   White icicle radish

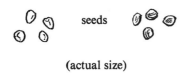

seeds

(actual size)

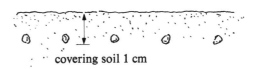

covering soil 1 cm

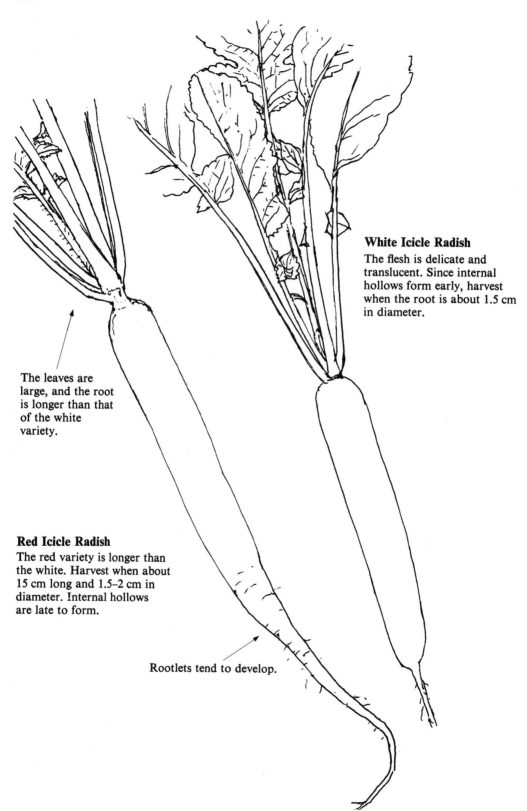

White Icicle Radish
The flesh is delicate and translucent. Since internal hollows form early, harvest when the root is about 1.5 cm in diameter.

The leaves are large, and the root is longer than that of the white variety.

Red Icicle Radish
The red variety is longer than the white. Harvest when about 15 cm long and 1.5–2 cm in diameter. Internal hollows are late to form.

Rootlets tend to develop.

Turnips

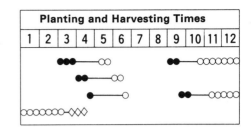

Planting and Harvesting Times											
1	2	3	4	5	6	7	8	9	10	11	12

Another member of the mustard family, turnips bear yellow, cruciate blossoms in the spring. They do well in cool weather and grow in temperatures of 59°–68°F. The small, fleshy roots have already begun to form by the time the plant bears three or four true leaves. They are fairly tolerant of acidity and thrive in moist and sandy, or clayey soil. They may be raised year round if planted in a cool, shady place in summer and in a sunny place in winter. Turnips grown from seed sown in the autumn are especially delicious and suffer little damage from insects.

Because they take little space and mature quickly, turnips are an excellent crop for the home gardener.

Sowing: If plenty of space is available, it is a good idea to sow turnips in several staggered batches. A large patch sown all at one time produces too many turnips for a small family to consume. And late harvesting results in waste and decreased quality.

Like weeds, turnips thrive in soil rich in organic matter if raised naturally without the harmful effects of agricultural chemicals and insecticides. Nutrients remaining in soil from compost used for a preceding crop are sufficient.

Preparation

Before sowing, mix ground limestone with the soil.

When using compost

Spread compost evenly over the bed and mix well with soil.

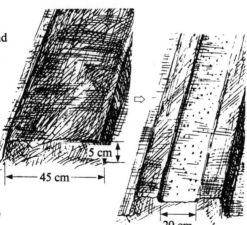

5 cm

45 cm

20 cm

When using dried guano

soil

Mix thoroughly with the soil two or three weeks before sowing.

Sowing

Make a trough in the sowing bed and water before sowing if the weather is dry.

Cover with a layer of soil two or three times thicker than the diameter of the seeds.

Germination and Thinning

Germination takes place from four to seven days after sowing. Thin out spindly or defective seedlings from overcrowded places.

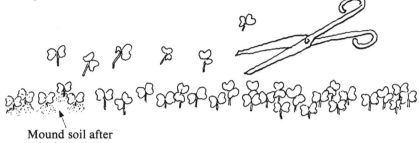

Mound soil after thinning.

Gradually thin out worm-eaten and defective seedlings.

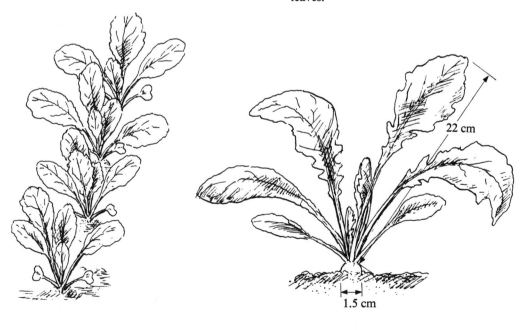

Tenth day after germination

The plant has developed 5 or 6 true leaves.

Twenty-fifth day after germination

The plant has developed 7 or 8 true leaves.

22 cm

1.5 cm

Fortieth day after germination

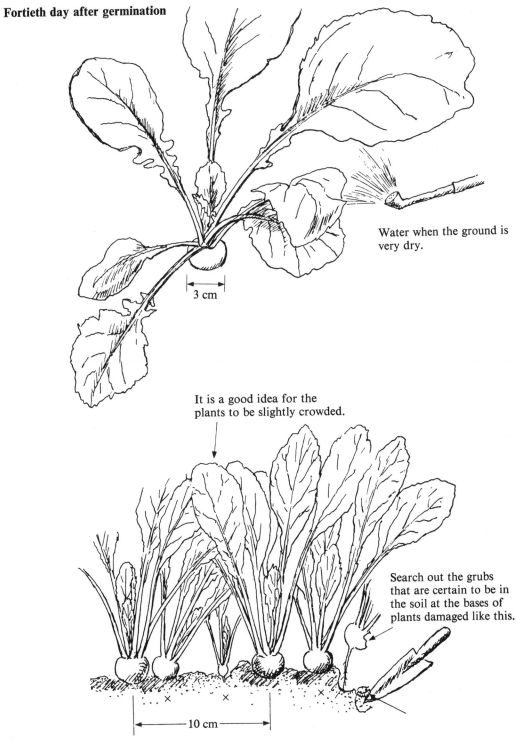

Water when the ground is
very dry.

3 cm

It is a good idea for the
plants to be slightly crowded.

Search out the grubs
that are certain to be in
the soil at the bases of
plants damaged like this.

10 cm

Thin out the turnips
marked ×. The ultimate
interplant interval
should be 10 cm.

Harvesting

Harvesting may begin when the turnips are 4–5 cm in diameter. When grown without fertilizers, turnips reach this stage in from fifty to sixty days, by which time they have about ten true leaves.

Leave slow-growing or unharvested turnips in the field to bloom in the spring. The buds of the blossoms may be boiled briefly and eaten with soy sauce as an appetizer.

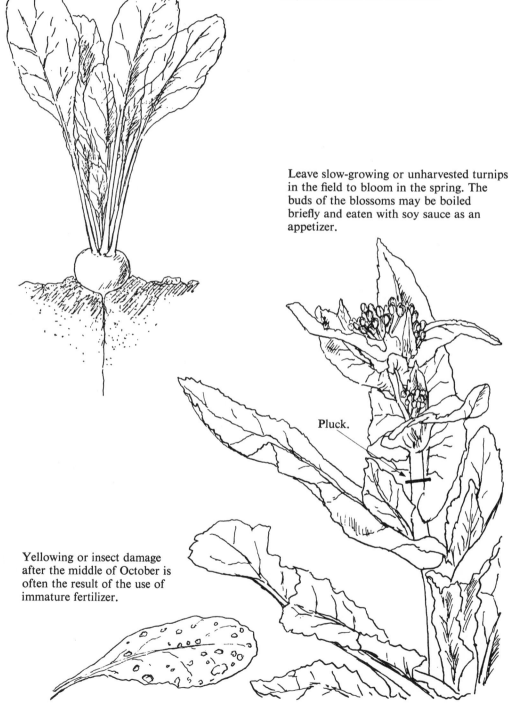

Pluck.

Yellowing or insect damage after the middle of October is often the result of the use of immature fertilizer.

Carrots

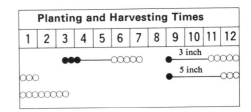
Better suited to home gardening than the long varieties, if sown in March, short strains of carrots may be harvested in the early summer. They may be harvested in the late fall and into the spring if sown in the early autumn. They are fairly tolerant of both high and low temperatures and will grow at even 80°–82°F. They thrive in the mild weather of spring and autumn and will grow in practically any soil that is moist and drains well.

If the soil was well fertilized for the preceding crop, there is no need to add fertilizer for carrots. They do, however, require more nutrition than *daikon* radishes and turnips; and the soil in which they are grown must be fertile.

Sowing: Since their germination ratio is low, sow carrot seeds abundantly. Choose a warm part of the day when soil temperatures are high and water the ground well beforehand. Spread straw on the ground to retain moisture.

Germination and thinning: Germination takes place in from six to ten days. Begin thinning when two or three true leaves have developed. Thin only in the most crowded places. Being dense enough for leaves of adjacent plants to touch stimulates carrot growth.

Sowing

No additional fertilizer is needed if the soil is still rich in organic matter from compost used for the preceding crop. If using dried guano, do not put it directly below the seeds but spread it between rows.

seeds

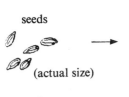

(actual size)

Spread straw on the ground to help retain moisture.

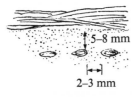

5–8 mm

2–3 mm

Seeds are covered with fine hairs. Press hairy seeds in the palm of the hands to remove the fuzz.

Germination ratios for carrot seeds are low. Cover with a layer of soil 5–8 mm thick and press lightly.

When soil is very acid, three to four weeks before sowing, add 200 g of ground limestone for each 1 m² of soil.

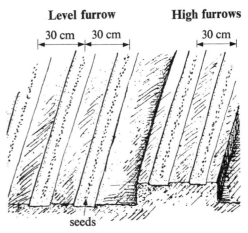

Level furrow

30 cm   30 cm

High furrows

30 cm

seeds

Plant in rows in prepared troughs.

Prepare high furrows if the soil drains poorly.

Cultivating and mounding: At thinning time, cultivate the soil and mound it around the bases of the plants to accelerate growth. Roots begin thickening about forty days after germination. At this time, make a shallow mound of soil around their bases to conceal the tops of the roots.

Weeding: Use no weed killers. Cut weeds at ground level and leave their roots in the soil.

Harvesting: So-called 3-inch carrots may be harvested in from 60 to a 100 days. The 5-inch variety will mature in from 90 to 120 days. Harvest early. If too much time is allowed to lapse, small side roots develop, reducing quality.

Germination

Germination takes place in from six to ten days.

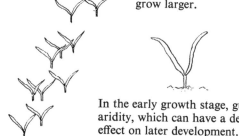

First the cotyledons emerge and grow larger.

Then the true leaves begin appearing.

Fifteenth day after germination

In the early growth stage, guard against aridity, which can have a decidedly bad effect on later development.

Thinning

First thinning is performed when two or three true leaves have emerged. After thinning, work the soil and mound it around the bases of the plants.

Leaves of adjacent plants should touch lightly.

Twenty-fifth day after germination

There is no need to work the soil further about forty days after germination.

By the time 5 or 6 true leaves have developed, the plants should be 10–12 cm apart.

A plant has been thinned out here.

After they begin thickening, cover the tops of the roots with a low mound of soil.

Harvesting

Carrots mature in from 60 to 120 days after germination. Pull out roots when they have grown to full maturity.

Burdock

Burdock, a biennial plant of the composite family, is sown in the spring, grows through the summer and autumn, and is harvested in the late fall, when leaves and stalks have died down. Allowed to remain in the ground, it sends out fresh buds in early March of the following year, puts out flower stalks in May, and blooms and bears seed in the heat of July. The unprepossessing, thistlelike flowers reveal only a few lavender petals from their prickly calyxes.

The long (sometimes 1 m) root is the part of the plant harvested and eaten. As early as two days after germination, the root is already 10 cm long and will be 40 cm long by the twentieth day. At germination, the two cotyledons open 180 degrees for maximum exposure to sunlight. If soil conditions are poor, they do not open fully, causing a reduction of light exposure and consequent drop in photosynthesis.

Leaves and petioles are excellent indicators of plant condition. In the case of burdock, as long as the young petiole rises straight, the root is in good shape and growing well. When the petiole droops to describe a semicircle, however, aging has set in. If, when viewed from the direction of the petiole, the leaves form a V with the main vein at its base, the plant is thriving. As long as this condition can be maintained until summer and with sound, natural soil conditions, ideal, thick burdock roots may be expected.

Preparations

If the soil is lean, make a compost trough beside the furrow. Do not put compost immediately below the seed rows. If the soil is fertile, compost may be simply spread on the ground on one or both sides of the furrow.

Rotate burdock crops at intervals of four or five years. The damage from serial planting is reduced, however, as the soil is enriched with natural composts.

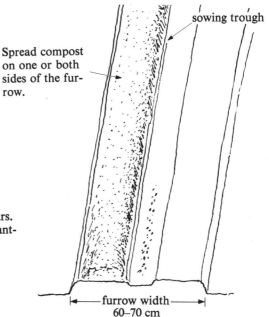

sowing trough

Spread compost on one or both sides of the furrow.

|← furrow width →|
60–70 cm

The depth to which the soil has been loosened and worked is often cited as the principal factor in producing long, thick burdock roots. But, as observation of plants that have sprung up between furrows from fortuitously dropped seeds makes clear, this is of much less importance than plenty of sunlight and natural soil conditions.

Cotyledons and young leaves pulled up during July and August in the thinning process are fragrant and delicious. But true harvesting begins in November. At that time, dig a hole 60 cm deep beside the furrow parallel with the plant and, carefully removing the surrounding soil, lift the root free. Harvest as needed. Even left in the ground, burdock maintains its quality until it sends out new buds the following spring. Seeds may be harvested from middle till late August of the second year. One plant produces an ample quantity.

Sowing

Sow in rows with 2–3 cm between seeds. Since they are photophilous and will not germinate without sensing light, burdock seeds must be barely covered with soil.

seeds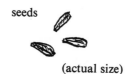

(actual size)

Since the covering layer is thin, care must be exerted to prevent soil from drying out before germination.

(Germinates between 50°–86°F; Grows between 68°–77°F)

Germination and Thinning

Germinate in from five to eight days. When germination is complete, thin until plants are 3 cm apart.

Fourteen days after germination

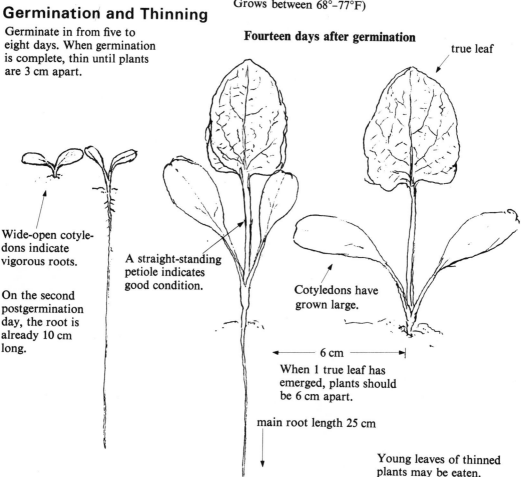

true leaf

Wide-open cotyledons indicate vigorous roots.

On the second postgermination day, the root is already 10 cm long.

A straight-standing petiole indicates good condition.

Cotyledons have grown large.

|← 6 cm →|

When 1 true leaf has emerged, plants should be 6 cm apart.

main root length 25 cm

Young leaves of thinned plants may be eaten.

Thinning

When 2 or 3 true leaves have developed, thin so that plants are 9 cm apart. Continue thinning until an ultimate interval of 15 cm is attained.

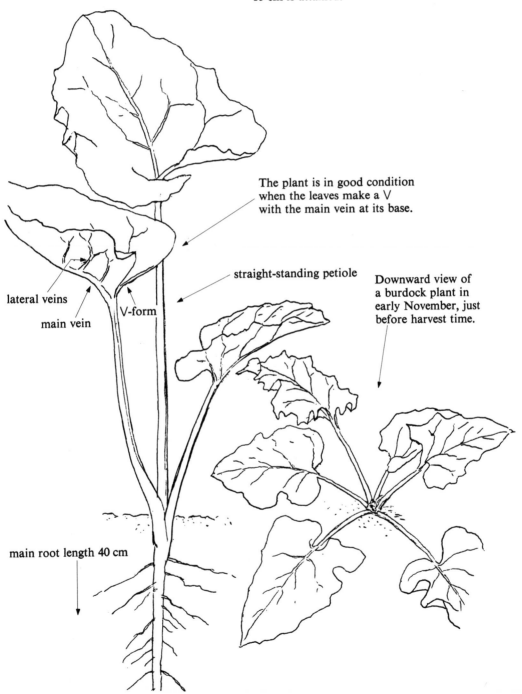

The plant is in good condition when the leaves make a ∨ with the main vein at its base.

lateral veins

main vein

∨-form

straight-standing petiole

Downward view of a burdock plant in early November, just before harvest time.

main root length 40 cm

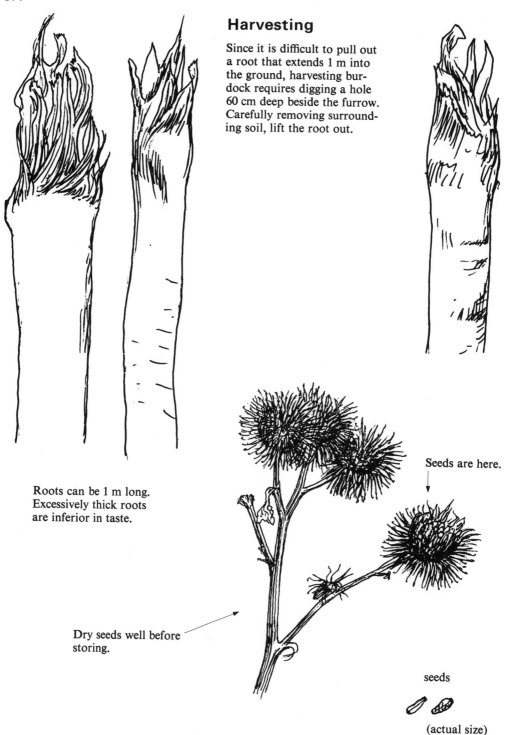

Harvesting

Since it is difficult to pull out a root that extends 1 m into the ground, harvesting burdock requires digging a hole 60 cm deep beside the furrow. Carefully removing surrounding soil, lift the root out.

Roots can be 1 m long. Excessively thick roots are inferior in taste.

Seeds are here.

Dry seeds well before storing.

seeds

(actual size)

Harvesting Seeds

(Middle to late August of the second year)

Taro

Plant stems occur in many variations. Some, like those of the legumes, are vines. Some, like those of such plants as onions, are bulbs developed from leaf sheaths. The kohlrabi forms a rounded corm at the root line. The lotus has underground rhizomes, and the squashes and cucumbers have stem modifications in the form of tendrils. Potatoes are underground stems called stolons. The edible underground stem of the taro is of the type known as a tuber, which is a developed, dwarf stem.

Taros are intolerant of dryness. Their wide-spreading, tautly stretched leaves not only catch a maximum amount of sunlight for the purpose of photosynthesis, but also shade the ground and in this way help reduce evaporation and retain moisture. As long as soil moisture is sufficient, taro leaves stretch out practically horizontally. When the soil drys, however, they turn down at the edges to allow silvery drops of water accumulated on their surfaces to fall to the ground. This drooping, however, has the undesirable effect of contributing to soil dryness by allowing sunlight to reach the bases of the plants.

Taros thrive in sunny places under conditions of high temperature and humidity and, if raised together with weeds, require practically no attention.

They take space. But, if other vegetables are raised together with them—in place of weeds—they can be fitted into domestic gardens. Use ample compost to raise soil temperatures and retain moisture. Taros will grow even in very acid soil (pH 4 or pH 3).

Seed taros
Select hearty, undamaged taros.

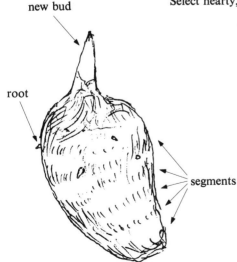

new bud

root

segments

The one shown here was left in the ground from the preceding year's crop. When it was dug up, in late April, the bud and roots had already started growing.

In tubers of the taro, lateral buds emerge from the segments. The parent taro develops from the dwarf stem at the top of the corm. Offspring develop from the lower to the higher segments of the parent and then generate offspring of their own.

Plant seed taros at intervals of 30 cm in rows 60 cm apart, or 80 cm apart if space permits. Set the seed taros in the ground, bud end up, at a depth of 7–8 cm. A compost ground covering absorbs sunlight and stimulates growth. Buds begin to grow at temperatures of more than 59°F (in May, under natural conditions in the Tokyo region). Keeping the ground covered to minimize evaporation and retain moisture throughout the summer ensures a delicious taro crop.

Planting

Set the seed taros in the earth bud-end up. Growth begins at a minimum temperature of 59°F. For continued growth, 77°–86°F are suitable.

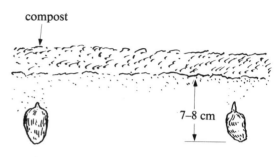

compost

7–8 cm

interplant inteval 60 cm

Initial Growth

Even though planted early, taros will not begin growing until the temperature rises above 59°F.

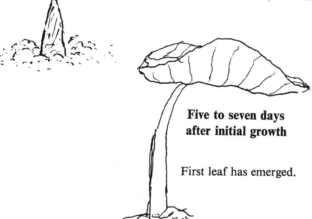

Five to seven days after initial growth

First leaf has emerged.

If the plants are raised with a stand of weeds that help retain moisture, leaf edges will not droop; and large drops of water will form inside the leaves. Photosynthesis proceeds smoothly in leaves in this condition.

Fourteen days after initial growth

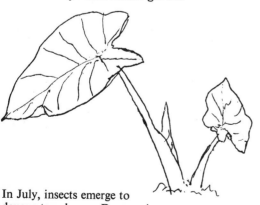

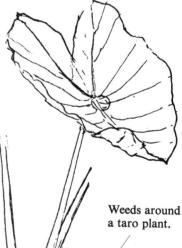

Weeds around a taro plant.

In July, insects emerge to devour taro leaves. Damage is reduced, however, if the taros are grown together with weeds.

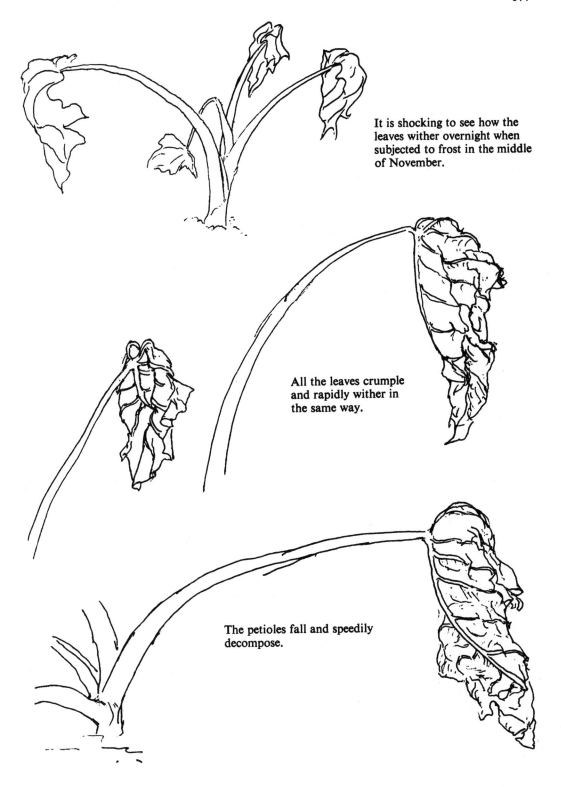

It is shocking to see how the leaves wither overnight when subjected to frost in the middle of November.

All the leaves crumple and rapidly wither in the same way.

The petioles fall and speedily decompose.

Harvesting

Dig taros up gently and carefully with a shovel. If they are
to be returned to the earth for
storage, do not break the
clusters.

parent tuber

offspring

seed tuber

This drawing shows five offspring
growing from the lower segments of
the parent tuber. Two small ones
are growing from the second segment, on the upper right. A still
younger generation of offspring is
represented by the taro arising from
one of the three new tubers on the
left.

The more numerous the new tubers,
the more nutrients are dispersed.
Taros are most delicious if allowed
to produce from five to six new
tubers.

Sweet Potatoes

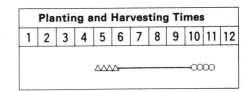

Planting and Harvesting Times

1	2	3	4	5	6	7	8	9	10	11	12

This convolvulaceous member of the morning-glory family is a native of Central America; thrives in hot weather; and, in tropical regions, grows year round. It has well-developed lateral roots on which tuberlike accumulations of starch and other nutrients, form. Since in Japan they generally die in the winter, sweet potatoes are usually raised from commercially available seedlings purchased in May or June and are harvested before first frost. Regarded as a self-sufficiency food and a famine-relief crop, sweet potatoes require very little care if heat and sunshine are available.

Prepare furrows 60 cm wide and 20 cm high and plant seedlings at a 30-cm interval. High furrows provide a richer soil-oxygen supply and thus help produce more and larger sweet potatoes. Avoid nitrogen fertilizers, which increase foliage that deprives the plants of sunlight. Vegetable ash mixed with the soil to a depth of 30–40 cm is enough. Unless the soil is very lean, no other fertilizer is required.

Preparations

In a sunny place, prepare mountain-shaped furrows 60 cm wide and 20 cm high. Plant seedlings at a 30 cm interval.

interplant interval 30 cm

height 20 cm

furrow width 60 cm

In general, plant in May or June, after all danger of late frost is over and when temperatures have risen to 64°–66°F. Try to set the seedlings out a day before a rain. Seedlings should have seven or eight true leaves. In such a case plant them so that the leaves are horizontally oriented. If leaves are fewer in number, incline the seedling somewhat. The main stalk should be set 3 cm into the ground. In seven to ten days, the plants will be firmly rooted. Sweet potatoes are tolerant of aridity, but a suitable amount of rain for the first two or three months stimulates root development. In about thirty days, the vines will begin developing.

If heat and sunlight are abundant during the determining phase of growth, in August and September, crops will be good and individual sweet potatoes large. Harvest as soon as possible because, if left too long in the fields, sweet potatoes are unsuitable for storage and rot if exposed to temperatures lower than 41°F. After harvesting, dry the sweet potatoes in the shade for about a week to allow the starch to break down partially and to increase sweetness.

Planting Seedlings

When true leaves are few in number, set the seedling in the ground at an angle with leaves and buds above the soil. Leaves wilt after planting but revive and begin to grow in about ten days.

Though a member of the convolvulaceous family, the mature sweet potato vine has leaves resembling those of the medicinal herb *Houttuynia cordata*.

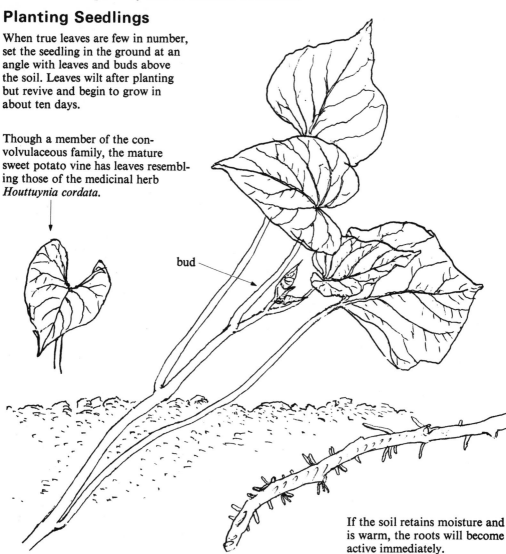

bud

If the soil retains moisture and is warm, the roots will become active immediately.

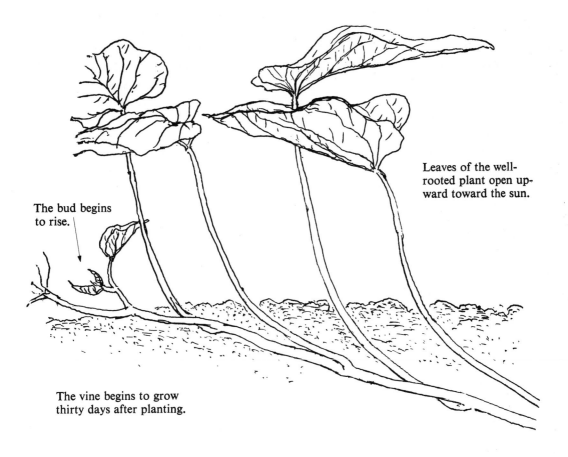

Leaves of the well-rooted plant open upward toward the sun.

The bud begins to rise.

The vine begins to grow thirty days after planting.

Young, tender vine tips are good to eat.

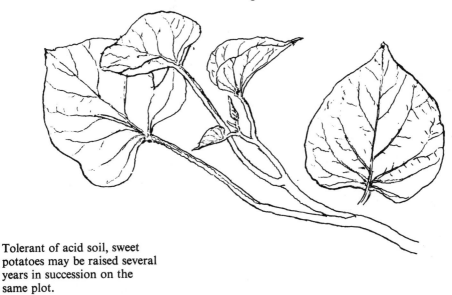

Tolerant of acid soil, sweet potatoes may be raised several years in succession on the same plot.

182

Carbohydrates resulting from the process of photosynthesis are stored in sweet potatoes.

Consequently, plucking leaves reduces the numbers of new lateral roots which develop into sweet potatoes.

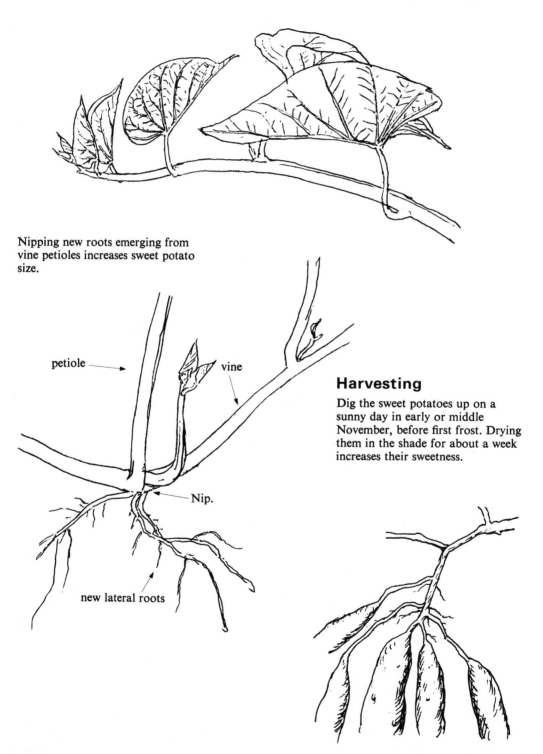

Nipping new roots emerging from vine petioles increases sweet potato size.

petiole

vine

Nip.

new lateral roots

Harvesting

Dig the sweet potatoes up on a sunny day in early or middle November, before first frost. Drying them in the shade for about a week increases their sweetness.

Potatoes

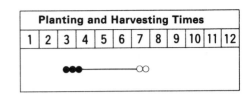

Planting and Harvesting Times											
1	2	3	4	5	6	7	8	9	10	11	12

Potatoes are suited to cool climates and thrive at temperatures of 59°–75°F. They grow large at about 63°F, but growth ceases when temperatures exceed 85°F. On the other hand, they are intolerant of cold and wither if hit by frost. In temperate zones, they are easiest to raise in the spring. They tolerate acid soil fairly well.

Planting: Obtain seed potatoes raised in cold regions, where low temperatures minimize the danger of damage from viruses. If seed potatoes are unobtainable, use potatoes sold commercially for food. But remember that potatoes will not sprout unless they are allowed to rest for a certain period after harvest. There are, of course, many different varieties of white potatoes, some of which are better for baking and others of which are better boiled.

To give them plenty of time to grow large before the hot summer weather withers their leaves, plant potatoes in late March or early April at the latest.

Protection from the cold: Potatoes that have just sprouted must be protected from evening frost. When they have begun to push their way up from the ground, mound earth over them to a depth of from 5–6 cm.

When the sprouts are 5–6 cm long, pluck off all but the most vigorous one or two. If you leave only one sprout, the potatoes harvested from the plant will be large. If you leave two, they will be slightly smaller but more numerous.

Rotation: Leave from three to four years between crops of potatoes and such other members of the nightshade family as tomatoes, eggplant, and green bell peppers.

Cutting Seed Potatoes

Cut so that all pieces have ample sprouts, or eyes.

Preparations

Choose a plot in which potatoes have not been raised for three or four years. Potatoes thrive even in acid soil.

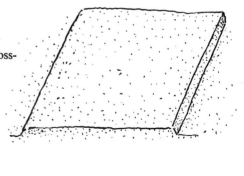

Quarter a seed potato weighing more than 100 g.

Halve a seed potato weighing 60–80 g.

Cut long potatoes cross-wise to minimize the area of the wound.

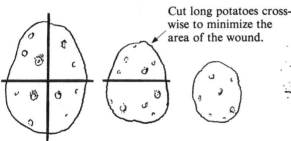

Plant seed potatoes weighing 30–40 g whole.

Planting

Press the seed potato into the soil, cut side down.

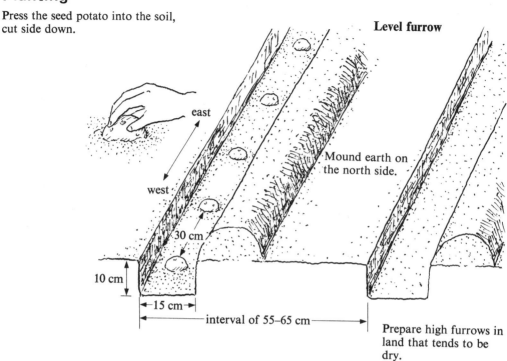

Level furrow

east

west

Mound earth on the north side.

30 cm

10 cm

15 cm

interval of 55–65 cm

Prepare high furrows in land that tends to be dry.

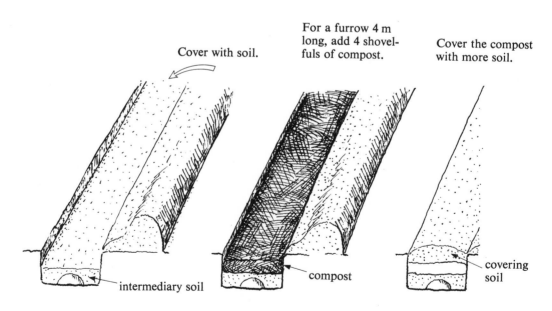

Cover with soil.

For a furrow 4 m long, add 4 shovelfuls of compost.

Cover the compost with more soil.

intermediary soil

compost

covering soil

Covering the seed potatoes with compost facilitates ventilation and retention of warmth.

Covering the soil with vinyl speeds germination. But this is unnecessary for potatoes planted after the end of March.

Mounding

When sprouts are beginning to push their
way up through the ground, protect them
from cold by mounding 5–6 cm of soil on
top of them.

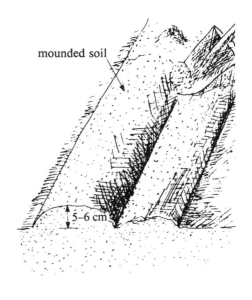

mounded soil

5–6 cm

Sprouts raise the soil as
they push their way up
through it.

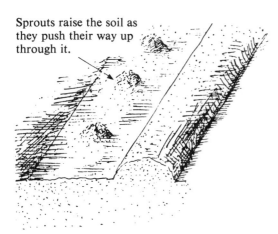

Plucking Sprouts

When sprouts are 5–6 cm
long, pluck off all but the
most robust 1 or 2.

seed potato

Holding the base of the sprout
to be preserved between the
fingers of one hand, pluck off
the others.

186

Cultivating and Weeding

Combine weeding, cultivating, and mounding until the plants bloom. Discontinue all three thereafter to prevent damaging roots.

Harvesting

The best time to harvest is when the lower leaves of the plant turn yellow and after five or six days of rainless weather.

Dig up potatoes when the soil has been dried by a few days of continuous sunny weather.

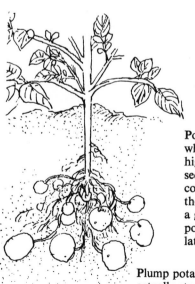

Bottom leaves have withered and turned yellow.

Potatoes cease growth when temperatures rise higher than 85°F. Consequently, harvest time comes too quickly for the potatoes to reach a good size if the seed potatoes are planted too late in the spring.

Plump potatoes are actually stems developed from underground stolons.

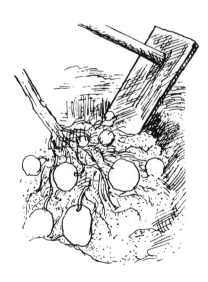

When large crops are to be stored, dry the potatoes in the shade for two or three days.

Tacai

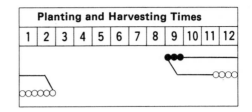

Planting and Harvesting Times

1	2	3	4	5	6	7	8	9	10	11	12

A classic example of the phenomenon, seen in winter dandelions and winter spinach, in which plants adapt themselves to obtain a maximum of sunshine during short, cold days by assuming a ground-hugging, rosette leaf arrangement in which no leaves overlap, *tacai* (pronounced tatsai) has glossy, spoon-shaped, blackish-green, crinkled leaves with edges that curl under. Like winter spinach and *komatsuna, tacai* is most delicious in cold weather when it strives to take in the most sun possible allows it to store up nutrients. The very color of *tacai* suggests abundance of vitamins. It becomes sweeter for being exposed once or twice to frost. No other leafy vegetable tolerates cold better. In addition, aside from some damage from grubs, it is robust and highly insect-resistant.

No additional fertilizer is needed if soil is fertile. Space may be economized by planting low *tacai* on the south sides of long, east-west rows and growing crops of taller vegetables on the north sides.

Sow in rows with 1–2 cm between seeds and barely cover with a thin layer of soil. If sowing is in clusters, leave an interval of 25 cm between each.

Seedlings grow slow at first and begin to expand from side to side after one or two exposures to frost. Stabilize the crop by thinning early to prevent competition among plants after frost.

To preserve the flavor of *tacai*, limit cooking time.

Sowing (Late September)
Sow in rows or clusters.

Germination
Germination occurs in three days; cotyledons are extremely small.

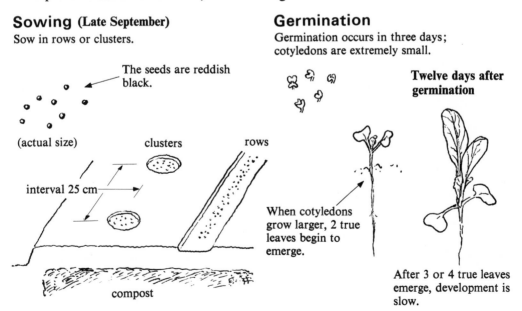

The seeds are reddish black.

(actual size)　　　clusters　　　rows

interval 25 cm

compost

Twelve days after germination

When cotyledons grow larger, 2 true leaves begin to emerge.

After 3 or 4 true leaves emerge, development is slow.

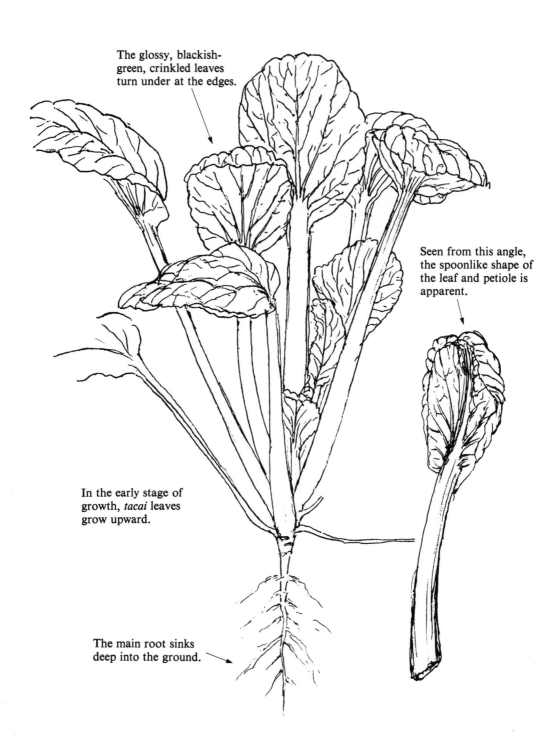

The glossy, blackish-green, crinkled leaves turn under at the edges.

Seen from this angle, the spoonlike shape of the leaf and petiole is apparent.

In the early stage of growth, *tacai* leaves grow upward.

The main root sinks deep into the ground.

This drawing shows the plant immediately before its first exposure to frost, after which it will assume its ground-hugging posture.

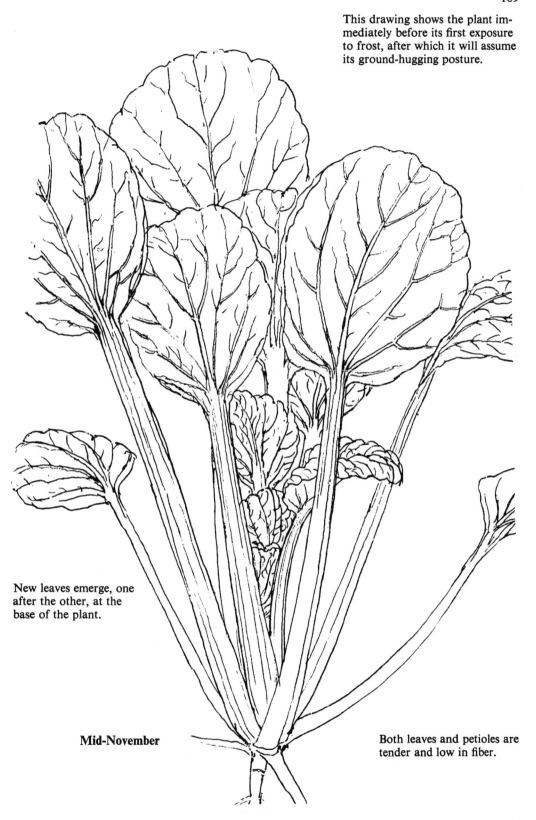

New leaves emerge, one after the other, at the base of the plant.

Mid-November

Both leaves and petioles are tender and low in fiber.

The handsome rosette form assures maximum exposure to sunlight.

Harvesting

The plants may be pulled up by hand after exposure to frost has resulted in the characteristic flattened, ground-hugging form.

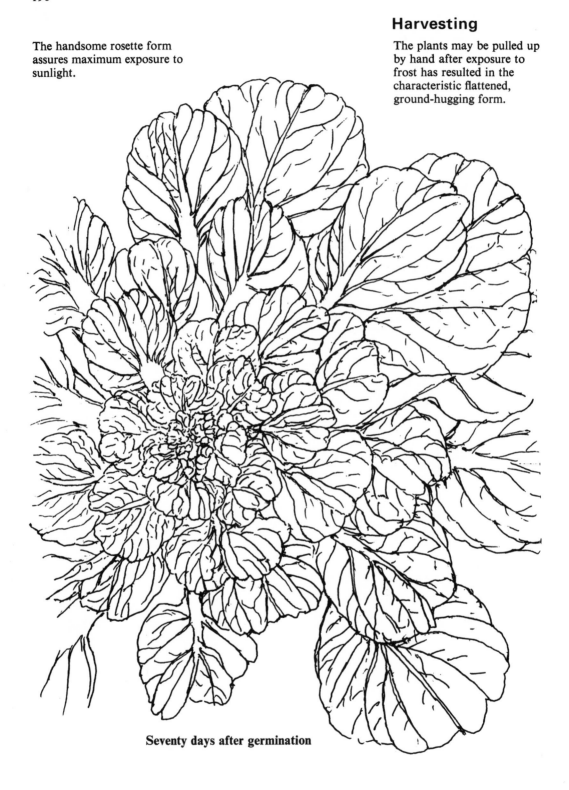

Seventy days after germination

Shaoxing Cabbage (*Takenoko* Chinese Cabbage)

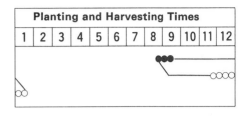

Planting and Harvesting Times

1	2	3	4	5	6	7	8	9	10	11	12

Another of the distinctively delicious Chinese vegetables currently gaining wide popularity, Shaoxing (pronounced shaoshing) cabbage is native to the eastern part of Hebei Province, the weather of which is influenced by the severe continental climate and the aridity of Inner Mongolia. Consequently, Shaoxing cabbage tolerates a wide variety of climatic conditions. Because of the shape of the unusual head, which reaches a diameter of 15 cm and a height of 45 cm, the Japanese call this vegetable *takenoko* (bamboo-shoot) cabbage. Unlike the ordinary variety of white Chinese cabbage, Shaoxing cabbage is bright green to the core. The leaves appear to twist around the head they form. It is very insect- and cold-resistant and is delicious in sautéed and simmered dishes or pickled.

Since heading of Shaoxing cabbage demands plenty of sunlight, plant in a sunny place in soil that is rich in organic matter. Sow early enough to give the plants time to root and grow strong before first frost.

In long, east-west rows, plant tall Shaoxing cabbage on the north side and low *qing-gen-cai* and *tacai* on the south. This way all the plants get adequate sun, and the lower ones prevent drying out of soil around the bases of the taller ones. Shaoxing cabbage may be planted on the north side of snow peas or broad beans, which they can protect from the cold. This is especially convenient for city gardeners, who often find it difficult to obtain bamboo or branches to construct windbreaks.

Sow in clusters of four or five seeds at intervals of 30 cm to prevent overcrowding. If thinned plants are to be eaten, sow in rows. In such a case, sowing may be later.

Sowing

Sowing in rows is easier if an interval of about 2 cm is left. Cover with a thin layer of soil because the seeds are photophilous and so small that a thick layer is too great a burden for the newly germinated seedlings.

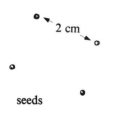

2 cm

seeds

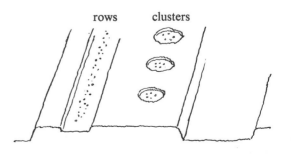

rows   clusters

192

Spreading compost or cut weeds and grass on top of the soil protects from aridity and freezing.

In small city gardens where there is no space for a compost pile, bury cut weeds and kitchen scraps between vegetable rows.

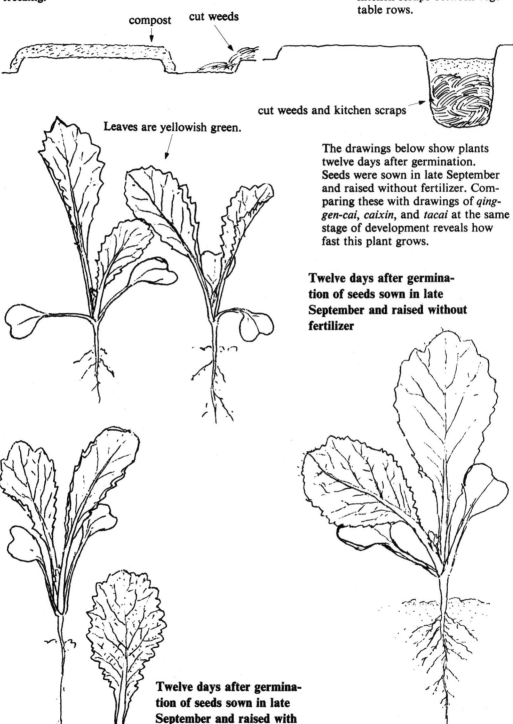

compost   cut weeds

cut weeds and kitchen scraps

Leaves are yellowish green.

The drawings below show plants twelve days after germination. Seeds were sown in late September and raised without fertilizer. Comparing these with drawings of *qing-gen-cai*, *caixin*, and *tacai* at the same stage of development reveals how fast this plant grows.

Twelve days after germination of seeds sown in late September and raised without fertilizer

Twelve days after germination of seeds sown in late September and raised with a little fertilizer

To stimulate heading, prevent
overcrowding by repeatedly
thinning so that leaves of
neighboring plants touch
lightly.

Growth accelerates in October.
This drawing was made of the
same plant six days after the
drawing on the preceding page,
lower right.

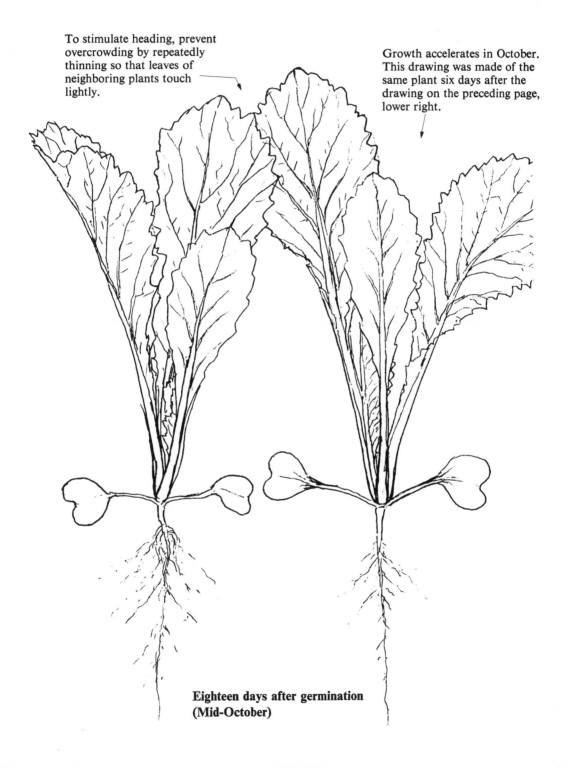

**Eighteen days after germination
(Mid-October)**

194

Twenty-two days after germination

Grubs and caterpillars emerging from the soil in the evening eat the leaves. Using a flashlight, find and destroy them.

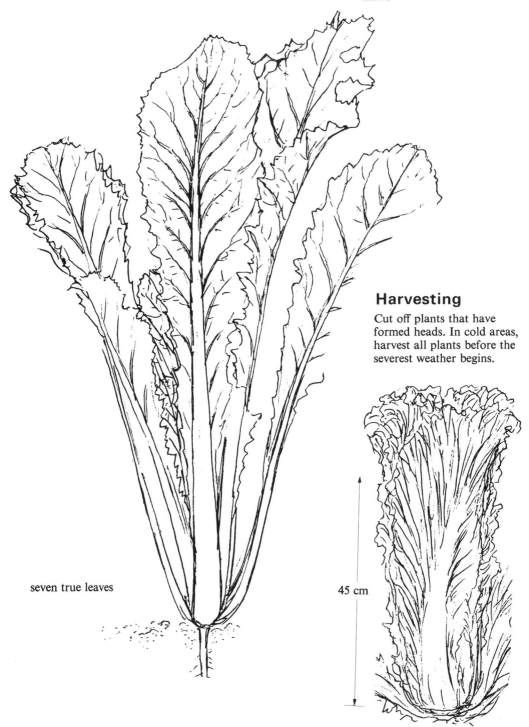

Harvesting

Cut off plants that have formed heads. In cold areas, harvest all plants before the severest weather begins.

seven true leaves

45 cm

Caixin

Planting and Harvesting Times											
1	2	3	4	5	6	7	8	9	10	11	12

This Chinese vegetable, the flower stalks of which are eaten, grows quickly and is very easy to raise. It is rich in the nutrients that will be required for blooming and later the production of seeds. Buds of many plants are valued foods in China, where legend has it that eating pollen ensures long life. It grows well at temperatures of about 68°F and is relatively tolerant of summer heat. It may be sown in fall and spring.

Though it makes no great demands for fertilizer, if raised in lean soil, *caixin* (pronounced tsaishin) produces slender flower stalks with tough fibers. Providing a natural environment with soil rich in organic matter and animal life ensures good growth, freedom from plant disease, and the production of delicious, slightly bitter-sweet flower stalks.

In general, seeds sown in the autumn produce thick flower stalks. Those sown in April or May produce slenderer stalks with fibers that soon grow tough. But, if planted in semishade among rows of such plants as *shiso*, corn, or eggplants, *caixin* seeds will do well even sown later than May.

Sowing

Fertilize lean soil beforehand. Sow in clusters of from 4 to 5 seeds at an interval of 20 cm or in rows 25–30 cm long.

Germinates in three or four days.

Four days after germination

seeds (actual size)

Barely cover seeds with soil.

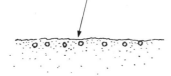

In a reasonably good environment, insect damage will be slight.

One true leaf has emerged.

Caixin may be harvested either during the thinning process, whole, plant by plant, or from large clusters created by plucking the growth bud early and thus stimulating the production of numerous lateral buds. In the former case, sow plenty of seeds in rows and thin by cutting plants off at the ground line. In the latter case, sow seeds in clusters.

Parboiled, *caixin* may be seasoned with soy sauce or other dressings and eaten cold as an appetizer. Or it may be used in miso soup, pickles, or sautéed foods. Cooking does not destroy its pleasant texture or its color and form.

Thinning

Avoid overcrowding. Thin as needed so that the leaves of adjacent plants touch lightly.

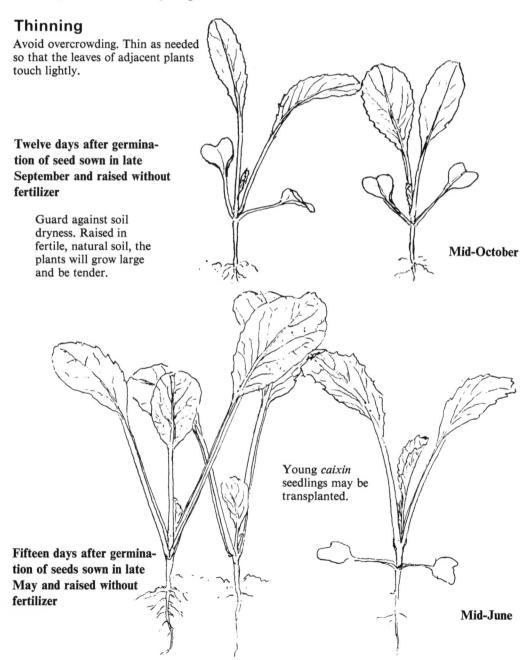

Twelve days after germination of seed sown in late September and raised without fertilizer

Guard against soil dryness. Raised in fertile, natural soil, the plants will grow large and be tender.

Mid-October

Young *caixin* seedlings may be transplanted.

Fifteen days after germination of seeds sown in late May and raised without fertilizer

Mid-June

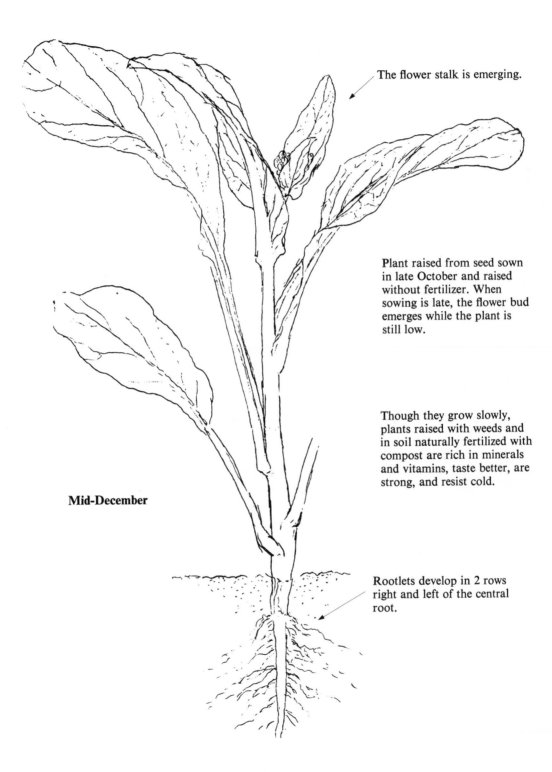

The flower stalk is emerging.

Plant raised from seed sown in late October and raised without fertilizer. When sowing is late, the flower bud emerges while the plant is still low.

Though they grow slowly, plants raised with weeds and in soil naturally fertilized with compost are rich in minerals and vitamins, taste better, are strong, and resist cold.

Mid-December

Rootlets develop in 2 rows right and left of the central root.

198

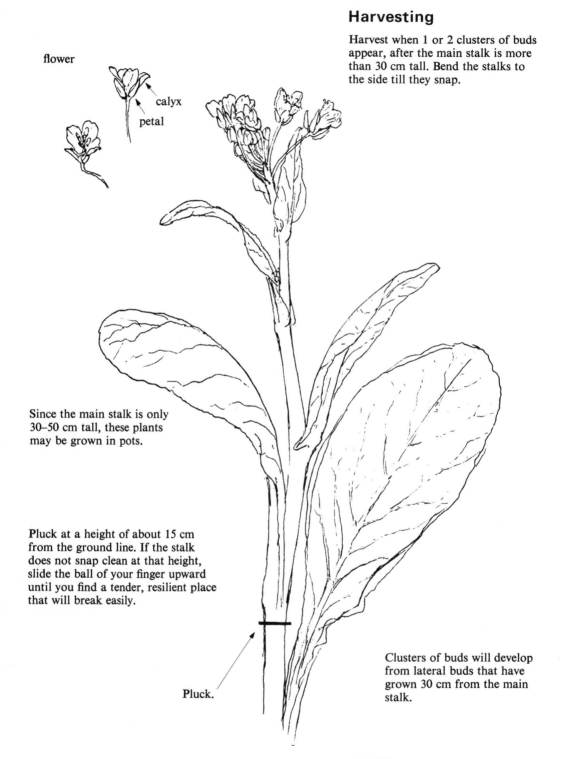

flower

calyx

petal

Harvesting

Harvest when 1 or 2 clusters of buds appear, after the main stalk is more than 30 cm tall. Bend the stalks to the side till they snap.

Since the main stalk is only 30–50 cm tall, these plants may be grown in pots.

Pluck at a height of about 15 cm from the ground line. If the stalk does not snap clean at that height, slide the ball of your finger upward until you find a tender, resilient place that will break easily.

Clusters of buds will develop from lateral buds that have grown 30 cm from the main stalk.

Pluck.

Mid-December

Hengcaitai

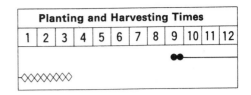

Planting and Harvesting Times

1	2	3	4	5	6	7	8	9	10	11	12

Another of the numerous plants the Chinese raise for their edible, tender, young flower stalks, *hengcaitai* (pronounced hengtsaitai) is native to the Wuhan region in the middle reaches of the Yangtze River. It is sown only in the autumn, and its stalks of buds may be harvested in January. They are best when one or two of the buds in the cluster have bloomed. With its dark, lustrous, purple-green leaves, reddish-purple petioles and veins, and yellow flowers, it is a very handsome plant. It grows 40–50 cm in height and puts out more lateral buds than *caixin*.

Easy to grow, it thrives in fertile soil but has a long growing period in which to develop and become strong, thick, and tender by harvest time.

Seeds may be sown from the middle of September until late October. But, if no fertilizer is to be used, it is better to ensure that the plants are well-rooted, large, and hardy when winter comes by sowing no later than the latter part of September. Sowing earlier than the first part of September invites disease. Sowing later than the end of October deprives plants of time to grow strong before winter damage occurs. Furthermore, such plants produce small harvests because they bloom while still small and then age quickly.

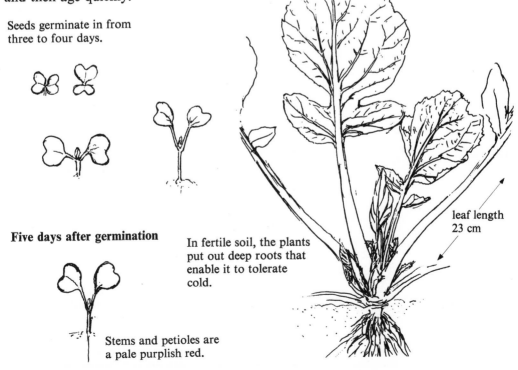

Seeds germinate in from three to four days.

Five days after germination

In fertile soil, the plants put out deep roots that enable it to tolerate cold.

Stems and petioles are a pale purplish red.

leaf length 23 cm

Hengcaitai tolerates transplanting and may be moved when four or five true leaves have developed. Sow in clusters of four or five seeds at a fairly large interval of 40 cm and barely cover with soil. If the soil in which they are to be planted has never been used for agriculture before, prepare compost of cut weeds and kitchen scraps from the spring. When it is mature, fertilize the plot with it before sowing.

Parboiled in lightly salted water, the reddish purple stems of *hengcaitai* turn deep green; and the liquid in which the vegetable is cooked becomes a transparent cobalt color. Its characteristic sticky texture, tenderness, and sweetness make it delicious cold as an appetizer or in soups or sautéed foods.

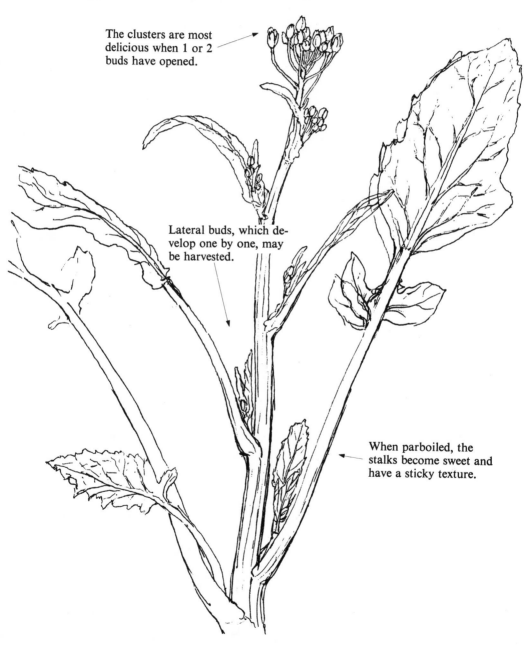

The clusters are most delicious when 1 or 2 buds have opened.

Lateral buds, which develop one by one, may be harvested.

When parboiled, the stalks become sweet and have a sticky texture.

Bok Choy

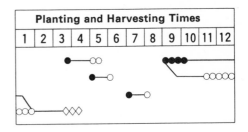

Planting and Harvesting Times

1	2	3	4	5	6	7	8	9	10	11	12

Native to the Guangdong (Canton) region, bok choy which has thick, fleshy, pure white stalks and fresh green leaves, is a small, nonheading kind of Chinese cabbage, the leaves of which are only about 20 cm long.

Since it grows well in cool climates, it is best to sow bok choy in the middle of September. Sowing it earlier than this runs the danger of damage from such things as heat and dryness. Sowing later deprives the plants of time to become well-rooted and stunts development. Nonetheless, spring and summer sowings too are possible.

Though it is relatively intolerant of severe cold, it is made stronger by being raised in soil that has been enriched with compost. Seeds sown in the ground where compost has been prepared are much hardier and thrive better than plants raised in artificially produced furrows.

Bok choy grown from seeds sown in the spring does not reach the size of plants from seeds sown in the autumn and should be harvested about thirty days after germination to prevent going to seed. Since it matures quickly and can be grown on small plots, it is well-suited to home gardens. Like most Chinese vegetables, it is insect-resistant and grows strong and hardy if raised in a natural environment free of immature compost and agricultural chemicals.

Sowing

In the autumn, make small holes at a 20 cm interval and sow in clusters.

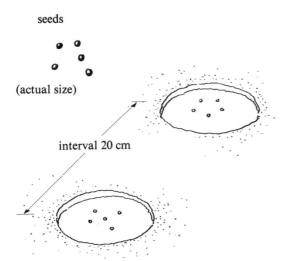

seeds

(actual size)

interval 20 cm

Germination

Germinates in from three to four days.

Immediately after germination, cotyledons are small.

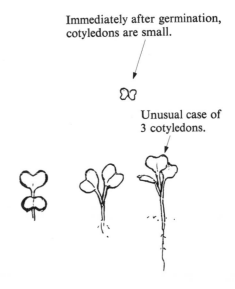

Unusual case of 3 cotyledons.

Spring and summer sowing: Bok choy, which goes to seed quickly, may be sown in spring or summer since it is relatively heat-resistant. In summer, sow in semi-shaded places among rows of other vegetables and reduce the danger of insect damage by sowing during rainy weather. Either sprinkle or sow seeds in rows. Barely cover seeds with a thin layer of soil; they germinate in three or four days.

Autumn sowing: In the autumn, to ensure firmly rooted, hardy plants, avoid overcrowding by planting in clusters of four to five seeds at intervals of 20 cm and thin regularly to ensure that the leaves of neighboring plants touch lightly. The plants become very handsome as their petioles broaden and their bases grow large and white.

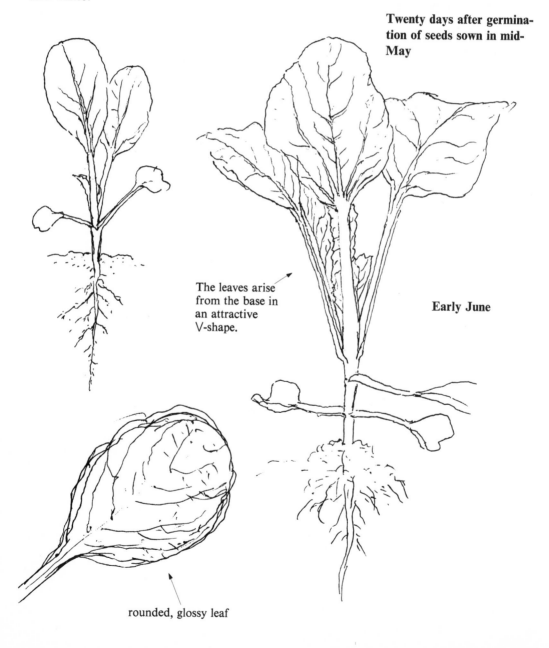

Twenty days after germination of seeds sown in mid-May

The leaves arise from the base in an attractive V-shape.

Early June

rounded, glossy leaf

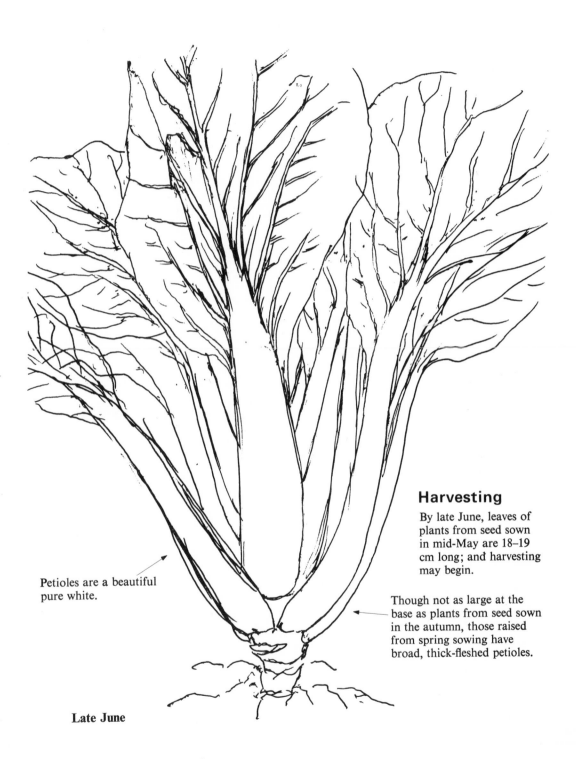

Petioles are a beautiful
pure white.

Harvesting

By late June, leaves of
plants from seed sown
in mid-May are 18–19
cm long; and harvesting
may begin.

Though not as large at the
base as plants from seed sown
in the autumn, those raised
from spring sowing have
broad, thick-fleshed petioles.

Late June

Harvesting Bud Clusters

Clusters of buds arising from
each axil may be harvested
and eaten.

stalk of buds and flow-
ers of a plant grown
from autumn sowing

Low soil temperatures in
winter reduce root water intake. This, combined with
wind-caused evaporation from
leaf surfaces, results in
dehydration.

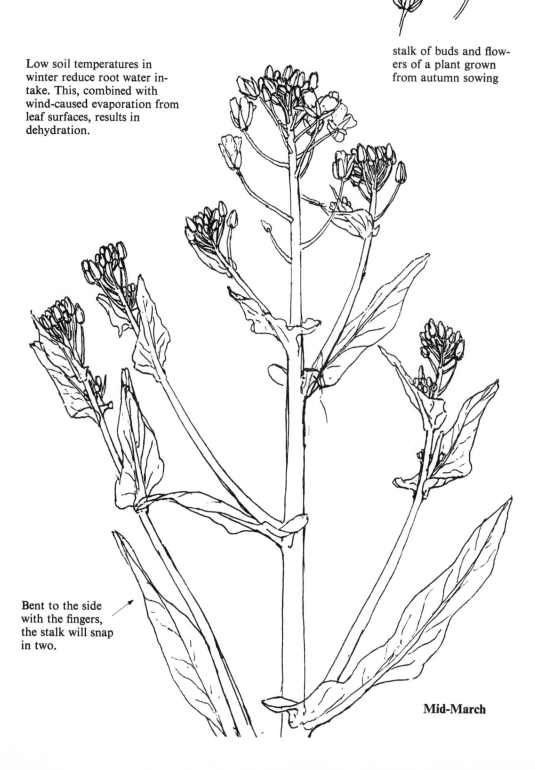

Bent to the side
with the fingers,
the stalk will snap
in two.

Mid-March

Qing-gen-cai

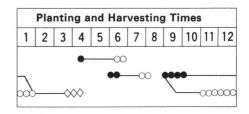
Another of the small varieties of Chinese cabbage, related to *tacai* and bok choy, which it resembles in leaf form, texture, and flavor, *qing-gen-cai* (pronounced ching-gen-tsai) has delicate green petioles and ovoid, fresh-green leaves. The petioles are larger than those of bok choy. Some are perfectly straight, and some curve inward. With the sweetness characteristic of many Chinese vegetables, it is prized in soups, sautéed dishes, cold appetizers, and pickles. It stands up well to boiling, and its already lovely color is actually enhanced by sautéing.

Relatively heat- and cold-resistant, it thrives in cool weather and may be sown in autumn or spring.

If plenty of compost is mixed with the soil, enabling them to become firmly rooted before the severe cold sets in, *qing-gen-cai* plants survive most winter damage except actual freezing of the ground.

Regular thinning during the seedling stage to prevent overcrowding is essential if the petioles, the most succulent and delicious part of the plant, are to grow thick and broad. Thin periodically to maintain an interval in which the leaves of neighboring plants touch lightly. By the time the leaves are 9–10 cm long, there should be only one plant in each location. Crowding is less important after the plants have gained some size: at that stage, an interval of 12–13 cm is suitable.

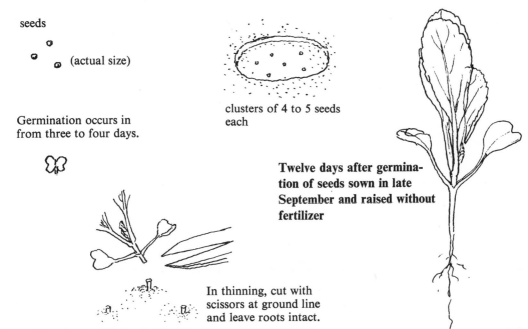

seeds

(actual size)

Germination occurs in from three to four days.

clusters of 4 to 5 seeds each

Twelve days after germination of seeds sown in late September and raised without fertilizer

In thinning, cut with scissors at ground line and leave roots intact.

Because the plants are low and small, large harvests may be obtained from plots of limited size. In a furrow 50 cm wide make two rows of clusters (from four to five seeds each) at an interval of 15 cm. Barely cover with a thin layer of soil. Seeds germinate in three or four days. The plants grow well in semishade, mature quickly, suffer very little from insects, and go to seed late. Once harvested, they should be used quickly since the petioles spoil rapidly. They may be safely parboiled and kept for a longer period refrigerated.

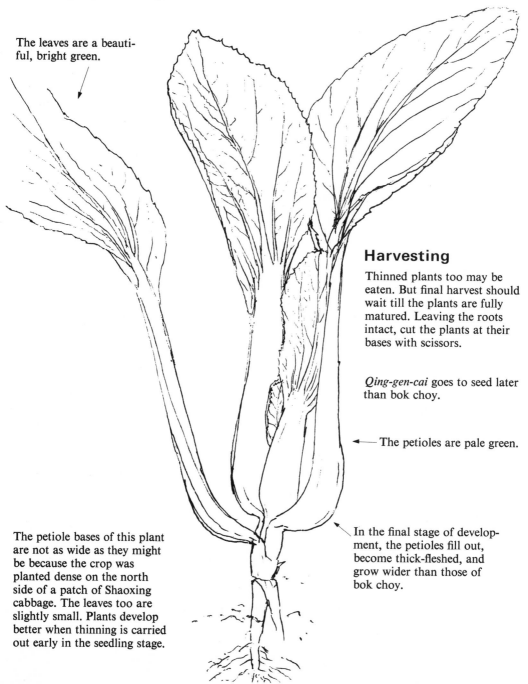

The leaves are a beautiful, bright green.

Harvesting

Thinned plants too may be eaten. But final harvest should wait till the plants are fully matured. Leaving the roots intact, cut the plants at their bases with scissors.

Qing-gen-cai goes to seed later than bok choy.

The petioles are pale green.

The petiole bases of this plant are not as wide as they might be because the crop was planted dense on the north side of a patch of Shaoxing cabbage. The leaves too are slightly small. Plants develop better when thinning is carried out early in the seedling stage.

In the final stage of development, the petioles fill out, become thick-fleshed, and grow wider than those of bok choy.

Ensai

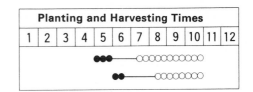

Planting and Harvesting Times											
1	2	3	4	5	6	7	8	9	10	11	12

This annual member of the convolvulaceous family resembles the morning glory and has hollow stems. Cultivated in a wide tropical region including central southern China, it is very insect- and heat-resistant and, like so-called Java spinach, is welcome in the summer when leafy vegetables are scarce. Even blazing sunlight causes it no damage, and it is robust enough to put out new shoots continuously.

Fresh vine tips and tender leaves may be washed and used raw in salads and sandwiches. Or they may be quickly parboiled and served with dressings as a side dish or appetizer. *Ensai* is especially good chopped and sautéed with minced garlic and ginger. It is richer in vitamins A and C than spinach and contains plenty of calcium and iron. It must be cooked quickly, as overcooking spoils its color and flavor.

Since it thrives in heat and humidity and dislikes aridity, choose a sunny place and use plenty of moisture-retaining compost. Aridity can be prevented by allowing a moderate stand of weeds to grow around the plant. *Ensai* itself puts out lateral shoots and leaves that shade its base and reduce evaporation.

In addition to its value as a food, arranged artlessly in a vase, it creates a cooling, exotic mood.

The seed case is hard. To ensure that the earth comes into direct contact with it, press the ground lightly with the hand after covering the sown seeds.

It may be harvested into late October. In November, however, when temperatures drop, its leaves wither. Like taro and sweet potato, the *ensai* plant shrivels suddenly with the first frosty morning. Interestingly, however, these three plants survive even typhoon-strength storms unscathed.

seeds

 Seeds are coffee-colored.

(actual size)

About seven days after germination of seeds sown in mid-May

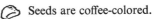

The seed case remains attached after germination.

The first 2 true leaves are pressed together in this way when they emerge.

The cotyledons are deeply cleft.

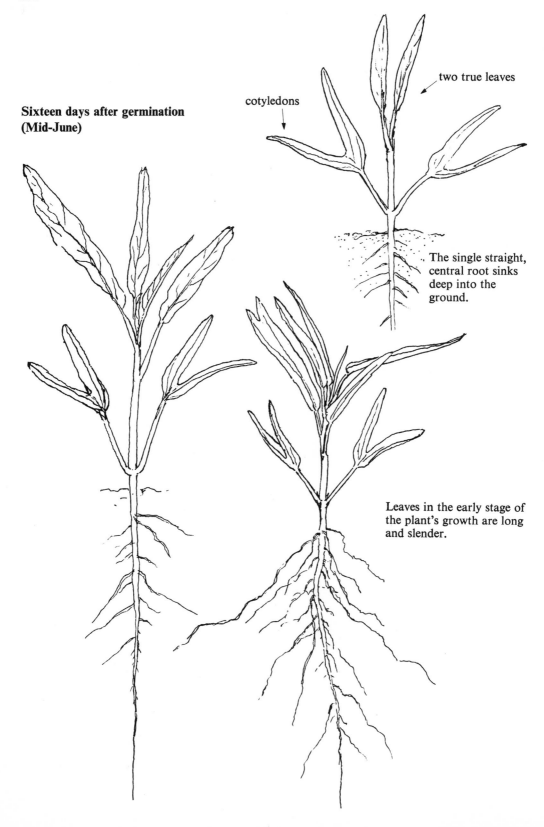

**Sixteen days after germination
(Mid-June)**

cotyledons

two true leaves

The single straight,
central root sinks
deep into the
ground.

Leaves in the early stage of
the plant's growth are long
and slender.

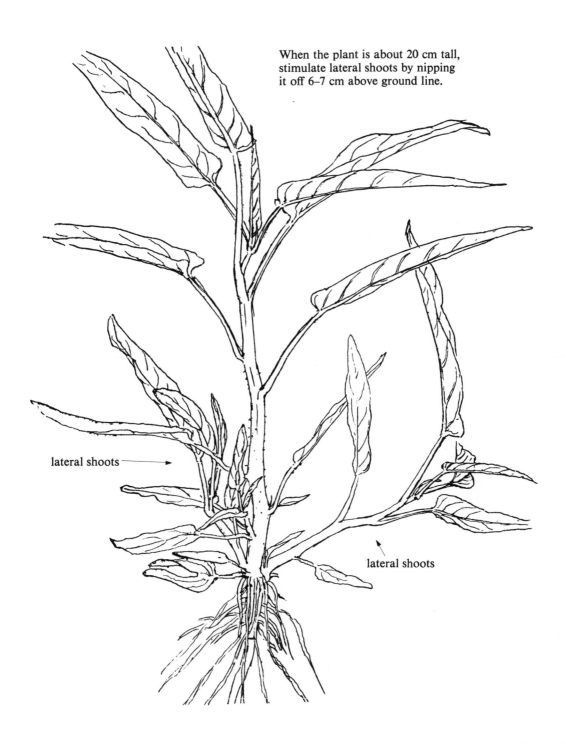

When the plant is about 20 cm tall, stimulate lateral shoots by nipping it off 6–7 cm above ground line.

lateral shoots

lateral shoots

Forty days after germination (Late June)

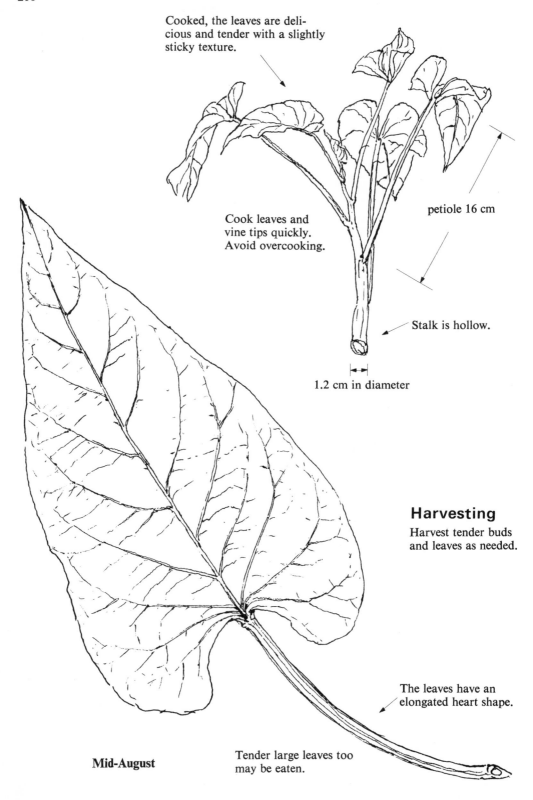

Cooked, the leaves are delicious and tender with a slightly sticky texture.

Cook leaves and vine tips quickly. Avoid overcooking.

petiole 16 cm

Stalk is hollow.

1.2 cm in diameter

Harvesting

Harvest tender buds and leaves as needed.

The leaves have an elongated heart shape.

Mid-August

Tender large leaves too may be eaten.

Java Spinach

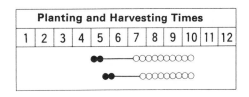

Not a true spinach at all but an annual member of the amaranth family, like the cocks-combs, Java spinach occurs in several varieties, some of which have red and some green leaves of round or willow-leaf shapes. A pale-green, round-leafed variety from Taiwan is of good quality. It is very tolerant of blazing heats and aridity and is widely grown throughout China and Southeast Asia. It is half again as rich in vitamins as spinach and contains abundant iron and magnesium. It may be eaten raw in salads, parboiled and served as an appetizer with various dressings, in sautéed dishes, and in batter-fried foods. The bud clusters are delicious fried in the tempura fashion. But Java spinach should as a rule be combined in some way with garlic, which masks its strong odor.

Thinned small plants may be eaten until five or six true leaves have developed. When the plants are about 20 cm high, nip the growing bud to stimulate lateral shoots. Then harvest tender young leaves as they develop, always leaving three or four on a shoot. Continue harvesting this way until the young bud clusters that appear in late summer have been harvested. Young plants are delicious, but the older they grow, the less palatable they become. Use the leaves quickly after harvest, as they spoil readily.

If soil is lean, add eight shovelfuls of compost for each 3.3 m². If compost is unavailable, about a month before sowing, add a handful of ground limestone for each anticipated plant. If it is raised after legumes or nonleafy vegetables, no fertilizing is needed.

It requires no more care than weeds and reseeds itself each year.

enlarged

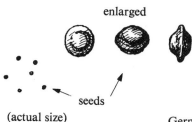

seeds

(actual size)

The small, gleaming black seeds look as if they had been lacquered.

Sow in clusters of 5 to 6 seeds at an interval of 20 cm.

Germinates in three days.

Four days after germination

212

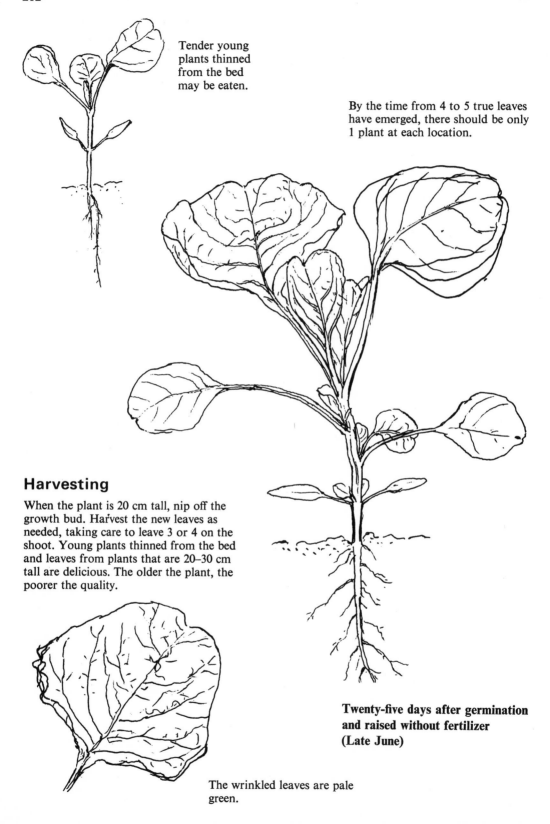

Tender young plants thinned from the bed may be eaten.

By the time from 4 to 5 true leaves have emerged, there should be only 1 plant at each location.

Harvesting

When the plant is 20 cm tall, nip off the growth bud. Harvest the new leaves as needed, taking care to leave 3 or 4 on the shoot. Young plants thinned from the bed and leaves from plants that are 20–30 cm tall are delicious. The older the plant, the poorer the quality.

Twenty-five days after germination and raised without fertilizer (Late June)

The wrinkled leaves are pale green.

Indian Spinach

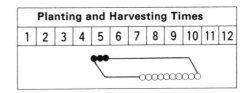
The annual *Basella rubra*, which is known as Indian or Ceylonese spinach, is not actually spinach at all but resembles it in flavor. It is a native of tropical Asia and occurs in two varieties: one in which the stalks are green and the other in which they are purple. The latter variety, with its dark green leaves and purple stalks, petioles, and veins is especially attractive visually.

Supported on poles, these vines reach lengths of 2–3 m. Six of them planted by a window double as edible crop and awning in the hot summertime.

Do not harvest until the plant is 1 m tall. Then, beginning at the bottom, with scissors, cut off every other leaf, petiole and all. At first, lateral shoots are very slow to appear. When the plant is 50 cm tall, encourage them by cutting off the growing tip, about 20 cm from its extremity. Leaves from the lateral shoots too may be harvested. In the autumn, flower buds appear at the axils of leaves. They too may be eaten.

When boiled, the glossy, fleshy egg-shaped leaves (7–10 cm long) become soft and viscous. Available in summer, when leafy vegetables are scarce, they are welcome for use in soups, as appetizers, in sautées, or topped with a sesame-seed sauce. They are rich in iron, calcium, and vitamins.

Tolerant of heat, these plants are disease- and insect-resistant and thrive as long as soil and environment approximate their requirements. They may be raised in pots in which compost has been added to the soil.

Sowing

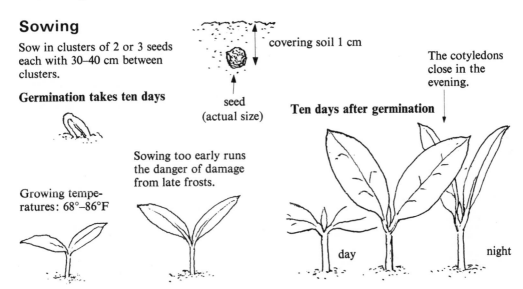

Sow in clusters of 2 or 3 seeds each with 30–40 cm between clusters.

covering soil 1 cm

The cotyledons close in the evening.

Germination takes ten days

seed (actual size)

Ten days after germination

Sowing too early runs the danger of damage from late frosts.

Growing temperatures: 68°–86°F

day

night

Sowing: In soil that has already been spread with compost, sow in clusters of from three to four seeds each with 30–40 cm between clusters. Cover with a fairly thick layer of covering soil since these seeds will not germinate in contact with sunlight. Guard against aridity. Because the seed cases are tough, either sow after a rain or water thoroughly after sowing.

Cotyledons open to 180 degrees during the day and close, like hands in prayer, from night till morning.

After four or five true leaves have developed thin, leaving only one plant in each location. A stand of weeds will retain soil moisture, enabling the plant to put out new leaves, one after the other.

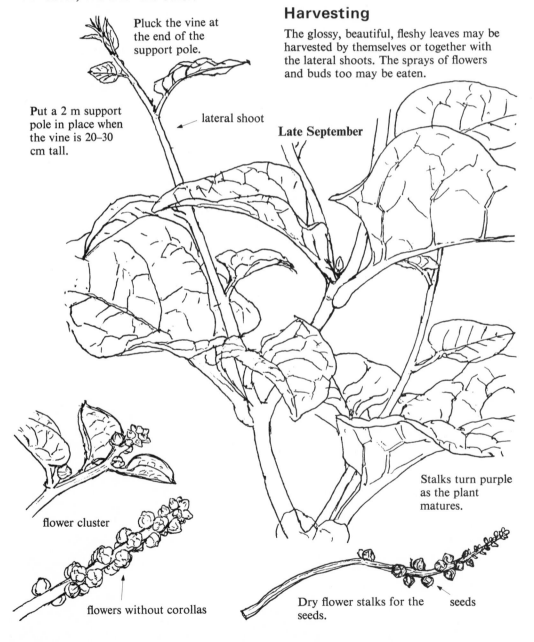

Pluck the vine at the end of the support pole.

Put a 2 m support pole in place when the vine is 20–30 cm tall.

lateral shoot

Harvesting

The glossy, beautiful, fleshy leaves may be harvested by themselves or together with the lateral shoots. The sprays of flowers and buds too may be eaten.

Late September

Stalks turn purple as the plant matures.

flower cluster

flowers without corollas

Dry flower stalks for the seeds.

seeds

Chinese Wolfberry

Planting and Harvesting Times											
1	2	3	4	5	6	7	8	9	10	11	12

Cuttings △----- Any time ----△

△---------- Any time --------△
Planting roots ----△----------○○○○○○○○○

Later than second year
----○○○○○○○○○○○○○○○○○○○○○○○---

Chinese wolfberry (*Lycium chinense*), a deciduous member of the nightshade family known as *gouqi* in Chinese and *kuko* in Japanese, is fond of water and is found by paddy fields, rivers, creeks, and ditches throughout Japan. It is inconspicuous in winter, when its leaves fall, and in summer, when it is concealed by weeds. But its translucent, pearly, egg-shaped berries catch the eye in autumn.

Long used in popular Chinese medicine, the plant produces both leaves and berries that may be eaten. The leaves are good in soups and sautéed foods, steamed together with rice, or dried for infusion as a beverage. The berries are used as a flavoring for sakè. Rice topped with tender, young wolfberry leaves parboiled in salted water is especially delicious.

The numerous, thick, gray-green branches that appear from the base of the clump in spring are free of them; but, as the branch grows woodier, slender, and gray, thorns appear at each leaf axil.

From Rooted Plants
(March to November)

Plant at an interval of 60 cm in a sunny, well-ventilated place. The drawing shows a newly planted wolfberry in March. New lateral shoots and buds have already developed.

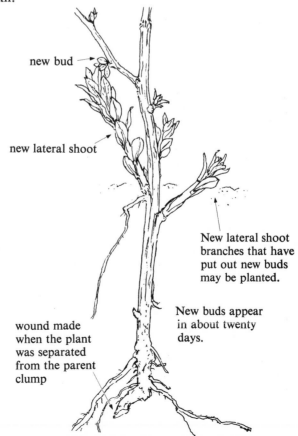

new bud →

new lateral shoot

New lateral shoot branches that have put out new buds may be planted.

New buds appear in about twenty days.

wound made when the plant was separated from the parent clump

In the summer, the plant blooms small lavender flowers, similar to those of the eggplant. Berries, which appear in the fall, develop in an unusual way: after the flowers fall, small gray protuberances emerge beside the peduncles and later develop into berries.

Either have someone who raises them give you plants separated from a parent cluster or take one or two cuttings about 30 cm long and plant them, horizontally, so that about 5 cm protrude above the surface of the ground. If weeds grow nearby, no fertilizing is needed. If care is taken that the soil does not dry out for the first ten days after they are planted, the cuttings will take root and begin to grow. Chinese wolfberry thrives and puts out abundant fresh shoots if planted in a sunny, well-ventilated place.

Wait to harvest plants grown from cuttings until the second year. Those grown from rooted plants, however, may be harvested, leaf by leaf, from four to five months after planting. Do not cut the branches as this inhibits the formation of berries. Furthermore, if berries are your aim, do not harvest leaves before blooming.

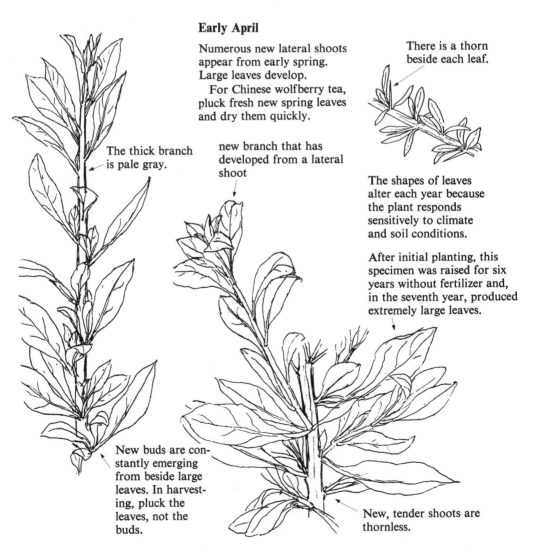

Early April

Numerous new lateral shoots appear from early spring. Large leaves develop.

For Chinese wolfberry tea, pluck fresh new spring leaves and dry them quickly.

There is a thorn beside each leaf.

The thick branch is pale gray.

new branch that has developed from a lateral shoot

The shapes of leaves alter each year because the plant responds sensitively to climate and soil conditions.

After initial planting, this specimen was raised for six years without fertilizer and, in the seventh year, produced extremely large leaves.

New buds are constantly emerging from beside large leaves. In harvesting, pluck the leaves, not the buds.

New, tender shoots are thornless.

Comfrey

Planting and Harvesting Times

1	2	3	4	5	6	7	8	9	10	11	12

Root cuttings
△---- Any time ---△
Planting roots
△-------- Any time -------- △
Later than second year

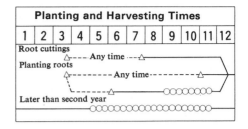

A perennial member of the borage family, comfrey will supply a family's needs for years planted in a sunny corner of field or garden. Native to the Caucasus, comfrey is extremely rich in vitamins, iron, calcium, and manganese. In addition, it contains vitamin B_{12}, which, occurring in some shellfish, is found in no other vegetable.

Comfrey dies down in winter to put out a dense growth of leaves from a short, hard stalk from the beginning to the middle of March. At full growth, the leaves are about 40 cm long. Young tender leaves from bud tips are good to eat. Dipped in batter and deep-fried, larger leaves that are still tender and that have developed a coat of fine hair make delicious tempura. Comfrey is used in salads and may be combined in a juicer with such other leafy vegetables as kale, *komatsuna*, cabbage, *shiso*, and parsley to make a refreshing green drink.

Obtain seedlings from a garden supplier. Or have someone who raises them separate a plant from a clump and give it to you. The root may be cut and planted as cuttings or the separated plant may be set out whole. Cut thick roots (about 1 cm in diameter) into pieces 5–10 cm long, set them horizontally in the ground, and cover with a layer of soil 4–5 cm deep. Whole plants will take root if simply returned to the soil.

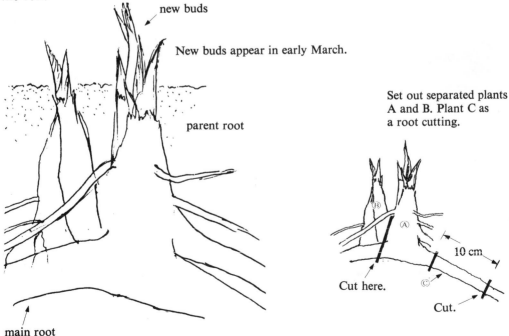

new buds

New buds appear in early March.

parent root

Set out separated plants A and B. Plant C as a root cutting.

10 cm

Cut here.

Cut.

main root

Since they are vigorous, comfrey plants may be allowed to grow by themselves in a corner of the garden as long as there is a stand of weeds nearby. Since, like all thick-rooted plants, comfrey absorbs plenty of nutrients from the soil, it is essential to set it in soil uncontaminated by agricultural or any other chemical substances. It never does to run risks with vegetables that we eat to sustain our own good health.

Bees abound in the neighborhood when comfrey puts out its nectar-rich pinkish-lavender blooms, from May to July. The bell-shaped flowers, which bloom one by one in a whorl, are especially attractive in summer at twilight.

Planting (March to November)

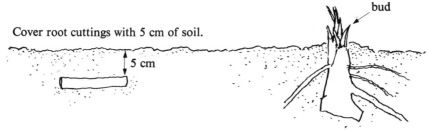

Set whole plants so that the tip of the bud protrudes above the ground.

bud

Cover root cuttings with 5 cm of soil.

5 cm

Development of a New Bud

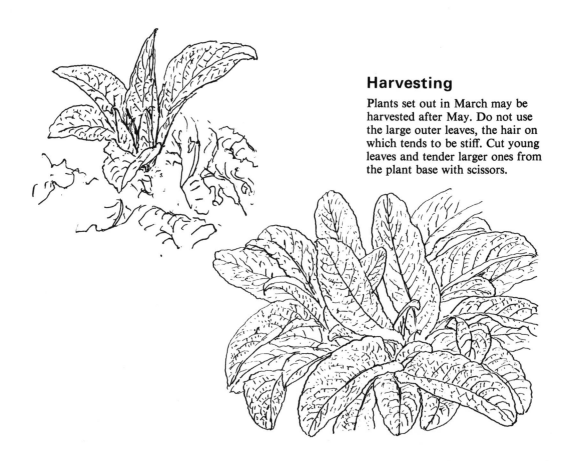

Harvesting

Plants set out in March may be harvested after May. Do not use the large outer leaves, the hair on which tends to be stiff. Cut young leaves and tender larger ones from the plant base with scissors.

Scallions

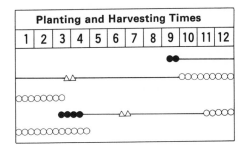
In the past, onions of this kind were cultivated for the green parts of the leaves alone. Today, the variety called *hanegi* is used in this way. The long white scallion was developed in cold regions where soil was mounded around the plants to protect them from frost, thus keeping considerable sections of the plant from the sun and preventing the development of green color. Scallions like sun and well-drained soil with a suitable degree of moisture. Growth drops at temperatures above 86°F, but the plants tolerate cold well.

Sowing: After scallion seeds have germinated, seedlings are allowed to develop to a certain stage and then are transplanted to their permanent location, where soil is mounded around them to encourage the growth of long, white lower sections. Soil in the seedling bed must be thoroughly worked. Compost is spread over the entire surface, and seeds are planted in rows. It is important to keep the soil moist until germination.

Thinning: When the seedlings are 10–12 cm long, thin crowded places to an interval of 2–3 cm. At thinning time too, water the soil.

Permanent planting: Seedlings from seeds sown in the spring are planted permanently in June or July; those from seeds sown in the autumn, in March or April. Furrows for permanent planting should be oriented east and west. Dig a deep trough and mound the soil on the north rim. Plant the seedlings against the south wall of the trough at an interval of 5–10 cm. Make a 5-cm layer of soil in the bottom of the trough. Press this soil to fix the seedlings in place. On top of this soil add a 5-cm layer of compost.

Although the scallions should grow well without additional fertilizer, if it is available, you may add a small amount of vegetable ash around the plant bases.

Sowing

If the soil is lean or if chemical fertilizers have previously been used on it, spread about three shovelfuls of compost over the whole surface and mix well. In the seedling bed make a trough about 20 cm wide. Sow seeds in rows. If the soil is highly acidic, use a small amount of ground limestone to neutralize it.

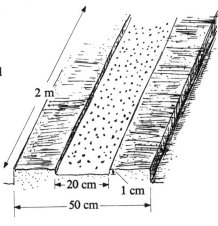

Since aridity impedes germination, after sowing spread chopped straw on the ground and water it.

Remove the straw immediately after germination begins.

Mounding: This process is very important in growing scallions. The best time for first mounding is forty to fifty days after permanent planting, when the roots should be active and the plant should be growing vigorously. Performed too early, mounding can retard growth. Thereafter, mound at intervals of from two to three weeks to conceal the white parts that appear above the ground line.

Diseases: Chemicals do not prevent diseases in scallions, which have a waxy leaf surface to which such substances cannot adhere. But this is no source of concern since nature cures practically all diseases afflicting scallions.

Germination

Germination occurs in from ten to fifteen days.

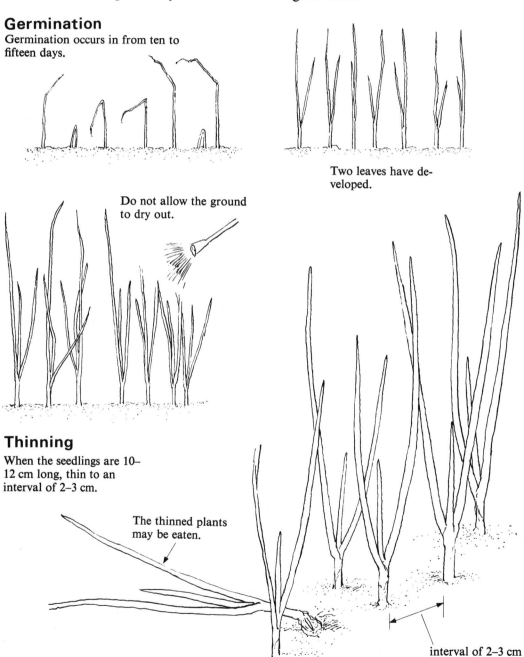

Two leaves have developed.

Do not allow the ground to dry out.

Thinning

When the seedlings are 10–12 cm long, thin to an interval of 2–3 cm.

The thinned plants may be eaten.

interval of 2–3 cm

Permanent Planting

Transplant seedlings from seeds sown in the spring in June or July. Transplant those from seeds sown in the autumn in March or April.

Stand the seedlings against the south wall of the trough. Return soil to the bottom of the trough to make a layer 5 cm deep. Spread compost on top of this layer and allow the scallions to grow for from forty to fifty days.

Ideally, at this time, seedlings should have an overall length of 30–40 cm.

Mound soil on the north rim of the trough.

20 cm

15 cm

grasses, straw, compost

soil

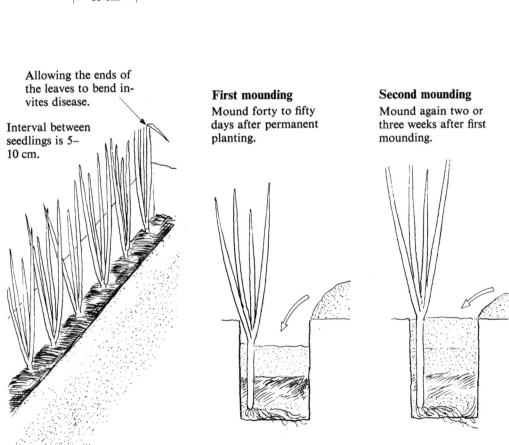

Allowing the ends of the leaves to bend invites disease.

Interval between seedlings is 5–10 cm.

First mounding

Mound forty to fifty days after permanent planting.

Second mounding

Mound again two or three weeks after first mounding.

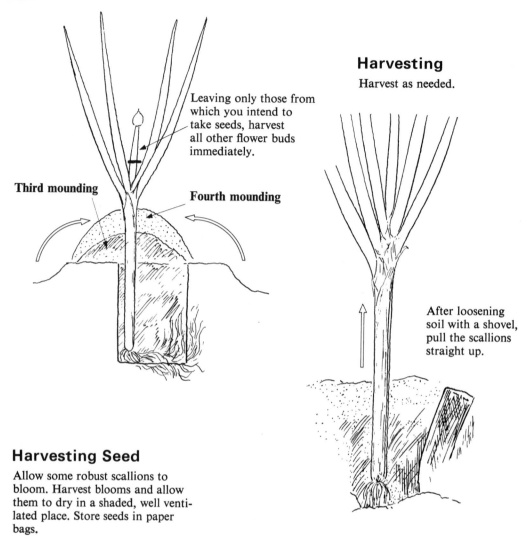

Leaving only those from which you intend to take seeds, harvest all other flower buds immediately.

Third mounding

Fourth mounding

Harvesting

Harvest as needed.

After loosening soil with a shovel, pull the scallions straight up.

Harvesting Seed

Allow some robust scallions to bloom. Harvest blooms and allow them to dry in a shaded, well ventilated place. Store seeds in paper bags.

Harvest.

seeds

(actual size)

Hanegi

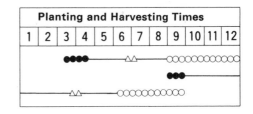

Planting and Harvesting Times											
1	2	3	4	5	6	7	8	9	10	11	12

Very ancient crop plants, though today they are more widely employed as garnishes and, in Japan, in such popular one-dish casserole meals as sukiyaki, various varieties of long onions were once used as medicinal herbs. For instance, hot plasters made with onions were once a favorite remedy for a cold. Their versatility meant that onions were always given a part of the domestic vegetable patch.

Sowing: Though much easier to raise, *hanegi* are sown in beds prepared as for scallions with the single difference that compost is not necessarily required. *Hanegi* can thrive without fertilizing. Sow in rows in well-worked, level ground. Since aridity impedes germination, after sowing, cover the ground with wet straw.

Thinning: Thin crowded places to an interplant interval of 2–3 cm.

Permanent planting: The trough need not be as deep as is required for scallions: a width of 15 cm and a depth of 10 cm are sufficient. Stand the seedlings in clusters of two or three along one wall of the trough. Intercluster interval should be about 15 cm. Return enough excavated soil to the bottom of the trough to make a layer 5 cm deep. Cover this with compost. Press the ground lightly with the palms of the hands to hold the seedlings in place. Water.

Sowing and Germination

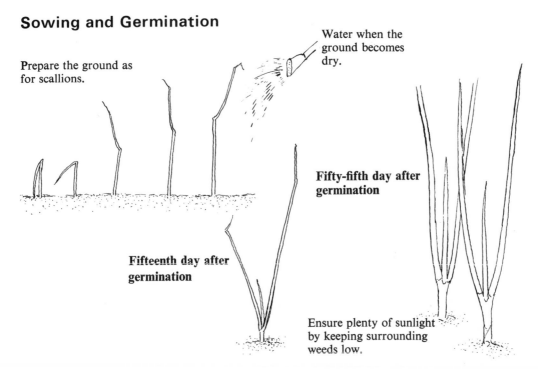

Prepare the ground as for scallions.

Water when the ground becomes dry.

Fifteenth day after germination

Fifty-fifth day after germination

Ensure plenty of sunlight by keeping surrounding weeds low.

Diseases: Like all the other onions, *hanegi* have a waxy leaf coating that repels liquids, including agricultural chemicals. Any insecticides sprayed on them drop to the ground, where they have a polluting, decidedly harmful effect.

Creating a natural environment is the way to prevent plant disease. Leaving things up to nature is the wisest policy. If the plants wilt, they wilt. But by and large nature will cure disease without our interfering.

Permanent Planting

Prepare a trough, plant the seedlings, and add compost. Lime is needed only in case of extreme acidity.

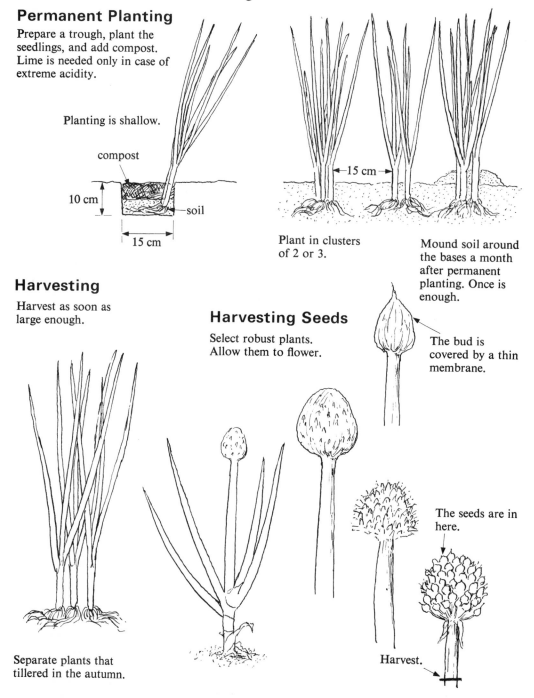

Planting is shallow.

compost

10 cm

soil

15 cm

Plant in clusters of 2 or 3.

Mound soil around the bases a month after permanent planting. Once is enough.

Harvesting

Harvest as soon as large enough.

Harvesting Seeds

Select robust plants. Allow them to flower.

The bud is covered by a thin membrane.

The seeds are in here.

Separate plants that tillered in the autumn.

Harvest.

Bermuda Onions

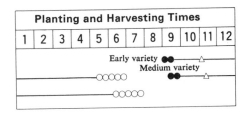

Planting and Harvesting Times											
1	2	3	4	5	6	7	8	9	10	11	12

Early variety
Medium variety

Leaves of the Bermuda onion, a member of the lily family, develop first. Later the bases of the leaf sheaths bulge to form the bulb. Though suited to moderate climates, the onions tolerate cold well enough to be planted in the autumn and harvested early the next summer.

Sowing: Always use new seed as the germination ratio of old seed is poor. Observing the weather conditions, sow either early (in the middle of September) or later (late September). If sowing is too early, the plants will become too large during the year and will bloom in the spring. If you sow too late, the roots will lack sufficient time to develop after permanent planting; and the plants will suffer from the cold.

Permanent planting: Transplant seedlings from seed sown in early September in early November and those from seeds sown in the middle of September in the middle of November. Choose a sunny place for the furrow, which should run east and west. The furrow should be 50 cm wide. In it make two rows of holes 10–12 cm apart. Be especially careful about watering. Onions like moist soil that drains well. Because they require much more nutrition than scallions or *hanegi*, use plenty of compost. In lean soil, leaves will fail to develop properly; and bulbs will be small.

Sowing

Using a furrow from which another crop has just been harvested, without adding fertilizer, sow to a width of about 20 cm.

seeds  (actual size)

Use new onion seeds; that is, less than a year after their harvest. Old seed will not germinate.

Cover seeds with 4–5 mm of soil, top with straw, and water.

Protect from drying with straw.

Germination

Germination occurs in from seven to ten days. Once it has begun, remove the straw covering.

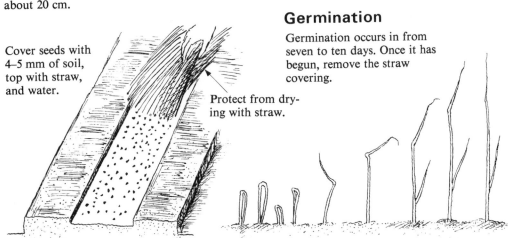

Protection from cold: Since cold weather, the time when roots are inactive, follows hard on transplantation to permanent beds, protect from dryness and frost by covering the furrow with straw. In cities, where straw is usually unavailable, substitute cut weeds. Tall grasses, like pampas, serve this purpose well.

Harvesting: Harvest when bulbs are full and leaves have drooped. Onions may be stored longer if harvested while the leaves are still green. With leaves still on, tie five or six onions together and hang them to dry in a well-ventilated, shaded place. Leaves of the Bermuda onion may be eaten while young.

Rotation: Rotate at a cycle of two or three years. Bermuda onions are especially sensitive to soil acidity.

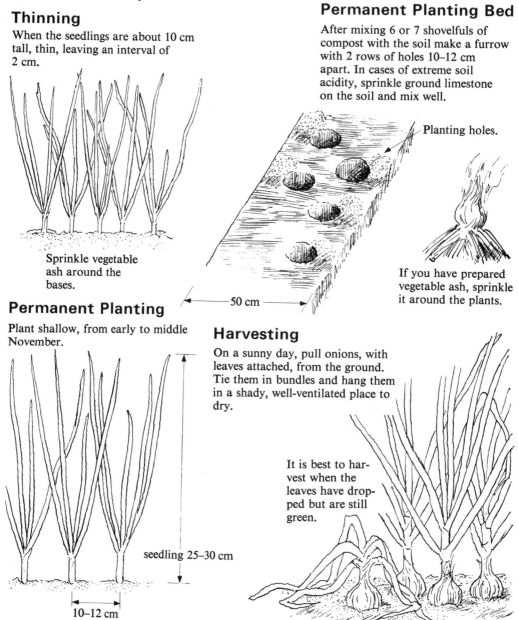

Thinning

When the seedlings are about 10 cm tall, thin, leaving an interval of 2 cm.

Sprinkle vegetable ash around the bases.

Permanent Planting Bed

After mixing 6 or 7 shovelfuls of compost with the soil make a furrow with 2 rows of holes 10–12 cm apart. In cases of extreme soil acidity, sprinkle ground limestone on the soil and mix well.

Planting holes.

If you have prepared vegetable ash, sprinkle it around the plants.

50 cm

Permanent Planting

Plant shallow, from early to middle November.

seedling 25–30 cm

10–12 cm

Harvesting

On a sunny day, pull onions, with leaves attached, from the ground. Tie them in bundles and hang them in a shady, well-ventilated place to dry.

It is best to harvest when the leaves have dropped but are still green.

Wakegi

Planting and Harvesting Times

1	2	3	4	5	6	7	8	9	10	11	12

A member of the lily family that is native to many parts of the world including Siberia, the Altai Mountains, Greece, and Southeast Asia, the onion that is known as *wakegi* in Japanese forms underground clustered roots and is dormant in the summer. It has long been cultivated in the western part of the main Japanese island Honshu and is widely used as a garnish for noodle dishes (*soba*) and *sashimi* and in soups, appetizers, and rice gruels.

Preparations: It thrives in temperate and warm climates, in sunny places where the soil is rich in organic matter. Since, like most other onions, it has a shallow root system, the *wakegi* is intolerant of aridity. On the other hand, too much moisture leads to disease. A fine, light soil with which chopped straw has been mixed is ideal. Kitchen scraps and dried weeds make suitable compost.

Wakegi can be raised in pots in a mixture of two parts compost to one part garden soil. If chemical fertilizer is used at planting time, seed onions may rot; and nitrogen fertilizers like ground limestone invite aphids. Pot cultivation is inexpensive, but the pot environment must approximate the natural one as closely as possible.

Harvesting: Leaves may be plucked and used thirty days after germination, when the plants should be 20 cm tall. Frost withers the leaf tips. Thereafter the above-ground part of the plant turns brown and drops. But beautiful, dark-green, new leaves begin appearing in March and are ready to harvest in April. When the top parts of the plants wither, in the middle of May, the seed onions may be dug up and dried. Store in a shady place till autumn.

Planting Seed Onions
(From late August till late September)

bud

Separate seed onions that have wintered one year into 2 or 3 cloves and plant at intervals of 20 cm.

Allow the pointed tip of the bulb to peep above the ground.

Separate into pairs.

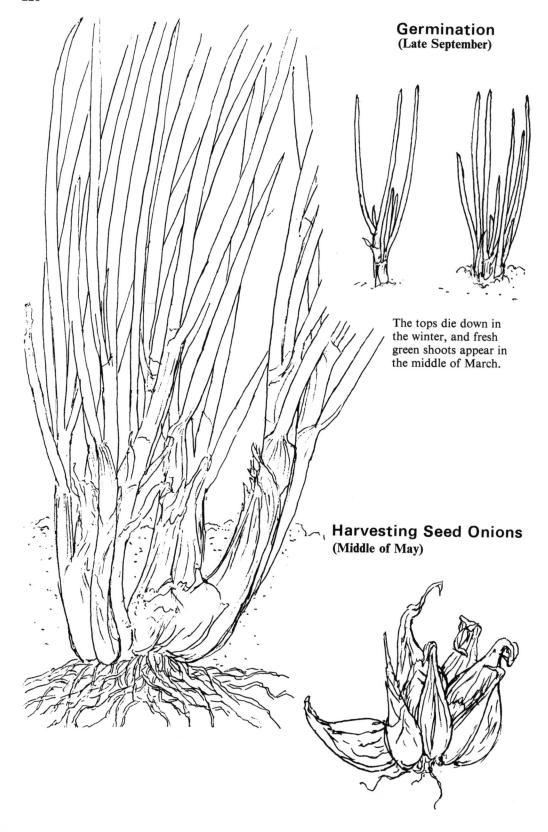

Germination
(Late September)

The tops die down in
the winter, and fresh
green shoots appear in
the middle of March.

Harvesting Seed Onions
(Middle of May)

Garlic

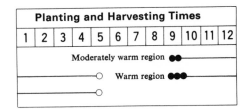

Planting and Harvesting Times

1	2	3	4	5	6	7	8	9	10	11	12

Moderately warm region ●●——

○ Warm region ●●●——

○

Though the fresh young leaves and stalks too may be eaten, it is the multiple bulb of this member of the lily family that is most widely used. Planting times for garlic vary subtly according to the source of the bulbs. When purchasing, be certain to investigate their origins and select bulbs that suit the climate in your region. In moderately warm regions, plant from the middle to late September. In warmer regions, plant until early October. If planted too soon, the stalks grow too large by winter; and the plants fall victim to the cold. If planted too late, the stalks will remain undeveloped; and the bulbs will not enlarge.

Dryness of soil in early spring retards bulb development. Since it is the time when garlic bulbs tiller, spring is the season when moisture and a maximum of soil nutrients are essential. For bulbs set out in the autumn, it is a good idea to rely on weeds and leaves to assist in providing nutrition and prevent moisture evaporation. Compost soaks up the warmth of the sunlight and thus helps keep soil temperatures high.

As this discussion makes clear, it is essential to guard against soil aridity at the season when garlic bulbs tiller. But heavy watering of soil in dry, cold, winter weather must be avoided since it invites freezing and makes moisture and nutrient intake impossible.

Select bulbs with pinkish flesh since white ones are prone to disease.

Plant so that the sprout end of the bulb is upward.

Planting

Plant at intervals of 10 cm in two rows in a furrow 50 cm wide.

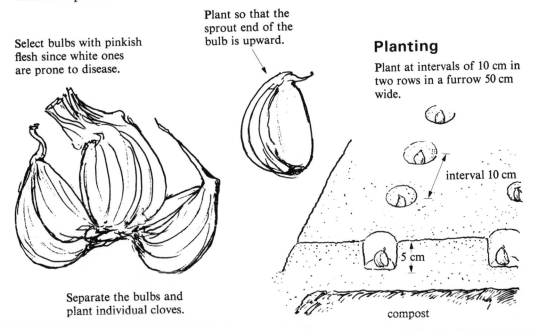

interval 10 cm

5 cm

Separate the bulbs and plant individual cloves.

compost

Though they survive winter, garlic is not necessarily cold-tolerant. Indeed in very chilly regions as much as half the lengths of the leaves will wither. The plants begin recovering and growing in April. Flowering stalks should be plucked at this time. When the stalks have withered about half their lengths, in May, dig up bulbs and dry them for two or three days in the shade. Delaying harvest has a detrimental effect on quality. Cutting bulbs without drying them invites rot and makes storage difficult.

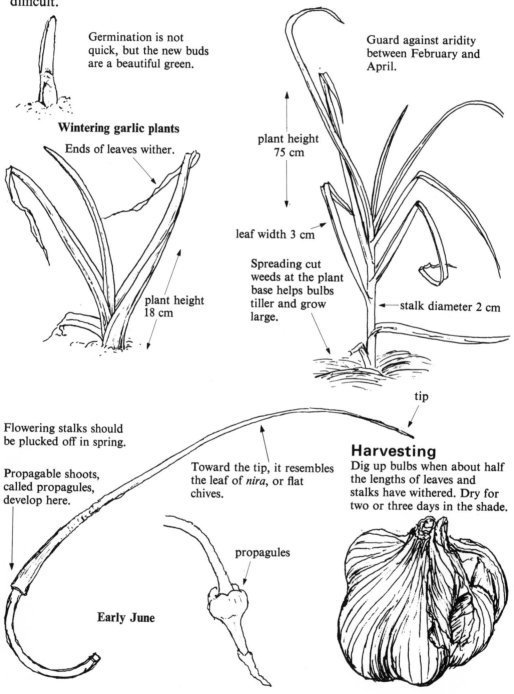

Germination is not quick, but the new buds are a beautiful green.

Wintering garlic plants

Ends of leaves wither.

plant height 18 cm

Guard against aridity between February and April.

plant height 75 cm

leaf width 3 cm

Spreading cut weeds at the plant base helps bulbs tiller and grow large.

stalk diameter 2 cm

tip

Flowering stalks should be plucked off in spring.

Propagable shoots, called propagules, develop here.

Toward the tip, it resembles the leaf of *nira*, or flat chives.

Early June

propagules

Harvesting

Dig up bulbs when about half the lengths of leaves and stalks have withered. Dry for two or three days in the shade.

Flat Chives (*Nira*)

Planting and Harvesting Times											
1	2	3	4	5	6	8	7	9	10	11	12

Second year

Later than second year

Permanent planting

Later than second year

This hardy member of the lily family is insect-resistant and therefore easy to grow. Once planted, it can be divided and raised for several years. Requiring no prepared field or bed, it can be grown around the fringes of areas planted with other crops or in a corner of the garden. Although it likes bright sun, it will thrive in half shade as well. Aside from its dislike of strong acidity, it makes no specific demands on soil and requires no fertilizing in ground rich in organic material.

Sowing: Flat chives may be raised from seed or from seedlings. In the first year of crops raised from seed, harvest should be moderate in order to give the plants time to grow strong. If you are in a hurry, plant seedlings in April. It will be possible to harvest in September of the same year. Sow seeds from March into April.

Thinning: After germination, plants are thinned. But, since chives like to be crowded, the interplant interval is only 1 cm.

Weeding: Weed according to the density of the plants. Although hardy, chives will not thrive if surrounded by tall weeds. The plants grow large and strong if given plenty of sun, but while seedlings are young, perform simple weeding early.

Sowing (March to April)

Sow seeds in rows in soil enriched beforehand with compost, guano, or pressed soy meal. Cover with a layer 2 or 3 times as thick as the seeds themselves.

seeds (actual size)

Germination and Thinning

After germination thin to an inter-plant interval of 1 cm.

↤1 cm

Do not harvest the first year after sowing but allow the plants time to grow strong.

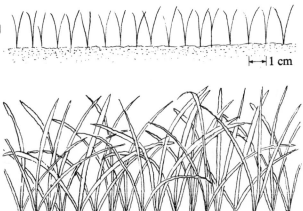

Supplement nutrition with pressed soy meal allowed to ferment in water and then diluted 1 part to 100.

Permanent planting: About ninety days after germination, gently pull plants from the ground. Cut off the top third of the leaves and plant permanently in clusters of four or five. Plant fairly deep so that roots are directed laterally and not downward.

Mounding: Mound soil around the bases of the plants to prevent exposure to the air of the roots, which grow upward and laterally.

Plant tops die down and disappear in winter. It is therefore necessary to mark or carefully remember the locations of the bulbs until fresh leaves appear in spring.

Harvesting: Cut leaves when fresh shoots have reached lengths of 20–30 cm. Robust plants will reach this stage in from ten to twenty days after germination and may be harvested from five to six times in a single year.

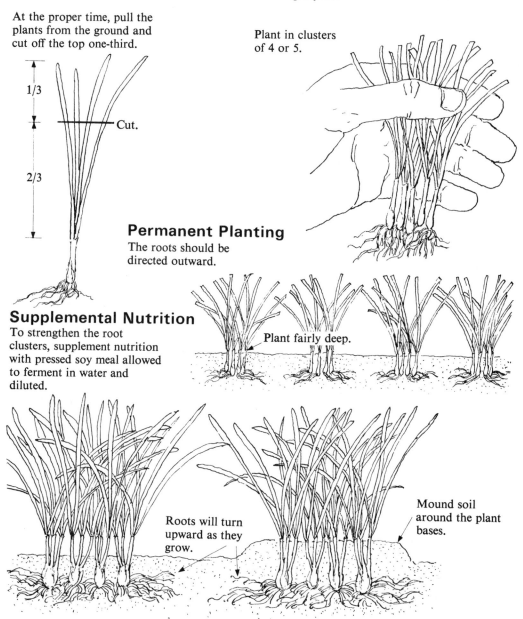

At the proper time, pull the plants from the ground and cut off the top one-third.

1/3

Cut.

2/3

Permanent Planting
The roots should be directed outward.

Plant in clusters of 4 or 5.

Supplemental Nutrition
To strengthen the root clusters, supplement nutrition with pressed soy meal allowed to ferment in water and diluted.

Plant fairly deep.

Roots will turn upward as they grow.

Mound soil around the plant bases.

Wintering

Upper leaves will die down in winter.

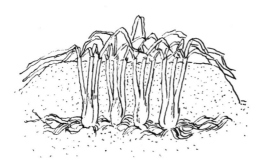

Spring Germination

New buds will appear in early March.

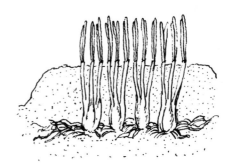

Harvesting

Harvest when the new shoots have grown to 20–30 cm in length.

Cut.

Leave 1–2 cm.

Flowering

Flowering weakens the bulb. Pluck buds early from all plants except those from which you intend to take seeds.

Pluck.

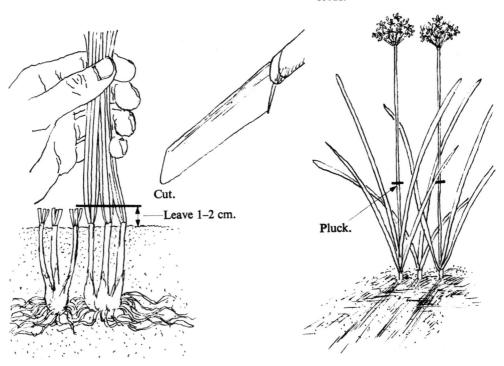

Separating

Separate bulbs that have tillered.

Permanent Planting

Plant permanently in clusters of
3 or 4.

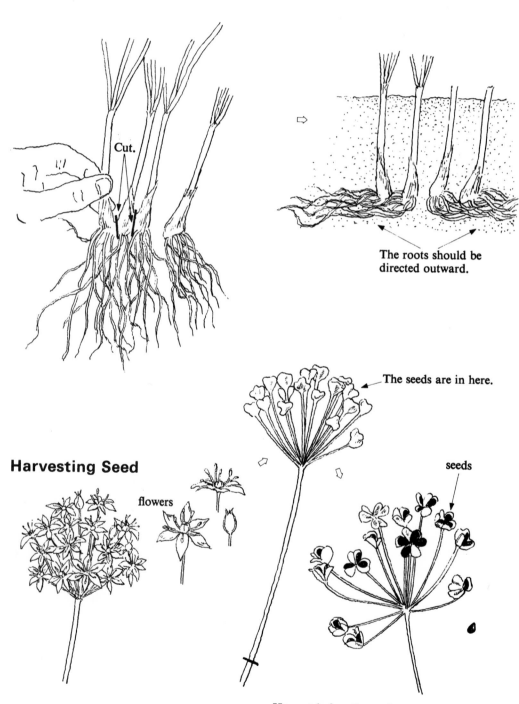

Cut.

The roots should be
directed outward.

The seeds are in here.

Harvesting Seed

flowers

seeds

Harvest before the seeds
are ejected.

Wild Rocambole

Planting and Harvesting Times											
1	2	3	4	5	6	7	8	9	10	11	12

⋀⋀⋀⋀⋀⋀⋀

⋀⋀⋀

Later than second year

○○○○○○○○

This perennial member of the lily family is one of the many wild herbs that, once an important part of the Japanese diet, have gradually disappeared from our dining tables. It still grows in open fields, where its small, pearllike bulbs may be dug up in the early autumn. In February, its fresh tender leaves, which appear in clumps when summer grasses die down, may be cut and eaten. With a flavor similar to that of *nira* flat chives, they are a welcome addition to tempura and soups and make a good garnish for various dishes. The bulbs, which are large enough to harvest between April and June, may be eaten raw with bean paste and have a strong, onionlike pungency.

Do not attempt to pull them up by the leaves, which are very slender (2–4 mm) and will certainly snap before the bulbs, which can be as deep as 20 cm underground, may be freed from the earth. Loosen the surrounding soil with a trowel first and then lift them out.

Harvesting Bulbs

Since in the wild the bulbs are often very deep underground, carefully loosen the soil around them before pulling them up.

Planting

Plant several together in a clump.

autumn planting

Germinating Bulbs

Returned to the earth, harvested bulbs will multiply the following year. They may be planted anywhere—among other crop plants or in a corner of the garden, for instance—and require no cultivation or fertilizers. As is the case with all other fundamentally wild herbs, however, they must be planted in places free of the danger of contamination from weed killers.

Plant harvested bulbs—the white part that was underground—in clumps at a depth of 4–5 cm.

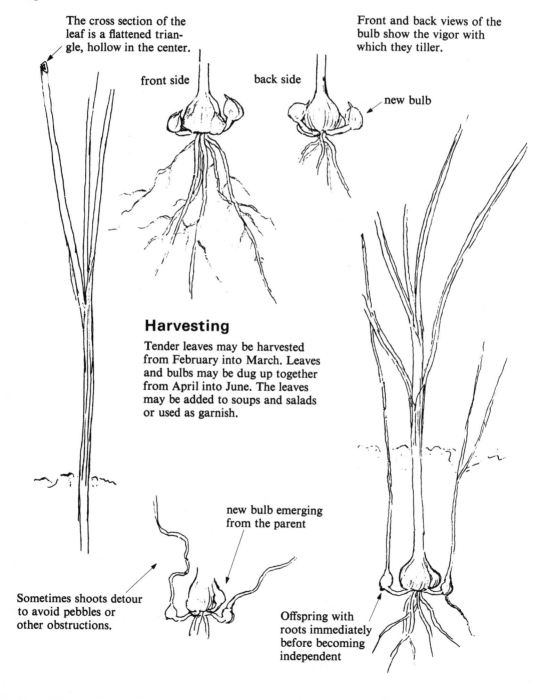

The cross section of the leaf is a flattened triangle, hollow in the center.

front side   back side

Front and back views of the bulb show the vigor with which they tiller.

new bulb

Harvesting

Tender leaves may be harvested from February into March. Leaves and bulbs may be dug up together from April into June. The leaves may be added to soups and salads or used as garnish.

Sometimes shoots detour to avoid pebbles or other obstructions.

new bulb emerging from the parent

Offspring with roots immediately before becoming independent

Fuki
(Wild Coltsfoot)

Planting and Harvesting Times											
1	2	3	4	5	6	7	8	9	10	11	12

Planting roots △△△△

Later than second year

Flower heads

The Japanese are said to eat about 180 different kinds of vegetables and herbs—more than any other people on earth. Some have been imported from China and other parts of the world; but many Japanese vegetable delicacies are purely indigenous and seasonal. One of the native ones especially relished by the people of Japan is *fuki* (*Petasites japonicus*), a composite perennial related to the butterbur. Although *fuki* petioles are cooked and eaten, the flower head (*fuki-no-tō*), which, encased in several layers of bracts, thrusts itself from underground stems with great vigor early in spring, is most highly prized. It is fifteen times richer in vitamin A than the stalk and leaves and, in addition, contains abundant protein; potassium, which accounts for its slight bitterness; and carbohydrate. With this great store of nutritional elements, it is an ideal food for spring, when people need energy to recover from the comparative inactivity of winter. Male and female reproductive organs are found in different plants; the pistils and ovaries occur in plants that produce flower heads.

Planting

Dig up a clump of *fuki*.
Separate the roots by
cutting underground
stems and plant each
separately at a 40 cm
interval.

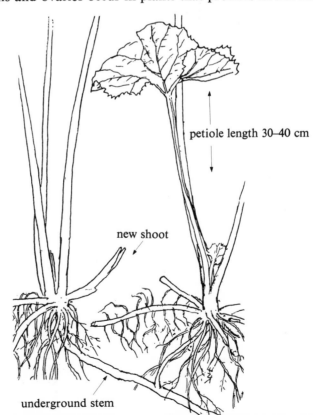

petiole length 30–40 cm

new shoot

underground stem

Cooking should be minimized to avoid spoiling the delicate, refreshing flavor. The flower head may be parboiled and served as an appetizer with a half-and-half mixture of soy sauce and vinegar. Or it may be halved or chopped and added to *miso* soups. Small natural ones are more fragrant and delicious than the larger commercially grown and marketed varieties.

Fuki is intolerant of aridity and direct sunlight; but, given the kind of environment suited to it—moisture and semishade—it may be grown without fertilizing or any other special care. In a temperate climate, like that of the Pacific side of Japan, petioles from plants with large, taut, dark-green, undamaged leaves may be harvested from April or June into October. They should be rubbed with salt, unpeeled, to remove their astringency, then boiled, chilled, and scraped—like celery. Indeed, *fuki* resembles celery in flavor.

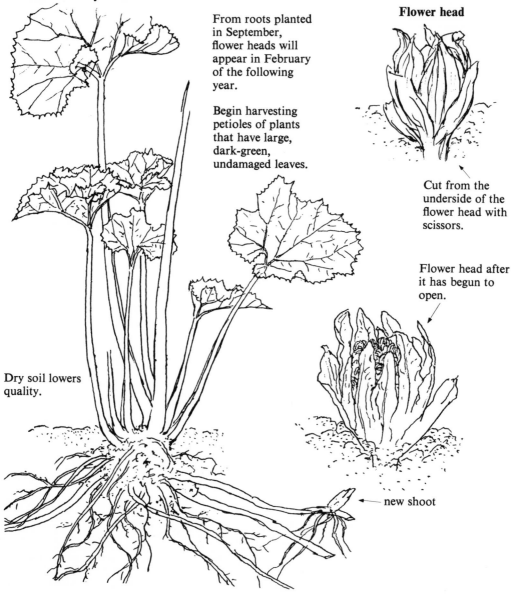

From roots planted in September, flower heads will appear in February of the following year.

Begin harvesting petioles of plants that have large, dark-green, undamaged leaves.

Flower head

Cut from the underside of the flower head with scissors.

Flower head after it has begun to open.

Dry soil lowers quality.

new shoot

Sesame

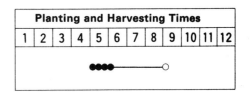
66,30 inches

If it grows properly, sown in May or June, sesame reaches a height of about 170 cm. Each of the roughly sixty leaf axils above the fifth one bears three pods, in which are located the seeds, which may be white, black, or golden. The golden variety is difficult to obtain. Black sesame is more fragrant, but white produces more oil. Both are alkali in nature, have high fat content, and are rich in minerals. Sesame grows well in most, even acid, soils and is disease- and insect-resistant.

Sowing: Between April and June, sow in rows in furrows 50–80 cm wide. Cover the soil with straw to retain moisture and protect seeds from birds.

At first, seedlings grow somewhat slowly. Caution is needed at weeding time since the plants closely resemble weeds.

Thinning: Thin steadily as the plants grow until, by the time they are about 20 cm tall, they are 20–30 cm apart.

Sesame requires little fertilizing. It grows with greater vigor in the warmth of the summer sun. Pluck off lateral buds that begin emerging when plants are 20–30 cm tall.

Ultimately, at each leaf axil above about the fifth one, three tubular, lavenderish-white blossoms will appear.

Preparation

A week or two before sowing, sprinkle from 2 to 3 shovelfuls of mature compost on each 1 m² of ground and mix well with the soil.

Sowing

Either water the ground or sow after a rain. Sow in rows, cover with a layer of soil 4–5 mm thick, and press lightly with the fingers.

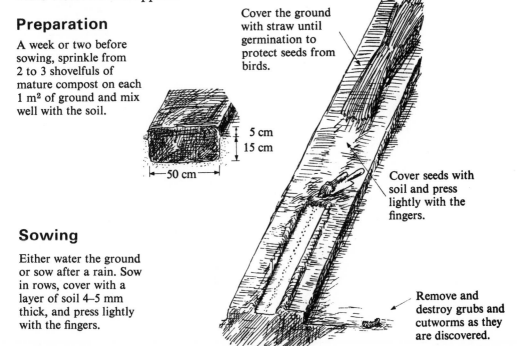

Cover the ground with straw until germination to protect seeds from birds.

5 cm
15 cm

←—50 cm—→

Cover seeds with soil and press lightly with the fingers.

Remove and destroy grubs and cutworms as they are discovered.

Harvesting: In late August, leaves will begin withering in conspicuous numbers. When, in September, lower pods begin to pop open, it is time to cut the plants at ground line. Cut stalks to lengths of 30–40 cm, put them in paper bags, and dry them in a shady place. When they have dried thoroughly, remove seeds from pods and store in a dry place. Toast in an unoiled frying pan before using.

Germination

Thinning

Begin thinning as soon as 2 true leaves have emerged.

Weeds flourish at this time of year. Cut them to allow the sesame seedlings to get plenty of sunlight.

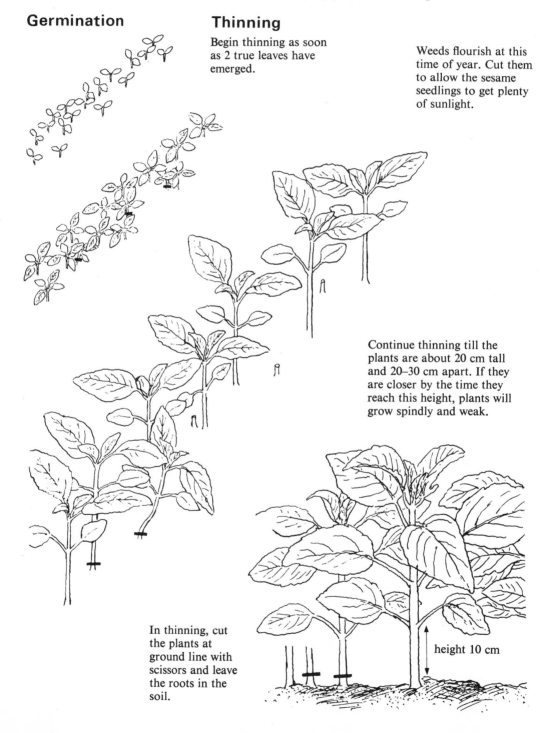

Continue thinning till the plants are about 20 cm tall and 20–30 cm apart. If they are closer by the time they reach this height, plants will grow spindly and weak.

In thinning, cut the plants at ground line with scissors and leave the roots in the soil.

height 10 cm

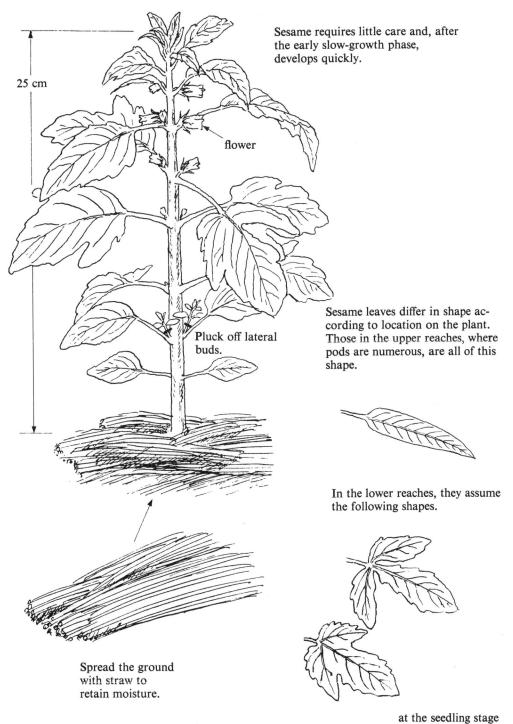

Sesame requires little care and, after the early slow-growth phase, develops quickly.

flower

Pluck off lateral buds.

Sesame leaves differ in shape according to location on the plant. Those in the upper reaches, where pods are numerous, are all of this shape.

In the lower reaches, they assume the following shapes.

Spread the ground with straw to retain moisture.

at the seedling stage

25 cm

Harvesting

By the time leaves begin withering, in
August, the plant will be laden with pods.

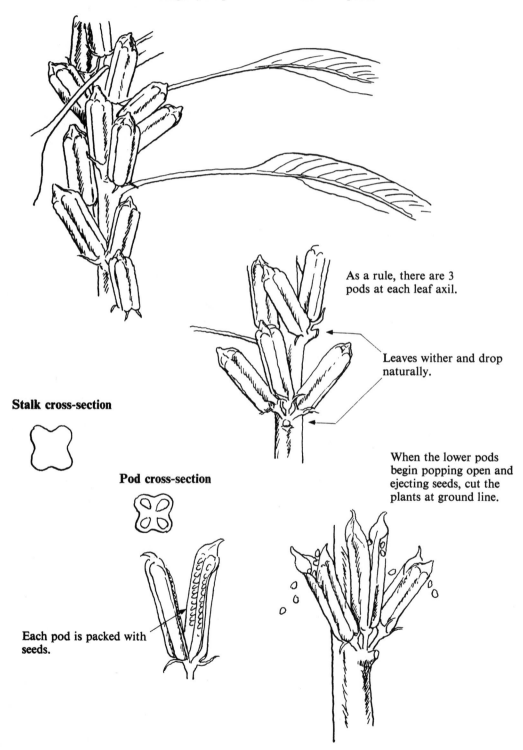

As a rule, there are 3
pods at each leaf axil.

Leaves wither and drop
naturally.

Stalk cross-section

Pod cross-section

When the lower pods
begin popping open and
ejecting seeds, cut the
plants at ground line.

Each pod is packed with
seeds.

Parsley

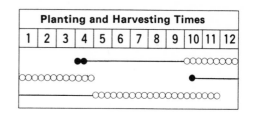

Planting and Harvesting Times											
1	2	3	4	5	6	7	8	9	10	11	12

Agricultural chemicals and insecticides are so violently toxic that they can kill human beings. Perhaps even more perilous, they are highly permeating and make their ways into the roots, stalks, and leaves of plants on which they are used. Degrees of permeation vary so drastically from chemical to chemical that even specialists cannot agree on the matter; and we ordinary vegetable growers cannot hope to discriminate among them in this connection. Consequently, our only recourse is to avoid using them, even in the interests of ridding plants of insect and bacterial pests, and thus to ensure that the vegetables we raise are perfectly safe to eat.

In harvesting parsley, to prevent the plant from weakening, make certain that at least ten leaves remain. Harvest outer leaves from stalk bases when a plant has developed more than thirteen or fourteen leaves.

Cultivation: In the early period, immediately after germination, parsley grows slowly. Parsley seeds are usually sown directly in the field or bed in which the crop is to be raised. If it must be transplanted, however, care is necessary. Since it puts out only one, straight, central, main root and tolerates high heats poorly, it must be moved before the plant has developed four or five true leaves.

Sowing

Plant in clusters in holes made in well-worked soil.

Leave an interval of 10 cm between clusters.

From two to three weeks before sowing, spread 2 or 3 shovelfuls of compost over the entire bed and mix well.

2 m

40 cm

hole for sowing

Sow 5 or 6 seeds in each hole and cover with 5–6 mm of soil.

Germination

Germination occurs about ten days after sowing.

The cotyledons grow larger.

two true leaves

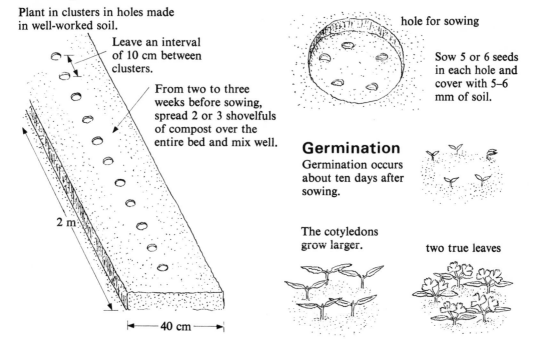

Seedlings grown from seed planted in the spring have a difficult time surviving summer heat without four or five true leaves, but allowing surrounding weeds to grow tall enough to offer shade protects them from withering. Seedlings grown from autumn-sown seeds develop flower buds if they have more than five true leaves at the time when they are exposed to winter cold. They will bloom early in the following summer. To inhibit blooming, seedlings should be small when winter comes. To protect from frost, spread straw on top of them. Neutralize soil with lime because parsley dislikes acidity.

Insects: Parsley is prone to illness if raised in poorly draining soil. With tweezers, or chopsticks, remove larvae of such butterflies as the *Papilio machaon*, which eat the leaves of parsley and of the beefsteak plant.

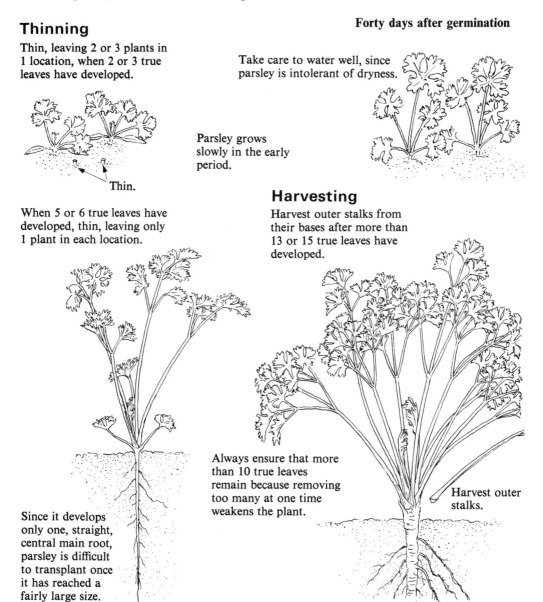

Thinning

Forty days after germination

Thin, leaving 2 or 3 plants in 1 location, when 2 or 3 true leaves have developed.

Take care to water well, since parsley is intolerant of dryness.

Parsley grows slowly in the early period.

Thin.

When 5 or 6 true leaves have developed, thin, leaving only 1 plant in each location.

Harvesting

Harvest outer stalks from their bases after more than 13 or 15 true leaves have developed.

Always ensure that more than 10 true leaves remain because removing too many at one time weakens the plant.

Since it develops only one, straight, central main root, parsley is difficult to transplant once it has reached a fairly large size.

Harvest outer stalks.

Beefsteak Plant (*Shiso*)

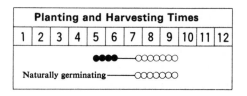
The beefsteak plant, which comes in green, red, and ruffled varieties, is a popular condiment in Japan. The green variety is highly fragrant. The red is used to color foods, and the ruffled variety is pickled together with the famous salted plums known as *umeboshi*. The seeds of the beefsteak plant are used as a condiment with *sashimi*. It is one of the numerous plants that, once planted artificially, seed themselves year after year.

Sowing: Beefsteak plant is raised between May and September. It grows best at temperatures of more than 77°F but is extremely intolerant of cold. Seeds may be sprinkled in a corner of the garden and covered with fine soil.

Germination: Newly germinated seedlings are so small that it is difficult to distinguish them from surrounding weeds. Those that come up in early June as a result of natural seeding are especially easy to overlook.

Sowing

Seeds require sowing the first year only. Thereafter, the plant will naturally seed itself. No compost is needed.

seeds

(actual size)

Plant from 8 to 10 seeds in 1 place.

soil

compost

Add about 2 handfuls of compost to the hole and mix well with soil.

15 cm

Thinning

When 5 or 6 true leaves have developed, thin, leaving 2 plants in 1 location.

Germination

In the early stage, the seedlings look like those of weeds.

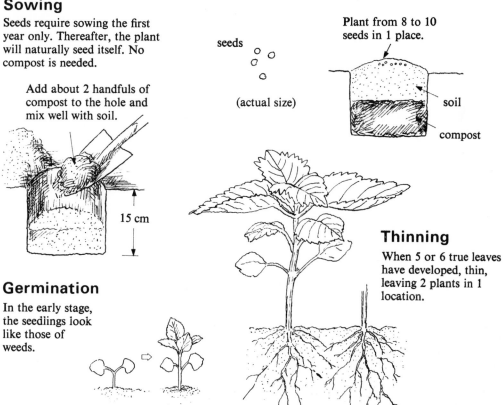

Harvesting: In rich soil, leaves and whole plants reach considerable sizes. At first combine thinning and harvesting. When plants are about 40 cm apart, harvest the large lower leaves first.

Harvest and eat fresh flower stalks that have begun to bloom, in the middle of August. In Japan, the seeds themselves are salted or simmered in soy sauce in what is known as *tsukudani*. The plants may be harvested through September but wither in the middle of October. Beefsteak plant is rich in the vitamins A, B₂, and C.

Harvesting

Harvest large, lower leaves from their bases when the plant has exceeded a height of 25 cm.

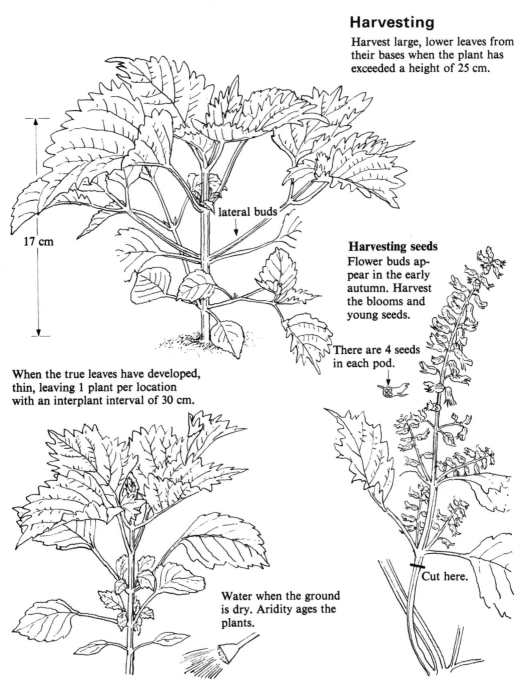

17 cm

lateral buds

Harvesting seeds
Flower buds appear in the early autumn. Harvest the blooms and young seeds.

There are 4 seeds in each pod.

When the true leaves have developed, thin, leaving 1 plant per location with an interplant interval of 30 cm.

Water when the ground is dry. Aridity ages the plants.

Cut here.

Ginger

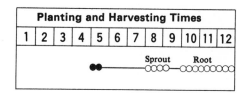
A perennial native to southwestern Asia, ginger likes high temperatures and humidity and ceases growth at low temperatures. Gingerroot cuttings are set out in May. Leafy sprouts are harvested in August and gingerroots in October.

Ginger prefers shady places in which the soil is fertile and moist and drains well. It is highly intolerant of aridity. Enrich lean soil with compost.

Setting out cuttings: Set cuttings of gingerroot in the soil with their buds upward. Since they will not sprout readily if temperatures are low, set them out in May, when high temperatures encourage quick sprouting.

Weeding: Since new ginger sprouts are so tender that they can be damaged by no more than a light touch, cut weeds around them before the sprouts emerge.

Harvesting: Harvest ginger sprouts in August, when a reddish bulb forms at the bottom. Using a transplanting trowel, dig up the sprout together with the root. Roots that remain in the soil will vigorously fork and grow and may be harvested as needed, starting in October. In December, cut off the stems and allow the roots to dry thoroughly for storage.

Root cuttings

Select pieces of gingerroot weighing 60–70 g and with 2 or 3 buds on each piece.

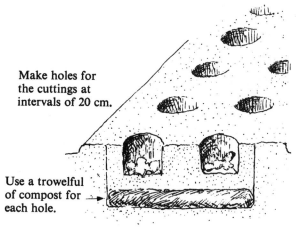

Make holes for the cuttings at intervals of 20 cm.

Use a trowelful of compost for each hole.

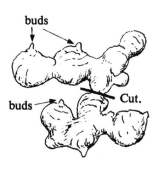

buds

buds   Cut.

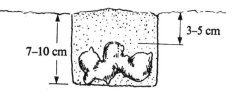

Position the cuttings so that the buds are upward and cover with a layer of soil 3–5 cm thick.

7–10 cm   3–5 cm

Germination

Though temperatures account for differences, in general ginger sprouts in from fifteen to twenty days.
actual size

Though it toler-
ates high temper-
atures, ginger
should be pro-
tected from direct
sunlight and raised
in semishade.

Weeding

Since the new sprouts are very delicate, weed early.

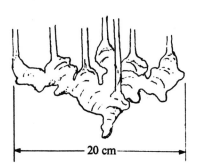

They snap off with the lightest touch.

Harvesting

Dig up sprouts and roots with a trowel. Harvest roots after October.

20 cm

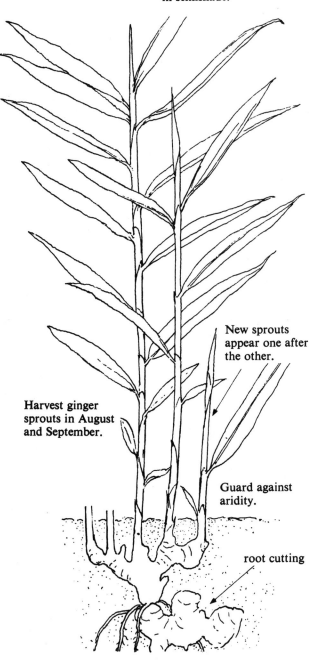

Harvest ginger
sprouts in August
and September.

New sprouts
appear one after
the other.

Guard against
aridity.

root cutting

Prickly Ash (*Sansho*)

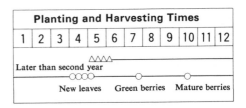

Planting and Harvesting Times											
1	2	3	4	5	6	7	8	9	10	11	12

Later than second year

New leaves Green berries Mature berries

Like the citrus trees a member of the rue family, the Japanese variety of the prickly ash (*Zanthoxylum piperitum*) grows in mixed forests all over the country and provides one of the two most popular sharp spices used in Japan—the other being *wasabi* horseradish. It is a deciduous tree native to Japan and Southeast Asia. Both its leaves and its berries have a distinctive aroma and pungency.

The fresh leaflets (*kinome*) appearing in April are used as a garnish with boiled new bamboo shoots or are pounded and mixed with *miso* to be spread on *tofu* and other foods broiled in a style known as *dengaku*. The green berries, simmered in a broth containing soy sauce and sugar, are used as a garnish for *sushi* and *sashimi*. The ripe berries are ground and used as a seasoning for grilled eel and other oily foods. The flowers are cooked in soy sauce, and the bark of the tree is ground to produce a seasoning spice. Many medicinal and preservative properties are attributed to the leaves, berries, and bark of the prickly ash. Moreover, from the distant past, people have thought that prickly-ash pestles for kitchen mortars ensured long life.

Planting a Sapling

No fertilizer is needed in places where fallen leaves enrich the soil and where there is a good stand of weeds. In lean soil, fertilize once with compost before planting.

A sapling that is 6–7 mm at planting time will be 2.5 cm in diameter in ten years. This is the ideal size from which to make good pestles for kitchen mortars.

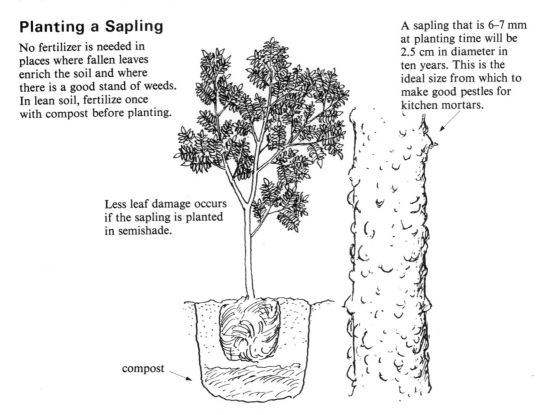

Less leaf damage occurs if the sapling is planted in semishade.

compost

250

The Japanese prickly ash may be raised from seed harvested in the autumn. But, since this takes longer, it is better to obtain a small sapling, which will thrive and produce good-quality leaves and berries if planted in a semishaded corner of the garden in soil that retains water well. Prevent dryness in autumn by leaving weeds to grow. The plant requires no other care and no fertilizing. These trees may be grown in pots.

Tender leaves (*kinome*) are harvested in late April. To release their fragrance, smack these leaves between the hands immediately before serving them.

Be cautious of the thorns at the bases of the petioles in all strains of this tree except *Asakura sansho*. Male and female reproductive organs develop on different trees. The berries, naturally, occur on the female plant.

Late March

The buds become active.

Middle of April

New, tender, leaves have appeared.

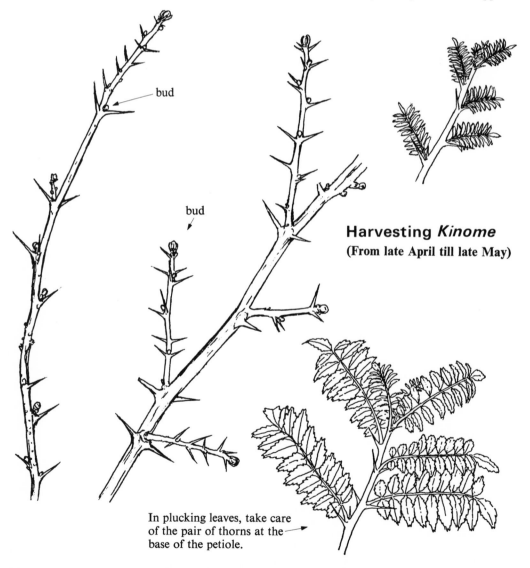

bud

bud

Harvesting *Kinome*
(From late April till late May)

In plucking leaves, take care
of the pair of thorns at the
base of the petiole.

Green Bell Peppers

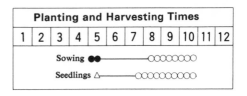
Green bell peppers thrive at higher temperatures than such vegetables as tomatoes, eggplants, and cucumbers. They dislike dryness and prefer plenty of sunshine. It is important to use abundant compost to keep the soil rich in organic matter. Inter-plant interval should be larger than in the case of eggplant.

Sowing: Seeds may be sown directly in the garden or in a pot, where the seedlings are grown until ready for transplanting. In either case, sow in clusters of about four seeds. Thin so that, by the time three or four true leaves have developed, only one seedling remains in each pot or each location.

Permanent planting: Whether home-grown or purchased on the commercial market, green-pepper seedlings should not be planted until after the middle of May, when temperatures are already fairly high. Seedlings planted when temperatures are low grow poorly and are subject to disease.

Plant green peppers last, after the breathing spell you can enjoy following the permanent planting of eggplant and tomatoes. Choose a sunny, windless day and plant them shallow to put the roots in the level of higher soil temperatures.

Support poles: Support poles are not needed until the peppers begin to form. Setting them too soon will cause the leaves to damage themselves by blowing against them in the high winds frequent in May. Low, sturdy, well-developed plants will not be toppled or uprooted by even strong winds.

Harvesting: Pluck first peppers before they have reached full maturity and then harvest others as they ripen, usually about twenty days after blooming. Green peppers will bloom until late October if supplemental fertilizer is provided and if caution is taken to prevent dryness and crowding, which deprives plants of adequate sunlight.

Using weeds: Cut weeds that overshadow plants and spread them on the ground at plant bases as a covering. Low weeds may be left in place to guard against dryness in the soil.

Sowing in Pots (Middle of May)

Sow in pots about 9 cm in diameter. Mix six parts compost with four parts soil. Water before sowing.

seed

(actual size)

Cover with fine soil.

252

Rotation: A member of the nightshade family, green peppers should not be planted in the same ground in successive years with any other members such as eggplant, tomatoes, and potatoes. A cycle of four or five years is recommended.

Germination

Germination takes place in from six to seven days. Too much water is a bad idea, but dryness must be guarded against.

First Thinning

Leaving 2 good seedlings, thin out straggling ones and those with leaves of unequal sizes.

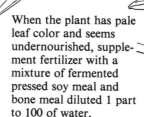

When 3 or 4 true leaves have developed, thin out all but the best single seedling.

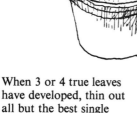

When the plant has pale leaf color and seems undernourished, supplement fertilizer with a mixture of fermented pressed soy meal and bone meal diluted 1 part to 100 of water.

Bed Preparation

(Two or three weeks before permanent planting)

Prepare the bed as for eggplant. But, since green peppers bear poorly in lean soil, spread more than 6 shovelfuls of mature compost on each 1 m² of ground. Then, digging to a depth of 20–30 cm, mix thoroughly.

Direct Sowing

Make furrows about 80 cm wide and 5 cm high. Seedlings should be set 65–70 cm apart; that is, somewhat farther than eggplant seedlings. Plants may be grown from seeds sown directly in such furrows.

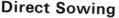

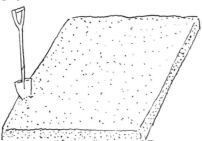

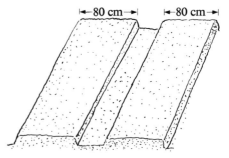

Permanent Planting

Choose a warm, windless day and
remove the seedlings from the pots
and set them out as for eggplant.

For permanent planting, select
seedlings that are 15–18 cm
tall and have 8 or 9 true leaves,
thick stalks with short interleaf intervals, and glossy
leaves. Commercially pur-
chased (in the middle of May)
seedlings too must meet these
requirements.

Pluck the first pepper
when it is 1.5–2 cm long.

15–18 cm

Green bell peppers dislike
dryness. Prevent it by spreading compost over the ground
around plant bases.

254

Harvesting

Harvest when large and ripe. A
hardy plant that grows properly
will yield more than 100 peppers.

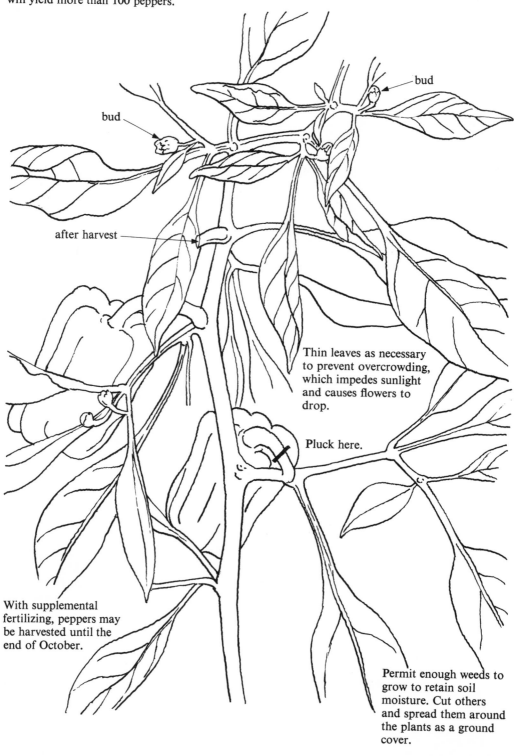

bud

bud

after harvest

Thin leaves as necessary
to prevent overcrowding,
which impedes sunlight
and causes flowers to
drop.

Pluck here.

With supplemental
fertilizing, peppers may
be harvested until the
end of October.

Permit enough weeds to
grow to retain soil
moisture. Cut others
and spread them around
the plants as a ground
cover.

Red Chili Peppers

Planting and Harvesting Times

1	2	3	4	5	6	7	8	9	10	11	12

Sowing ●●————————○○○

Seedlings △△————————○○

Peppers, members of the nightshade family, originated in Central and South America and come in three major varieties: very piquant peppers that are red when ripe; less piquant, small green peppers; and sweeter, large, green or red peppers (pimentos). One plant is enough for an ordinary household for a year, unless the leaves too are to be eaten, in which case two plants may be needed. In either case, a small corner of the garden is ample room.

Preparations: As is true in the case of large, sweet peppers, seeds for red chili peppers may either be sown in pots first and the seedlings later transplanted to the field or sown directly in the ground. Choose a sunny plot in which no member of the nightshade family has been grown for four or five years. Peppers grow well at temperatures of about 77°F but not at temperatures lower than 59°F.

Permanent planting: Taking care not to shake the soil from the roots, plant seedlings permanently during the daylight of a warm, fair day in late May. Plant shallow to ensure that the roots are at a level where soil temperatures are high. Though winds are often strong in May, avoid using support poles at this time since leaves and stalks may be damaged by blowing against them. Seedlings cannot easily be blown over as easily as the second day after planting.

Permanent Planting

Plant permanently when plants have developed about 10 true leaves. Good health is indicated by leaves positioned at 45° to the stem. Bear this in mind when purchasing commercial seedlings.

To prevent crumbling of the soil, water seedlings before transplanting.

Two or three weeks before permanent planting, dig a hole and mix the soil with 1 or 2 trowelfuls of compost.

Dig a suitable hole in the prepared plot. Remove the plant from the seedling pot and plant carefully.

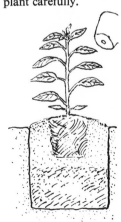

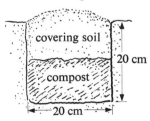

covering soil

compost

20 cm

20 cm

Harvesting: For edible leaves, pluck lateral buds, with leaves and buds, from late July. In the middle or late October, when about 80 percent of the peppers have turned red, harvest by cutting the plant at ground level. Leaving the peppers on, hang the branches upside down in a shady place to dry. Still leaving them on the branches, put the peppers in an empty vase indoors and use as needed.

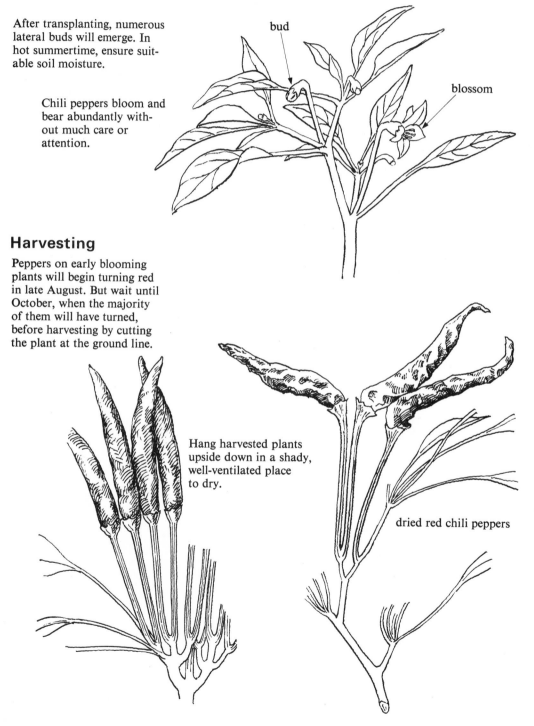

After transplanting, numerous lateral buds will emerge. In hot summertime, ensure suitable soil moisture.

Chili peppers bloom and bear abundantly without much care or attention.

bud

blossom

Harvesting

Peppers on early blooming plants will begin turning red in late August. But wait until October, when the majority of them will have turned, before harvesting by cutting the plant at the ground line.

Hang harvested plants upside down in a shady, well-ventilated place to dry.

dried red chili peppers

Sweet Green Chili Peppers

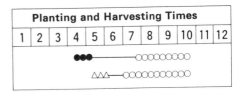
These members of the nightshade family, which are called lion head (*shishitō*) in Japanese because of an imagined resemblance between the tip of the fruit and the leonine head, are generally refreshing and mild in taste. Occasionally, however, one will be extremely fiery and peppery. This is more often caused by lean soil or some other factor impairing growth and development. Furthermore, such peppers generally occur on weak and aging plants. Still the condition of the soil does exert a delicate influence on taste since excess fertilization can result in chilies completely lacking in piquancy and flavor.

Choose a sunny place and use ample compost. The soil should drain well but must also retain a suitable amount of moisture. Insufficient sunlight, and not lack of nutrition, hampers blooming, causes flowers to drop, and robs peppers of color and luster. Use of improperly matured kitchen scraps or ground limestone causes the appearance of a stinkbug that inserts its proboscis into the stalks of the plants and sucks out sap. To prevent this, plant in a sunny place and use nothing but completely mature compost, which will have lost all unpleasant odor. The suitable degree of acidity is pH 6–6.5. Soil that has been prepared in this way will require no lime.

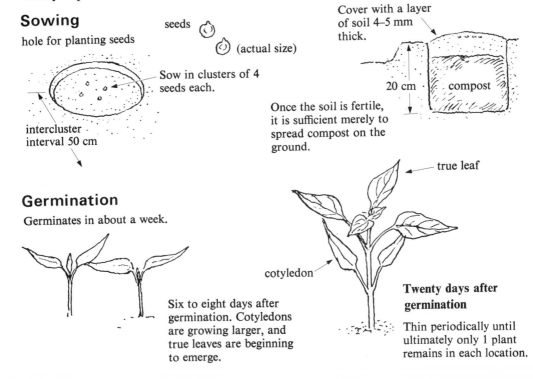

Sowing

hole for planting seeds

seeds

(actual size)

Sow in clusters of 4 seeds each.

intercluster interval 50 cm

Cover with a layer of soil 4–5 mm thick.

20 cm   compost

Once the soil is fertile, it is sufficient merely to spread compost on the ground.

Germination

Germinates in about a week.

Six to eight days after germination. Cotyledons are growing larger, and true leaves are beginning to emerge.

true leaf

cotyledon

Twenty days after germination

Thin periodically until ultimately only 1 plant remains in each location.

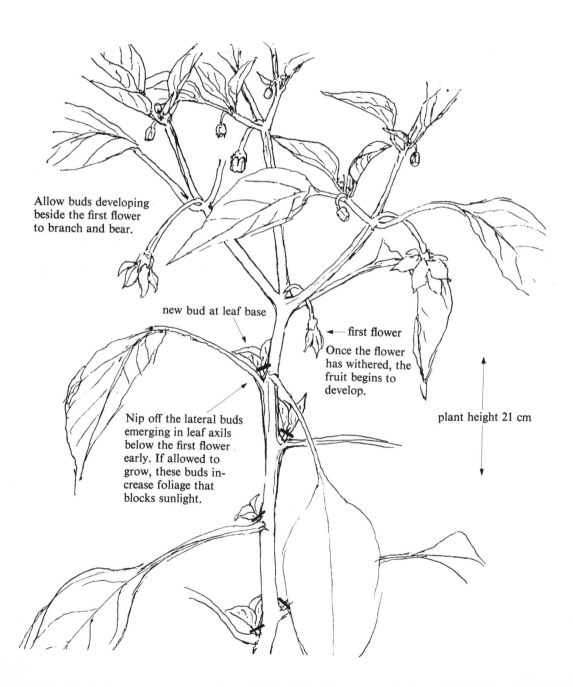

258

Rotate crops of chilies with other members of the nightshade family at a cycle of no less than four or five years.

Sow after the tomatoes and eggplant have been set out, in late May. Select a warm (more than 72°F), windless day and plant shallow. Chill and winds after planting greatly weaken plants. This is why the warmth of May is ideal. Spreading cut grasses and weeds around the plants retains moisture and facilitates intake of nutrients from the soil. Preventing aridity in this trouble-free way improves the flavor of the peppers and reduces the danger of insect damage.

Allow buds developing beside the first flower to branch and bear.

new bud at leaf base

first flower

Once the flower has withered, the fruit begins to develop.

plant height 21 cm

Nip off the lateral buds emerging in leaf axils below the first flower early. If allowed to grow, these buds increase foliage that blocks sunlight.

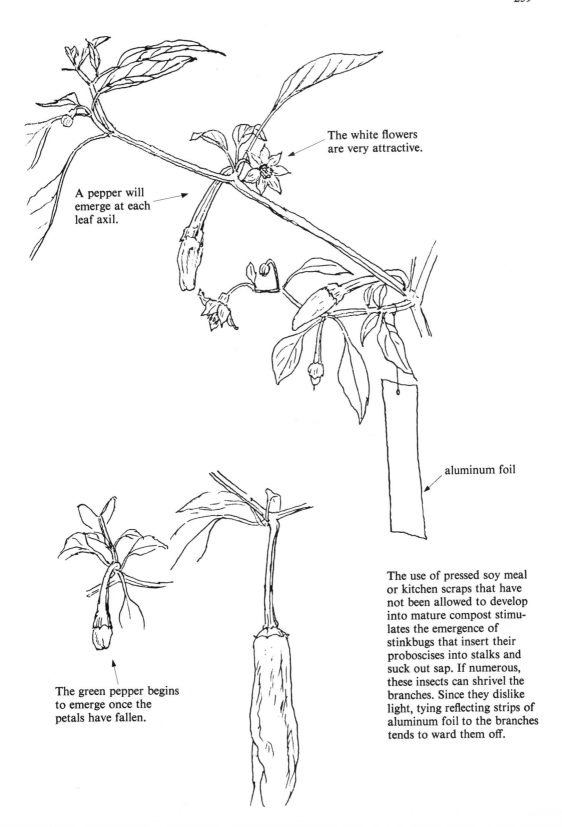

The white flowers
are very attractive.

A pepper will
emerge at each
leaf axil.

aluminum foil

The green pepper begins
to emerge once the
petals have fallen.

The use of pressed soy meal
or kitchen scraps that have
not been allowed to develop
into mature compost stimulates the emergence of
stinkbugs that insert their
proboscises into stalks and
suck out sap. If numerous,
these insects can shrivel the
branches. Since they dislike
light, tying reflecting strips of
aluminum foil to the branches
tends to ward them off.

260

Plenty of sunlight
stimulates development
of the peppers.

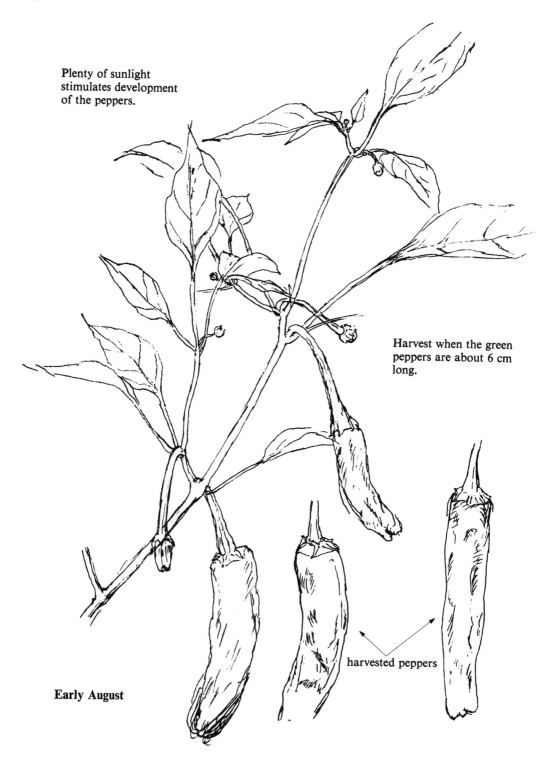

Harvest when the green
peppers are about 6 cm
long.

harvested peppers

Early August

Fushimi Peppers

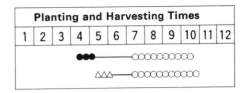

Planting and Harvesting Times											
1	2	3	4	5	6	7	8	9	10	11	12

Somewhat different from sweet green chilies, *Fushimi* peppers have a distinctive flavor resulting largely from thick flesh, which has the additional result of making these peppers unsuitable for the kind of drying usually called for with hot red chili peppers. Nonetheless, it is possible to dry and store peppers that have turned red on the plant by late autumn. Picked green, *Fushimi* peppers and their leaves are good in salads, broiled, or pickled.

A member of the nightshade family, they must not be planted in serial with such other family members as bell peppers, eggplant, tomatoes, or potatoes. In small city gardens, the need to rotate crops posed by plants of this kind often creates a space problem. A good way to solve it is to divide the available land into four equal plots and use a different quarter for nightshade crops each year.

These plants are generally raised from commercially sold seedlings, which have been raised in the warmth of a hothouse. Exposing them suddenly to a harsh natural climate has a very weakening effect. For this reason, plant them in windless weather after the middle of May in soil that has been enriched with compost. Select a warm day and plant shallow at intervals of 50 cm.

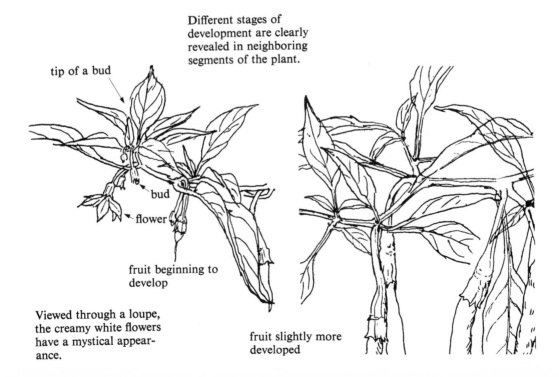

Different stages of development are clearly revealed in neighboring segments of the plant.

tip of a bud

bud

flower

fruit beginning to develop

Viewed through a loupe, the creamy white flowers have a mystical appearance.

fruit slightly more developed

At an early stage of growth, pluck off lateral buds developing below the first flower since they will become too luxuriant and block sunlight. Insufficient light causes blossoms to drop. Allow three buds beside the first blossom to develop and bear.

Constant moisture is more important than fertile soil in the cultivation of peppers. Allowing weeds to coexist with the plants reduces evaporation from the soil. In addition, spreading cut grasses and weeds on the ground around the plants retains moisture and protects the growing environment in many other ways.

If fruit-bearing branches become so heavy that they are in danger of falling to the ground, prop them up on posts. A good stand of weeds and cut grass on the ground too will protect the peppers from being soiled by splashing mud. One or two plants in a corner of the garden will provide both pleasure and an ample crop.

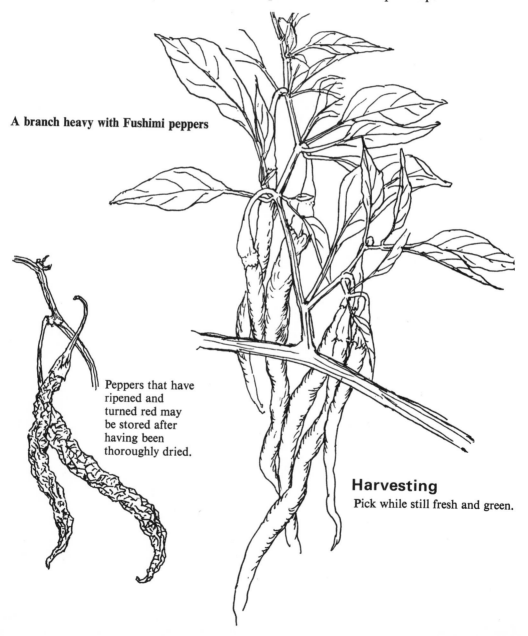

A branch heavy with Fushimi peppers

Peppers that have ripened and turned red may be stored after having been thoroughly dried.

Harvesting
Pick while still fresh and green.

Basil

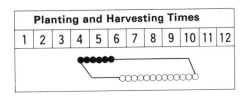
An annual member of the mint family, basil is one of a large number of fragrant herbs raised in gardens from ancient times for a wide range of purposes: seasoning for food, preservation of meat and fish, medicines, herbal liqueurs, herbal infusions, sachet, dyes, cosmetic bathing preparations, and even dried floral arrangements.

A native of India and Southeast Asia, basil reaches a height of 60 cm and has lovely, fragrant, glossy, pale-green leaves. Its piquancy and mild aroma combine wonderfully well with fresh tomatoes. Fresh, tender leaves may be harvested and used raw. Or entire branches may be cut and dried in semishade for use as a spice.

Basil may be grown in pots and thrives and puts out many lateral shoots if kept in a sunny place. Or it may be raised and harvested together with tomatoes. In this case, it is better to plant basil in a furrow adjacent to the tomato plants or among them in such positions that the poles supporting the tomatoes will not shade the basil and make it grow straggly.

Preparing Soil

Obtain unglazed pots 21–24 cm in diameter. Place a small piece of plastic screen over the hole in the bottom to keep out insects. Fill the pot to a depth of 3–5 cm with coarse, well-draining soil. Then fill the pot to about 80% full with a combination of 2 parts compost to 1 part soil.

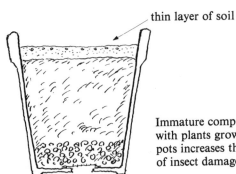

Soil

Two parts compost to one part garden soil, coarse red soil, or peat moss.

Coarse, gravely soil in the bottom improves drainage.

screen to keep insects out

Sowing

Water the pot well and top the contents with a layer of fine soil. Sow seven or eight seeds to a pot and cover with a thin layer of soil.

The seeds are dull, black, and lavalike.

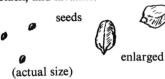

seeds

(actual size)

enlarged

thin layer of soil

Immature compost used with plants grown in pots increases the danger of insect damage.

Seeds should be sown from the middle of April until early June. Sow from six to seven seeds in one cluster in the ground or in a pot of about 21–24 cm in diameter. Thin until there are two plants for a 21 cm pot or three for a 24 cm pot. Young basil seedlings tolerate transplanting.

Leaves may be harvested about fifty days after germination. Nipping the growing buds stimulates the production of more lateral shoots. For drying, cut immediately before the plants bloom. Kept indoors, potted basil will live and stay fresh throughout the winter.

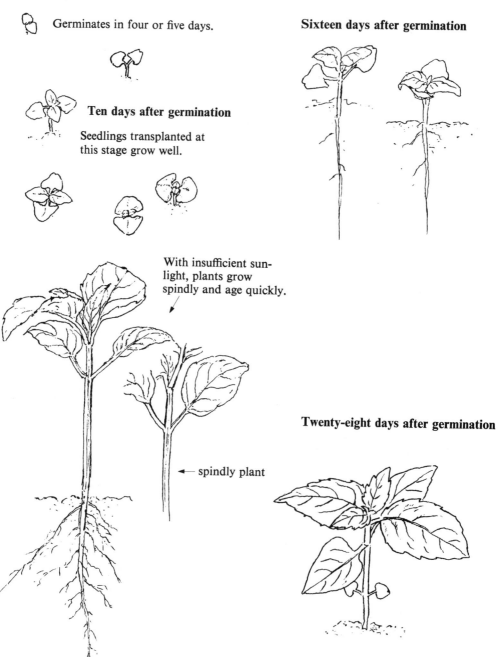

Germinates in four or five days.

Sixteen days after germination

Ten days after germination

Seedlings transplanted at this stage grow well.

With insufficient sunlight, plants grow spindly and age quickly.

← spindly plant

Twenty-eight days after germination

Harvesting

Leaves and lateral buds appearing
at leaf axils may be plucked and
used from about fifty days after
germination.

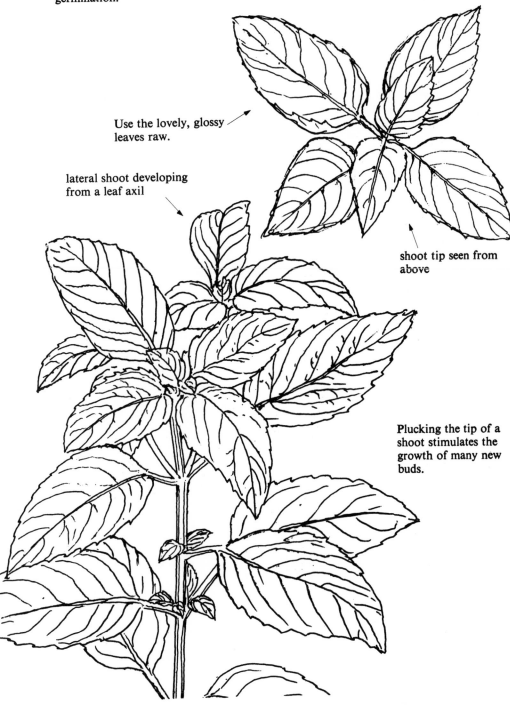

Use the lovely, glossy
leaves raw.

lateral shoot developing
from a leaf axil

shoot tip seen from
above

Plucking the tip of a
shoot stimulates the
growth of many new
buds.

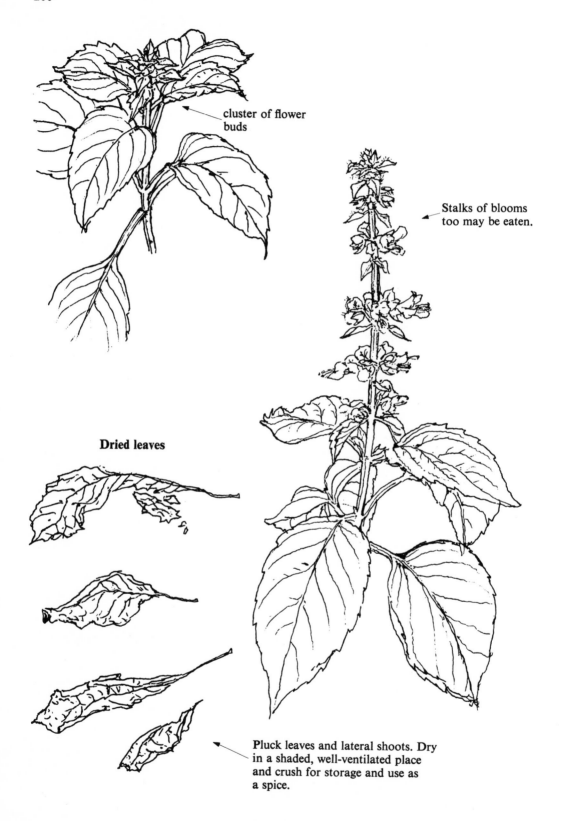

cluster of flower buds

Stalks of blooms too may be eaten.

Dried leaves

Pluck leaves and lateral shoots. Dry in a shaded, well-ventilated place and crush for storage and use as a spice.

Sage

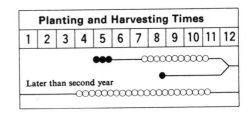
Another member of the mint family, sage (*Salvia officinalis*), which is native to Southern Europe and the Mediterranean region, has been grown as an important herbal medicine since the times of ancient Greece and Rome. Like the other garden herbs, aside from its culinary and medicinal functions, because of its lovely, graceful foliage and delicate fragrance, arranged in vases, it is a refreshing, ornamental addition to the daily-life environment. Sage's fleshy, silvery-gray leaves have a grainy, wrinkled surface that produces a very unusual tactile impression. The charming lavender blossoms resemble those of the beefsteak plant and basil.

Sage is chopped and used raw in salads and dressings or in the preparation of herb-seasoned butters and margarines. Dried and powdered it is used as a seasoning or in the preparation of herbal teas, said to be effective in treating coughs and colds.

Sage may be grown in pots as well as in the garden. But the narrow confines of the pot lead to considerable insect damage if chemical fertilizers are used. Such damage is greatly reduced if mature compost is used instead of chemicals.

Pluck the growing bud early to prevent the plant from growing too tall and to stimulate the production of lateral shoots.

Seeds may be sown directly in an unglazed pot 21–24 cm in diameter or in smaller pots first and then transplanted, one to each larger pot when about four true leaves have developed. Sift the soil to eliminate the finest particles and in this way to ensure good drainage. Place pots in a sunny place. Planted together in garden plots with Brussels sprouts or broccoli, sage will ward off butterflies and thus prevent the appearance of ravaging caterpillars.

For drying, pluck shoots bearing plenty of young leaves before the plants bloom. Dry in a shaded, well-ventilated place. Although leaves for immediate use may be plucked at any time, they are most fragrant in summer.

Sowing

Sow 2 or 3 seeds in a small, unglazed pot 9 cm in diameter. When 4 true leaves have developed, transplant each seedling to a larger pot 21–24 cm in diameter or directly into the garden.

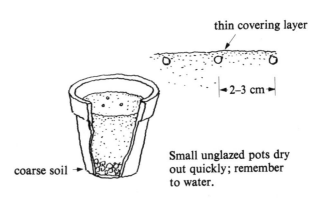

thin covering layer

2–3 cm

River sand used as a cover retards germination.

coarse soil

Small unglazed pots dry out quickly; remember to water.

Permanent Planting

Transplant each seedling to a larger, unglazed pot 21–24 cm in diameter.

seeds

(actual size)

Sown in the middle of May, seeds germinate in ten days.

On top of a layer of coarse soil, add a layer of cultivation soil (1 part soil to 2 parts mature compost) that fills the pot about 40%. Set the seedling in the center and add more cultivation soil around it. Avoid immature compost and chemical fertilizers.

coarse soil

Twelve days after germination

Transplanting is safe by this stage. Use a fork to transplant without breaking the bole of soil around the roots.

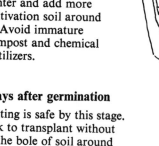

When 4 true leaves have developed, transplant seedlings to a larger pot or into the garden.

Insufficient sunlight and overcrowding cause plants to grow straggly.

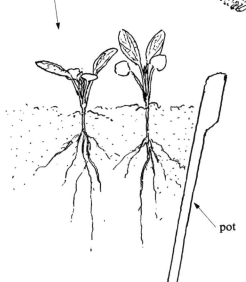

pot

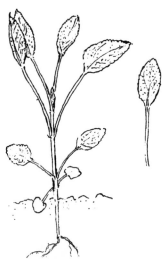

Harvesting

Pluck and use lateral shoots that emerge after the growing bud has been nipped off. The leaves are most fragrant in summer immediately before the plants bloom. This is the best time to harvest for drying.

Often sage does not bloom in its first summer.

Nip off the growing bud.

Nipping the growing bud stimulates the production of many lateral shoots.

lateral shoot

lateral shoot

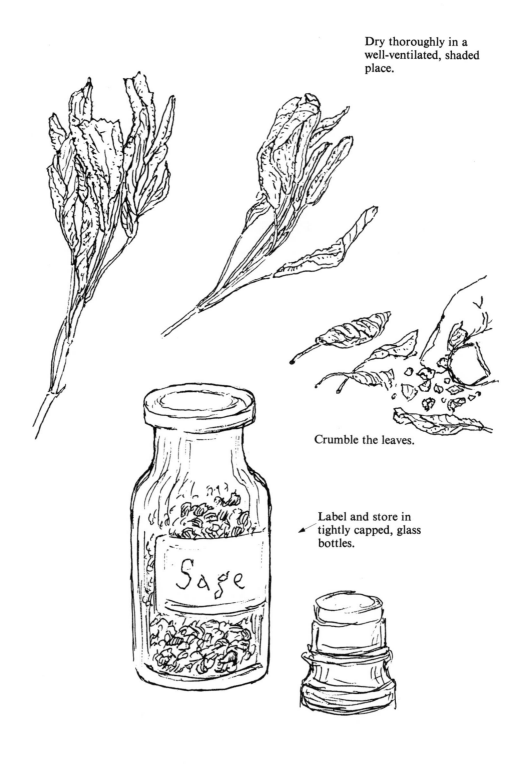

Dry thoroughly in a
well-ventilated, shaded
place.

Crumble the leaves.

Label and store in
tightly capped, glass
bottles.

Sage

Coriander

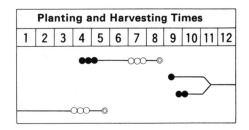

Planting and Harvesting Times

1	2	3	4	5	6	7	8	9	10	11	12

The familiar herbs—basil, sage, thyme, dill, anise, rosemary, savory, mint, caraway, marjoram, chives, tarragon, lavender, and so on—are of course delicious fresh. But dried too, they are fragrant, long-lasting, and important natural seasonings. In addition, they are lovely to look at even after being dried.

Another of these plants, coriander, a biennial member of the parsley family native to Southern Europe, produces tender, young leaves that are good in soups, salads, and sandwiches and seeds that, with a sweet fragrance resembling the aroma of orange and a distinctive piquancy, is an important ingredient in herbal candies, liqueurs, sauces, and indispensable to curries. Young seedlings look very much like parsley. Though smelling like certain insects, mature leaves are elegant and beautiful.

Seeds may be sown in spring or autumn. Since they will not germinate until soil temperatures begin to rise, however, they cannot be sown before late April. Sow seven or eight seeds in a deep, unglazed pot (21–24 cm in diameter). They will germinate in about two weeks. Thereafter thin periodically until only one or two seedlings remain in each pot. Timely thinning prevents plants from growing straggly and falling over.

Raise in a sunny place with a southern exposure and avoid excess moisture. Though insects rarely cause trouble, aphids will emerge if too much fertilizer or immature compost is used or if the pots are kept in a poorly ventilated place.

Leaves may be harvested when the plant is more than 20 cm tall. Plants raised from seed sown in September bloom in late April; those raised from seed sown in May bloom in late July. Seeds, which, by then, have a thin brown coat, may be harvested thirty days after blooming. Hang indoors to dry.

Sowing

Sow 7 or 8 seeds in a pot 21–24 cm in diameter. Cover with a layer of soil 2 or 3 times as thick as seeds are wide. In garden plots, sow in clusters of 4 or 5 at an interval of 30 cm.

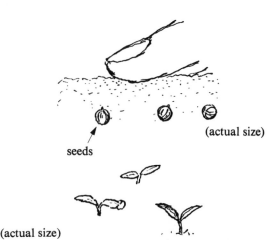

seeds

(actual size)

Germinate in from ten to fourteen days.

(actual size)

272

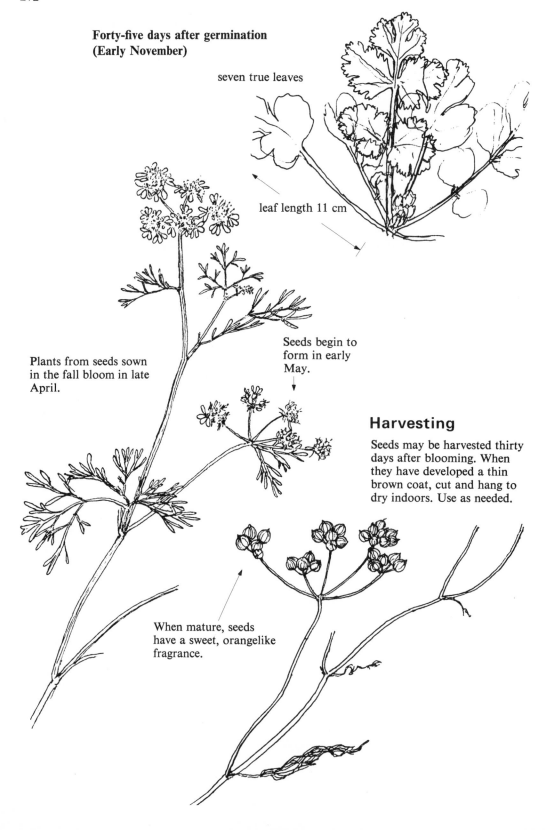

Forty-five days after germination (Early November)

seven true leaves

leaf length 11 cm

Plants from seeds sown in the fall bloom in late April.

Seeds begin to form in early May.

Harvesting

Seeds may be harvested thirty days after blooming. When they have developed a thin brown coat, cut and hang to dry indoors. Use as needed.

When mature, seeds have a sweet, orangelike fragrance.

Fennel

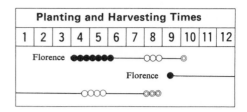

Planting and Harvesting Times											
1	2	3	4	5	6	7	8	9	10	11	12

Florence ●●●●●●● ——○○○—— ◎

Florence ●

——○○○○———— ◎○○

There are two varieties of fennel, an annual member of the parsley family native to Southern Europe and the Mediterranean region. One is common fennel, the seeds of which are used as a seasoning. The other is what is known as Florence fennel, which provides not only seeds, but also edible leaves and stalks and a bulbous swelling at the base of the stalks immediately above the root that may be sliced thin and simmered or used raw in salads.

It may be sown in either the autumn or the spring. Sown in the autumn, fennel will reach a height of 20 cm within the year. Its leaves die down in severe cold, but the plant begins to grow vigorously after about April.

Since it has a single straight root and therefore does not tolerate transplanting, it should be sown directly in the garden. It requires no additional fertilizer if grown in well-draining ground rich in organic matter. It shares the astonishing characteristic of many of the other herbs of being unpredictable in growth because of the strong influence exerted on it by yearly climatic and environmental changes.

Sow in clusters of from three to five seeds, about 3 cm from each other with an intercluster interval of 20 cm. Cover with a layer of soil two or three times as thick as the seeds themselves and press lightly with the hands to ensure close contact between seeds and soil.

Sowing

Sow directly in field or garden, as fennel does not tolerate transplanting. Cover with a layer of soil 2 or 3 times thicker than the seeds themselves.

If the soil is lean, add a shovelful of compost for each plant.

Like other herbs, including dill, borage, and coriander, fennel reseeds itself and comes up every year after having once been sown and raised to maturity.

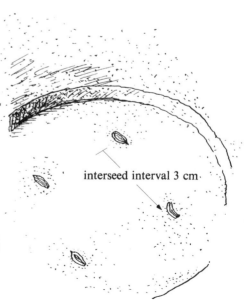

interseed interval 3 cm

Germination occurs in five days for seeds sown in mid-September and in about ten days for seeds sown in mid-April. Ensure full growth by thinning, after plants are 5–6 cm tall, until there is only one in each location. Leaves may be harvested as soon as the plant is about 40 cm tall. The edible bulbous swelling at the base of the stalks of Florence fennel may be harvested in April or May for plants raised from seed sown in September. Cut the plant free at the base line. The bulb disappears as the plant grows tall; and the plants bloom with yellow, umbrella-shaped flowers, like a larger version of dill flowers, in June. Seeds may be harvested in early August.

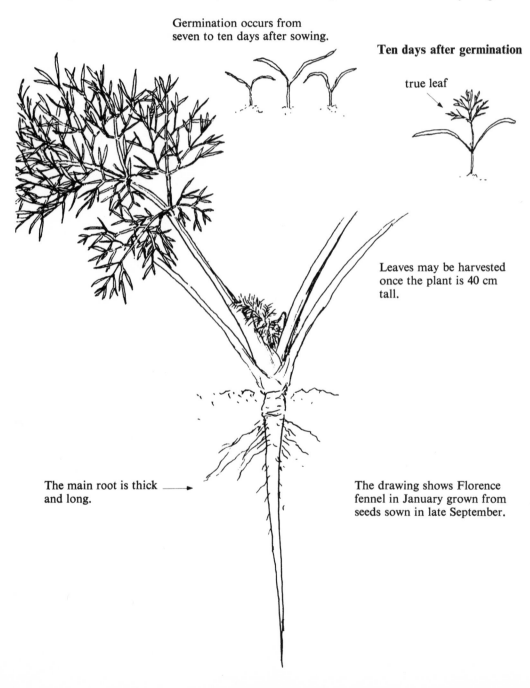

Germination occurs from seven to ten days after sowing.

Ten days after germination

true leaf

Leaves may be harvested once the plant is 40 cm tall.

The main root is thick and long.

The drawing shows Florence fennel in January grown from seeds sown in late September.

Fennel in early February

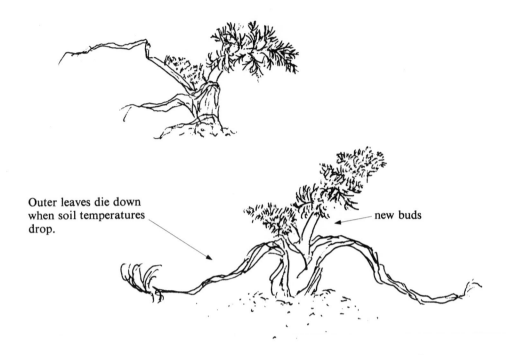

Outer leaves die down
when soil temperatures
drop.

new buds

Harvesting the Bulbous Stem

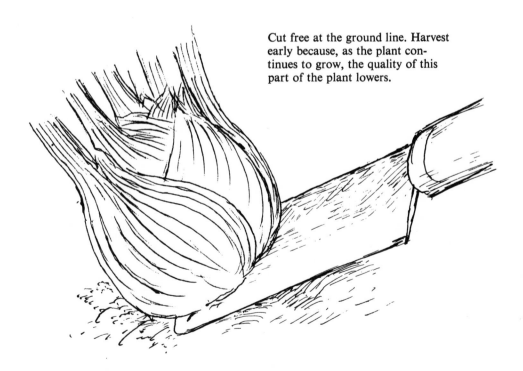

Cut free at the ground line. Harvest
early because, as the plant continues to grow, the quality of this
part of the plant lowers.

On plants that bloomed in
late June, green seeds appear
in mid-July. Harvest in early
August, when the green color
has faded.

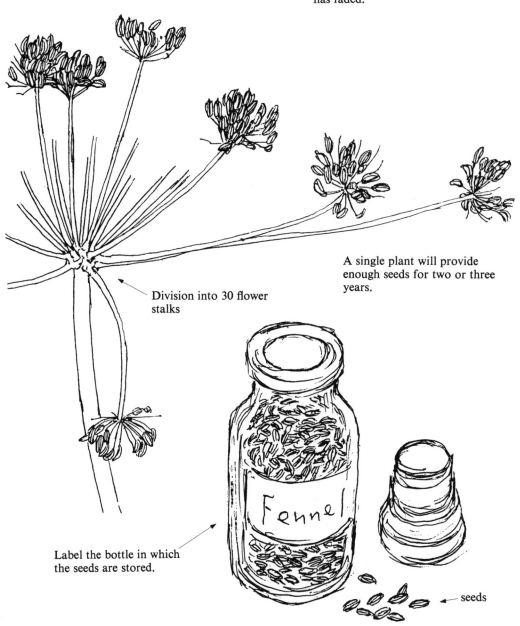

Division into 30 flower
stalks

A single plant will provide
enough seeds for two or three
years.

Fennel

Label the bottle in which
the seeds are stored.

seeds

Index